Deconstructing the Republic

Deconstructing the Republic

Voting Rights, the Supreme Court, and the
Founders' Republicanism Reconsidered

Anthony A. Peacock

The AEI Press

Publisher for the American Enterprise Institute
WASHINGTON, D.C.

To Gretchen and to the memory of our parents,
Julienne, Holley, and Tim

Distributed to the Trade by National Book Network, 15200 NBN Way, Blue Ridge Summit, PA 17214. To order call toll free 1-800-462-6420 or 1-717-794-3800. For all other inquiries please contact the AEI Press, 1150 Seventeenth Street, N.W., Washington, D.C. 20036 or call 1-800-862-5801.

NRI NATIONAL RESEARCH INITIATIVE

This publication is a project of the National Research Initiative, a program of the American Enterprise Institute that is designed to support, publish, and disseminate research by university-based scholars and other independent researchers who are engaged in the exploration of important public policy issues.

Library of Congress Cataloging-in-Publication Data

Peacock, Anthony A. (Anthony Arthur), 1959–
  Deconstructing the republic : voting rights, the Supreme Court, and the founders' republicanism reconsidered / Anthony A. Peacock.
    p. cm.
  ISBN-13: 978-0-8447-4263-2 (pbk.)
    1. Republicanism—United States. 2. United States. Voting Rights Act of 1965. 3. United States. Supreme Court. I. Title.

    JA84.U5P38 2008
    324.6'20973—dc22

                                                            2008000137

12 11 10 09 08   1 2 3 4 5

Printed in the United States of America

Contents

Acknowledgments

This book is the product of a number of years of work on questions of American republicanism and the Voting Rights Act. I have benefited from conversations and commentary on works of mine over that time from numerous individuals, too many to name here. I am grateful to all those who have taken their time to enlighten me on the subjects this book covers. Special thanks are due in particular to Ralph Rossum, Charles Kesler, Joe Bessette, Jeremy Rabkin, Robert P. George, Mark Rush, Brad Watson, Chris Manfredi, Rainer Knopff, Ted Morton, Barry Cooper, Tim O'Rourke, Jim Ceaser, and Peter McNamara. I would also like to thank the two reviewers the American Enterprise Institute had assess my manuscript. Their comments were very helpful in improving the text. Special thanks are also due to Henry Olsen, Sam Thernstrom, Karlyn Bowman, Laura Harbold, Lisa Ferraro Parmelee, and Kathy Swain of AEI. Their remarks on earlier drafts of this book were critical to making it a much better work than it otherwise would have been. Of course, the usual homily applies: I remain responsible for all defects that remain with the final product.

I would also like to thank Kim Dennis, Ryan Stowers, and Courtney Myers, whose early help with this project was instrumental to its completion.

The National Research Initiative at the American Enterprise Institute and the Earhart Foundation provided me generous financial assistance to conduct the research and the writing of this book. I give my sincere thanks to both organizations.

At Utah State I would also like to thank Peter and Carol McNamara, Randy Simmons, and Bobbi Herzberg for their assistance and support.

Finally, and above all, I must thank my wife, Gretchen, and our children, Hamilton, Spencer, and Holley, for their enormous support and toleration for all the time the old man spent in the "dungeon" working on this project. I owe them all big time and undertake here in print to pay up in full.

Introduction

About a month and a half before future Supreme Court Justice Samuel Alito's confirmation hearings in January 2006, Senator Joseph Biden, a Judiciary Committee Democrat, announced that a filibuster of Alito's nomination might be necessary because, in a 1985 application to the Reagan administration's Office of Legal Counsel, Alito had expressed "disagreement" with the Warren Court's reapportionment cases—the "one person, one vote" decisions which held that state and congressional electoral districts had to be equally populated.[1]

"The fact that he questioned abortion and the idea of [racial] quotas is one thing," Biden declared. "The fact that he questioned the idea of the legitimacy of the reapportionment decisions of the Warren Court is even something well beyond that."[2] Unfortunately, no serious discussion of the reapportionment cases took place during the confirmation hearings. Given the star-chamber-like atmosphere of Senate Judiciary Committee hearings, where Republican judicial nominees are expected to recant their conservative judicial philosophies, Alito wisely avoided contesting the issue. Had he done so, however, an examination of the constitutional foundations of the reapportionment decisions would likely have revealed just how thin they were.

The reapportionment decisions were intended to address what was no doubt an unseemly aspect of American republicanism: grossly disproportionate electoral districts. Like all constitutional holdings, however, these decisions would give rise to a universal legal rule that would apply not just to grossly disproportionate electoral districts, such as the Alabama districts in dispute in *Reynolds v. Sims* (1964),[3] but to all electoral districts in America. In Colorado in 1962, for example, voters had approved of a federal model of state government in which unequally populated electoral

1

districts would be tolerated in order to give voice to geographic units of representation, similar to the U.S. Senate.[4] Following the Court's decision in *Reynolds* requiring both houses of state governments to have equally populated electoral districts, such options would no longer be available.

This book describes the deconstruction of American republicanism that has been orchestrated by the Supreme Court through its interpretation of the Voting Rights Act (VRA) of 1965.[5] Although it has not acted alone in this exercise, having received significant support along the way from Congress, various administrations, civil rights groups, and academics, the Court has taken the most audacious steps toward challenging the Founders' republicanism. The reapportionment cases set the stage for this development by establishing that courts had both the legal authority and institutional capability to resolve complicated questions of representational "fairness."

In *Allen v. State Board of Elections* (1969), the Court incorporated the principle of "effective" representation from the reapportionment cases into its interpretation of the VRA—a very difficult task.[6] In the reapportionment cases, the Court required states drawing electoral maps simply to create electoral districts of numerically equal population. But how to define "effective" racial representation for those jurisdictions attempting to comply with the VRA? The *Allen* decision never specified an answer to that question beyond indicating that it was synonymous with a right to an "undiluted vote." This idea eventually evolved into a right of minorities "to elect their preferred candidates of choice" to office—a right now explicitly guaranteed in the VRA of 2006.[7] *Allen* set in motion a generation-long conflict between the VRA and the laws of equal protection, requiring states to classify voters on the basis of race—a constitutionally suspect activity—to achieve the right electoral outcomes.

This book proposes that we can understand the current law of the VRA as the product of two significant developments in American judicial politics. The first is the emergence of what I call "judicial rationalism," a judicial form of Friedrich Hayek's "constructivist rationalism." For Hayek, constructivist rationalism referred to a political vision that assumed all social institutions are (or ought to be) the product of deliberate design, and that the political branches of government possess the knowledge necessary to achieve that design.[8] Hayek's critique of socialism and of the planned economy—"rationalism"—was that the political branches do not have the moral, social, or political knowledge necessary to regulate social and economic life.[9] The presumption that they do had been the "fatal conceit" of socialists and social democrats, ranging from the early progressives to modern liberals.[10]

The first thesis of this book is that what Hayek said about the political branches of government is equally true of the judicial branch. Supreme Court jurisprudence through the last half of the twentieth century was distinguished, as much as anything, by the Court's fatal conceit that it could rationally reconstruct American republicanism from the top down in accordance with a preconceived vision of "fairness."

The most decisive origin for this new judicial rationalism was the reapportionment cases of the 1960s. These rulings displaced the Founders' idea of qualitative constitutional majorities—deliberative majorities that respected minority rights—with government by pure numerical majorities, a form of republicanism that too often did not respect minority rights. In doing so, they not only introduced a radically new democratic principle into the American political order; they also signaled a new judicial dispensation.

With the passage of the Voting Rights Act in 1965, a second definitive feature of modern judicial politics made its appearance: the politics of multiculturalism, one of the most determinative and, I believe, dangerous developments in American politics in the last half-century. An elite driven movement that originated in America's universities, the politics of multiculturalism now pervades virtually every aspect of American politics, law, and culture. It is reflected, on the one hand, in the volumes of literature on race produced (particularly since the 1960s) by the social science and legal academic community and, on the other hand, in the extent to which that literature has insinuated itself into public policy. The net effect has been to secure the significance of race well into the future by institutionalizing it.

The VRA has been crucial to this development, emerging as part of a broader civil rights strategy in which the meanings of equality and discrimination have been changed. The marriage of social scientific and legal academic opinion to voting rights advocacy created a powerful coalition. Like the reapportionment cases and other civil rights initiatives, the administration and adjudication of the VRA have wedded knowledge to power, academic expertise to administrative efficiency and judicial authority. Reflective of a theoretical shift of concern from discriminatory conduct to independent principles of distributive justice, the administration and adjudication of the VRA, particularly after 1969, transformed the law from a legal guarantee of protection from discrimination into a substantive equal-rights objective focusing on disadvantage and groups.[11]

In this book I define the politics of multiculturalism as a vision of America that considers race and ethnicity, not merely as sources of identity and of mutual interest, but also as legally determinative categories that afford legitimate foundations for claims to representation and political rule.[12] The multiculturalist vision was constitutionalized in the Supreme Court's recent affirmative action cases involving the University of Michigan, *Grutter v. Bollinger*[13] and *Gratz v. Bollinger*.[14] Three days after the release of those decisions in June 2003, the Court handed down *Georgia v. Ashcroft*,[15] a voting rights case involving the VRA that sought to institutionalize the same multiculturalist vision of America.

In all three decisions the question in dispute was that of "underrepresented minorities." In *Grutter* and *Gratz*, the Court heard arguments concerning underrepresentation in higher education. In *Ashcroft*, the argument involved underrepresentation in electoral redistricting. "Underrepresentation" was defined exclusively in terms of race and ethnicity. The classes recognized were those that John Skrentny has referred to as the handful designated as America's "official minorities": blacks, Hispanics, and Native Americans in the case of the University of Michigan's undergraduate and law school admissions policies, and blacks in the case of *Ashcroft*—a group recognized under the VRA.[16]

In *Grutter*, a majority on the Court created for the first time in constitutional history a "diversity" exception to the laws of equal protection, ruling that a public university had a compelling interest in promoting a racially diverse student body. Writing in response to the majority's opinion, Justice Clarence Thomas chided his colleagues: "The Court's civics lesson presents yet another example of judicial selection of a theory of political representation based on skin color—an endeavor" Justice Thomas had "previously rejected" in the case of the VRA.[17]

This book contends that the conflict between the VRA and the equal protection clause of the Fourteenth Amendment is symptomatic of the underlying incompatibility between what scholars and judges have referred to as "first-generation" and "second-generation" voting rights.

First-generation voting rights protect the right to cast a ballot. They are what the original VRA was designed to address.

Second-generation voting rights, by contrast, are not rights to cast a ballot, but rights to representation—specifically, rights to "effective" racial representation. They protect the right to an "undiluted" vote for racial groups. They originated in *Allen* and would be the focus of attention throughout the subsequent history of the VRA. Although voting rights advocates—and the majority in *Allen*—believe that these are simply an extension of first-generation voting rights, I do not agree: Second-generation voting rights are not only categorically distinct from first-generation voting rights; they are, in fact, their antithesis. Whereas first-generation voting rights are private or individual in nature and are colorblind, not requiring the identification of individuals with racial or ethnic groups for their vindication, second-generation voting rights are collective or group rights that are impossible to vindicate without taking cognizance of a voter's race and violating the rights of others. This difference is precisely why they are of such dubious constitutionality.

This conflict between the Constitution and second-generation voting rights is, to my mind, the conflict between Madisonian and multiculturalist understandings of equality and representation. The distinction between the two is crucial to appreciating how second-generation voting rights present a rationalist and multiculturalist threat to the Founders' republicanism.

I identify the Founders' republicanism with Madison's understanding of this term and use the terms "Madisonian republicanism" and "Founders' republicanism" interchangeably throughout the book. Madison was an ardent proponent of the Constitution's twin objectives of protecting private or individual rights and promoting the general welfare. He defended the Constitution's separation of powers, its principles of federalism, and its objectives of limited government. He also explained as well as anyone both the originality and the mechanics of the Constitution's institutional and noninstitutional safeguards against incidences of faction. Perhaps above all, Madison, along with Hamilton, understood that the Constitution and union, in addition to the concept of a uniform, singular citizenship based on constitutional union, were the key to American greatness. These elements of the Founders' republicanism are threatened by second-generation voting rights. How precisely they are and what they portend for American republicanism is discussed in the forthcoming chapters.

Plan of the Book

In chapter 1, I outline the basic elements of the Founders' republicanism as it is reflected in the thought of James Madison and *The Federalist*. I contrast Madisonian republicanism with the republicanism of second-generation voting rights, which, I contend, is a multicultural republicanism. This chapter also outlines the six distinct ways that today's VRA threatens Madisonian republicanism and summarizes the most significant way in which second-generation issues undermine what has been referred to as the Founders' "commercial republicanism."

Chapter 2 briefly summarizes the theoretical origins of the politics of multiculturalism, as well as its influence on modern political science and the challenge it poses to the Founders' conception of natural rights. The chapter suggests that the most discernable roots of the multiculturalist movement can be traced to the historicism of early twentieth-century progressivism. The Founders promoted individual rights and were skeptical of factions and group interests.[18] Multiculturalism, by contrast, glorifies group rights and minority identity. Like the progressives, the multiculturalists see as the very essence of American politics groups whose demands should be satisfied by legislation.

In chapter 3, I explore the historical backdrop to *Baker v. Carr* (1962),[19] from which the Supreme Court's judicial rationalism received its single most significant boost. In *Baker,* the Court held for the first time that a challenge to a state apportionment statute—here Tennessee's—was not a political question (best left to the political branches of government to decide) and was therefore appropriate for judicial review. I further discuss the constitutional arguments the Court raised in defense of its position in *Baker* and in later reapportionment decisions. We will see that extending the rationalism of the reapportionment cases became particularly problematic in the case of multimember electoral districts, where a tension arose between the individual and group dimensions of reapportionment law that would persist in the case of the VRA. We will also see that the reapportionment cases would set the stage for many of the issues the Court would have to address in its interpretation of the VRA.

Chapter 4 reviews the history of the VRA from the *Allen* decision to the end of the 1970s. Following *Allen*, as defensible as that decision may have been, the VRA increasingly became an instrument of the politics of multiculturalism. This development was apparent in the adoption of a racial class–warfare vision of America in *United Jewish Organizations Inc. v. Carey* (1977),[20] perhaps the most important Supreme Court ruling prior to the 1990s. Also examined in chapter 4 is the inclusion of "language minorities" in the 1975 VRA, a development that would further reinforce the multiculturalism of second-generation voting rights. I conclude with some thoughts on how the first fifteen years of VRA jurisprudence transformed the act into an instrument of multicultural politics, thus setting the stage for seminal amendments made to it in 1982 that entrenched even more deeply the multiculturalist rationalism of today's VRA.

Chapter 5 discusses the "results" test incorporated into the VRA by Congress in 1982, as well as *City of Mobile v. Bolden* (1980)[21] and *Thornburg v. Gingles* (1986),[22] two cases that reflected the Madisonian and multiculturalist visions of equality and representation at war with one another in American law. This leads to an investigation of the continuing expansion through the 1980s of the meaning of "discrimination" in the VRA. Issues respecting the burdens of proof that were debated and litigated throughout the 1980s raised questions about the ongoing objects of American civil rights law.

In chapter 6, I examine the Supreme Court's voting rights cases of the 1990s with a view toward illustrating that faction, and specifically the racial and ethnic fragmentation of American society, was at the center of attention throughout those cases. This very Madisonian theme once again pointed up the conflicting visions of equality and representation held, respectively, by Madisonian and multicultural republicanism.

In chapter 7, I review VRA law from 2001 to 2006. The cases I examine make clear that the Court's tentative recognition in the 1990s of the conflict between the VRA and the laws of equal protection would dissipate in a few short years. The Founders' republicanism may have been briefly resurrected in the 1990s, but the rationalist and multiculturalist assault on that republicanism would continue in force following the 2000 census.

The conclusion returns to the subject of the Founders' republicanism, this time in the context of what a Founders' VRA might look like. Today's VRA has converted the Founders' citizens' Constitution into a victims' Constitution. Second-generation voting rights, in this sense, are definitively un-American. A Founders' VRA would return the act to its original purpose of serving as an antidiscrimination measure, one that treats all Americans equally and solidifies a uniform concept of citizenship, rather than perpetuating the race entitlement initiative of second-generation voting rights.

Deconstructing the Republic concludes that, given the unsavory and intractable nature of vote-dilution law and the fact that Congress has now extended to 2032 two critical sections of the VRA that were set to expire in 2007, the only solution to the racial divisiveness incited by today's VRA would be for the Court to find the principal sections of the act unconstitutional. That possibility, however, is very unlikely, and American republicanism will likely be saddled with the burden they impose for decades to come.

1

Madisonian versus Multiculturalist Republicanism

Along with Alexander Hamilton, James Madison has rightly been acknowledged as the principal source for the intellectual foundations of the United States Constitution and, particularly, its theory of republicanism. Madison was instrumental at the Constitutional Convention in shaping provisions respecting congressional representation, and he wrote the most important *Federalist* numbers on this subject. To misinterpret Madison's conduct or ideas, as Lance Banning has observed, is to misunderstand the Founding.[1] This point is particularly true when it comes to the Founders' understanding of republicanism.

Madison defined the ends of the Constitution as twofold: "to secure the public good and private rights."[2] These two objects speak to the distinctive elements of Madison's understanding of rights and his concept of republicanism, both of which are related to first- and second-generation voting rights. For Madison the rights established in the Constitution, like those in the Declaration of Independence, were individual or personal in nature. They adhered to the *individual* and protected specific, cognizable claims against the state. As Madison emphasized, rights were "private," not public.[3] They were to be enjoyed equally by all, not just a few. Nor could a genuine right be transient or fluctuate over time. As the Declaration made clear, natural rights were eternal and prepolitical in the sense that they were inalienable, antedating the state. Constitutional rights were also prepolitical in the sense that they were beyond political dispute—whether or not they were inalienable.

Although the foundational and inviolable character of rights meant they could not be contested, they had to be limited. They could not apply to

9

political disputes or extend beyond those relations over which individuals had exclusive control: property, contract, claims of negligence, and even the right to vote, which individuals were free to exercise or not as they saw fit.[4] Rights were distinct from *interests*, which were not private in character but made claims on the public good, and were properly the subject of political contest.

The distinction between private rights and the public good had its constitutional embodiment in the distinction between the judiciary and the political branches of government. According to Madison's reading, the separation of powers was based on a functional distinction between the expertise and capability of the various branches of government as much as on a political anthropology that sought to counteract ambition with ambition.[5] The judiciary was charged with protecting the rights of individuals against encroachments from the political branches of government. The precondition for this power was that the judiciary itself not engage in political disputes or decision-making. It had to remain politically separate if it were to arbitrate neutrally on questions of rights.[6]

This idea of separation was at the heart of Justice Felix Frankfurter's objection in *Colgrove v. Green* (1946).[7] In *Colgrove*, Illinois voters had challenged congressional redistricting in a state in which the largest district was nine times the size of the smallest. The plaintiffs appeared to have a compelling case. Nevertheless, Justice Frankfurter objected on behalf of the Court that the federal judiciary did not have the constitutional authority to intervene in redistricting disputes because article 1, section 4 of the Constitution granted sole authority to decide such questions to state governments and to Congress.[8] What was being raised by the plaintiffs was a "wrong suffered by Illinois as a *polity*" rather than a claim relating to a "*private wrong*"—which was properly within the jurisdiction of the courts.[9] Should the Supreme Court agree to resolve questions of redistricting, as it was being invited to do in *Colgrove*, it would have to address distinctively "political questions," entering (in Frankfurter's well-known formulation) the "political thicket."[10] This involvement would be inconsistent with both the judiciary's institutional capacity and its constitutional authority—an assessment with which both Madison and Hamilton would have concurred and an understanding of the judicial role which, until the era of Chief Justice Earl Warren, had been virtually universal. The judiciary's role, as they imagined it, would certainly not involve questions of reapportionment or redistricting.

Madison's understanding of the public good also had important implications for current voting rights disputes. By his reading, although the majority *had* interests, it did not *represent* those interests; rather, it represented the public good.[11] In *Federalist* 10 Madison made clear that "when a majority is included in a faction, the form of popular government . . . enables it to sacrifice to its ruling passion or interest both the public good and the rights of other citizens." The inquiries in *Federalist* 10 and, more generally, the Constitution itself, were intended "to secure the public good and private rights against the danger of such a faction, and at the same time to preserve the spirit and form of popular government."[12] For our purposes, three of the many implications of these compact passages are particularly significant.

First, the form of popular government under the Constitution would have to be configured in such a way as to ensure that the majority could not sacrifice the public good or private rights to its ruling passion or interest. As the basis of American constitutionalism was the individual, so the object of the legislative process was to be the general welfare or public interest.

Second, Madison's republicanism was not intended to promote bargaining, logrolling (in which legislators exchange support for one another's proposals), or tradeoffs among discrete groups so they could have their interests satisfied.[13] Although representatives were certainly to be cognizant of constituent interests, legislators, he suggested, should not be "advocates and parties to the causes which they determine."[14] To do so would simply give preference to the legislator's personal interests or the interests of the legislator's constituents—a recipe for faction and for unlimited government, because the desires of legislators and constituents are potentially infinite.

The third implication of the above passages, following from the first two, was that the majority's ruling passions and interests were not synonymous with the public good; in fact, they were its antithesis.[15] As Madison's comments in *Federalist* 10 made clear, the public good was something distinct from mere particular passions or interests, including those of the majority.[16]

However much passions or interests might animate political actors— be they part of the majority or minority—the specific purpose of federal institutional process was to wean representatives from those interests to which they were drawn so passionately. Key here were the Constitution's institutional processes and limited objects, both of which would work to raise deliberations from mere interests to what would promote the general welfare.[17] Thus, Madison's republicanism poses problems for political observers and advocates who would reduce politics to a mere clash of interests.

Such an argument, as Hamilton demonstrated in *Federalist* 35 and Madison demonstrated in *Federalist* 55 and 56, misapprehended the nature of American republicanism. Representing all classes and all interests in society was both impracticable and unnecessary. It was impracticable because it was impossible to represent all interests in any representative body,[18] especially in the large republic envisioned by the Constitution. It was unnecessary because the objects of the federal government were limited to commerce, finance, military affairs, treaties, and other forms of "negotiation," all of which would be pursued with a view to the common good, not narrow constituent interests.[19] An election was not about representing interests or about capturing every shade of public opinion. It was, rather, about judging the character and the opinions of a representative and selecting a government that was the best available.

Madison's views are apropos to the VRA because the VRA suggests that minority representatives should be advocates of "the interests or prejudices of their respective constituents." Today's VRA more closely approximates the republicanism of *Federal Farmer* 7, which required electors to "chuse men from among themselves, and genuinely like themselves," than it does the republicanism of the Constitution. If the mandate of section 2 of the VRA, for instance, which entitles minorities "to elect representatives of their choice," is not intended to ensure that policy takes more cognizance of the interests of legally recognized minorities, then it is difficult to appreciate why specific constituencies are entitled to their own representation.

It might be argued that the VRA is simply intended to make sure that more minority "voices" are adequately accounted for in legislative deliberations, and that this action does not require common concerns to be sacrificed to minority demands. Indeed, this effort would be perfectly consistent with Madisonian republicanism, because the only minority interests of which cognizance would be taken would be those that comport with the common good. But this is generally not what the advocates of second-generation voting rights have in mind. What would be the point of ensuring minority electoral success if there were not some policy consequence for minority interests somewhere down the road? As Lani Guinier has remarked, this would simply mark the "triumph of tokenism."[20]

The Founders' Commercial Republicanism

The Constitution was intended to transform the nature of factional struggle in American politics through the creation of an extended commercial union that would, in the language of Hobbes, crush the children of pride and the spirit of vanity. It was also intended to extinguish politics understood as widespread and perennial contests over political and constitutional principles.[21] Although the ostensible objective of race-based representation may be to enhance deliberative and legitimate government, the introduction of race into the calculus of effective representation has undermined those very principles that were thought to be settled by the Constitution, the resolution of which was presumed by the idea of representative government itself.[22]

The race-based theory of representation that underlies current VRA law poses many problems to liberal democratic government. One in particular is its failure to demonstrate the existence of any fundamental interests that are not already protected against majoritarian rule by individual rights.[23] The very institutional changes introduced by the VRA have arguably threatened individual rights by exaggerating certain considerations in representative government—particularly considerations of race—to the disregard or exclusion of others.

This point was the substance of Justice Clarence Thomas's concurring opinion in *Holder v. Hall* (1994),[24] the most provocative and comprehensive indictment of second-generation voting rights ever written by a High Court justice. Thomas excoriated the Supreme Court for acting like Platonic guardians in its adjudication of vote-dilution disputes.[25] Not only had vote-dilution conflicts proved to be intractable, but the judiciary's preference for majority-minority districts had unjustifiably imposed a single theory of representation on jurisdictions throughout the country and could not have calculated a better way to exacerbate racial tensions, "segregating the races into political homelands."[26] Examining the potential for racial strife that voting rights practices had caused, Justice Thomas identified racial with religious faction, enlisting Justice William O. Douglas's admonition in *Wright v. Rockefeller* (1964): "'When racial or religious lines are drawn by the State, . . . antagonisms that relate to race or to religion rather than to political issues are generated; communities seek not the best representative but the best racial or religious partisan.'"[27] In *Shaw v. Reno* (1993) Justice Sandra Day O'Connor referred to this same passage from *Wright*, drawing many of the same conclusions.[28]

The identification of racial with religious partisanship and the distinction of racial and religious antagonisms from true political issues speak to two central themes of the Constitution's republican theory: the primacy of passion over interest in politics and the irrelevance of race and religion as legitimate categories of legal distinction in republican government. These issues were familiar to many of America's Founders, including James Madison. In *Federalist* 10, for instance, Madison distinguished factions "united and actuated by some common impulse of passion" from factions united and actuated by "interest."[29] Like many classical liberal thinkers before him, Madison understood that the most tempestuous and explosive factions were those animated by passion, particularly collective passion.[30] Governments whose object was the salvation of souls had fallen because they had incited the volcanic passions of rage that attached to differing religious opinions.[31]

The Supreme Court's concern in *Shaw* and its subsequent voting rights cases in the 1990s was that race might present many of these same incendiary pathologies. Indeed, the Court's own jurisprudence had suggested that the Constitution's proscriptions against racial classifications were even more emphatic than those against religious classifications. The First Amendment, for instance, recognizes the salutariness of promoting religious "identity" through the free exercise clause, the clause allowing for nonassimilationist or "difference-regarding" distinctions in law in those cases involving religious practice.[32] At least implicitly, the Constitution appears to recognize not merely religious freedom but the fact, acknowledged by numerous Founders such as George Washington, that religion promotes moral and civic virtue.[33] In contrast with the free exercise clause, the Constitution never condones the promotion of racial identity. Unlike the case of religious practice, the Constitution brooks no nonassimilation doctrines on the question of race.

The Founders' theory of republicanism was predicated on the recognition that the difficult question for representative institutions was not so much how to *receive* interests into the legislature, but rather how to *combine* them effectively for the general welfare.[34] How, and around what specific interests, would political bonds be formed? Classical liberal political science, developed by Hobbes and later refined by the likes of Locke, Montesquieu, and Hume, originated in a political anthropology that understood individuals to be divided naturally by their passions but capable of being united artificially by their interests.[35]

Property (for Locke) and commerce (for Montesquieu and Hume) were essential to this project of unification, the preconditions for stable and energetic government. Madison agreed with classical liberal theory that political conflict originating in emotion or passion was typically excited by frivolous, insubstantial causes. By contrast, political conflict originating in interest derived primarily from relations of property. Property interests were rational interests not only because they were necessary to the support of life and liberty, but also because, being tangible, they directed men's attention to concrete realities that might be improved. While they could result in conflict or even hostilities, they also directed men's attention to the longer-term view of political order and thus held out the promise of reconciliation and good government.[36] It was no accident that, when enumerating those "three descriptions of men" who would dominate representation in Congress, *Federalist* 35 outlined predominantly economic categories: "landholders, merchants, and men of the learned professions."[37]

By contrast, the most destructive and explosive factions were those anchored in passion—in pride, in hatred, and in vanity. These conflicts, above all, were to be avoided. As historians and political theorists have informed us, the new science of politics that provided the blueprint for the Constitution, and that the Constitution improved upon yet again, emerged against a backdrop of violent and tyrannical religious wars that marked the nadir of European politics throughout the seventeenth and eighteenth centuries. Commercial republicanism would provide a constitutional order founded on the recognition that factious conflicts, such as those based on passionate attachments to revealed religion or to ethnic and racial chauvinism, could be smoothed over, if not eliminated altogether, by anchoring political bonds in relations of property with a view to promoting security, well-being, civilization, and the other blessings of liberty.

The Founders' republicanism would check majority faction in government through institutional mechanisms, as well: the separation of powers, checks and balances, federalism, and the different modes of election for federal officeholders. These mechanisms would check the factionalism of oppressive majorities only *after* they had formed, however. Such factions also needed to be checked *before* they could form, through noninstitutional means. Madison implored citizens to see that the problem of faction needed to be addressed most fundamentally at the level of *society* before it could infiltrate the ranks of government.[38]

Key to this idea was the "extended sphere," that novelty in American republicanism that would combine the Constitution's complex institutionalism with a multiplicity of economic, social, and religious interests.[39] Understanding the operational features of the extended sphere is critical to appreciating precisely how the VRA threatens the Founders' republicanism, specifically the Constitution's design to address the problem of class conflict.

As Martin Diamond has observed, not just any large republic would do in forming the Constitution's designs against faction. Many large regimes were broken into simple classes, with the rich on the one side and the undifferentiated poor on the other. Only in a large *commercial* republic could propertied interests be sufficiently differentiated to avoid the class conflict that had been the bane of republics since time immemorial.[40] The "first object of government," Madison stressed, is to protect the "diversity in the faculties of men, from which the rights of property originate." But

> from the protection of the different and unequal faculties of acquiring property, the possession of different *degrees* and *kinds* of property immediately results; and from the influence of these on the sentiments and views of the respective proprietors, ensues a division of the society into different interests and parties. . . . Those who hold and those who are without property have ever formed distinct interests in society.[41]

The solution to the problem of faction, as far as *The Federalist* was concerned, lay in replacing divisions over *degrees* or *amounts* of property with divisions over *kinds* of property. As Diamond highlighted, the Constitution would offer up the prospect of doing so for the first time in history.[42]

The elimination of such critical social divisions was essential to the promotion of the general welfare, where the legislative process under the Constitution was predicated on a prelegislative softening, if not dissolution, of the effects of faction. Madison could thus conclude: "In the extended republic of the United States, and among the great variety of interests, parties, and sects which it embraces, a coalition of a majority of the whole society could seldom take place upon any other principles than those of justice and the general good."[43]

Six Ways Today's VRA Threatens Madisonian Republicanism

As the Constitution would subordinate racial and religious classifications to economic classifications, so the extended sphere would reduce the economic classifications themselves from the historically fatal class struggles that plagued premodern republics to the safe, even salutary, struggles among ever more differentiated kinds of propertied interests that would flourish under the Constitution.[44] The VRA threatens both of these elements of Madisonian republicanism by elevating race to a status of preeminence in American law and by institutionalizing racial class divisions that threaten the resurrection of preliberal forms of political conflict anchored in divisive notions of racial identity. The VRA converts political conflicts into racial class conflicts and does so by transforming the highly differentiated regime of predominantly political and economic interests contemplated by the Founders' republicanism into an artificially contrived confederation of what Justice Thomas referred to in *Holder v. Hall* as race-based "political homelands."[45]

A central theme throughout this book is that with the emergence of the politics of multiculturalism as a challenge to the original constitutional understandings of equality and representation, the American constitutional order now stands exposed to a form of sectarian conflict similar in nature to that of preliberal regimes. This situation is clearly what concerned Justices Thomas and Antonin Scalia in *Holder*. It is what concerned the Court in *Shaw v. Reno* (1993), where Justice O'Connor warned that "racial gerrymandering, even for remedial purposes, may balkanize us into competing racial factions."[46] It is what Justice Douglas warned of in *Wright v. Rockefeller* a generation earlier.

Both Madison and Hamilton provided graphic descriptions of the oppressiveness of those petty republics in which homogenous, majoritarian interests tyrannized over minorities. In *Holder*, Justice Thomas detailed how the multiculturalism of VRA law had worked to deconstruct America's large, dynamic commercial republic into an archipelago of discrete racial and ethnic constituencies, each with its own presumed homogenous interests and each, therefore, exposed to precisely that majoritarian tyranny Madison and Hamilton feared from small republics. President Bill Clinton's nominee to head the Civil Rights Division of the Department of Justice in 1993, Lani Guinier, was famously criticized for suggesting that it was legitimate to distinguish between "authentic" and "inauthentic" black representation.[47] But the VRA itself gave institutional legitimacy to that distinction. If black voters have distinct political interests—interests that have generally been identified as pro-Democratic, pro–big government, redistributionist interests by voting rights scholars[48]—and if these interests have been institutionalized by the VRA's mandates for their representation, it is only a small step to the conclusion that those blacks whose views do not comport with "black interests" are "inauthentic."

By legitimizing the idea that race is synonymous with political interest, the VRA has given institutional blessing to unsavory political identifications such as those indicated by Guinier. This unseemly side of the VRA and its race-preference policies is rarely, if ever, recounted in voting rights scholarship or jurisprudence. Yet it does remind us that the VRA, like the advocacy for special group rights to racial representation more generally, has transformed the Founders' republicanism into a regime of race-centric pluralism that at bottom breaks down even further to a regime of racial class warfare. At one level, then, the VRA has replaced the Founders' republicanism and James Madison's concern for securing "the public good and private rights" with the republicanism of John C. Calhoun, slavery's archtheorist, who denied the notion of a common good and considered "the community as made up of different and conflicting interests, as far as the action of the government is concerned."[49]

At another level, the VRA has gone further than this. Like the "diversity" rationale in education policy, second-generation voting rights can be understood as consistent with pluralist doctrine, the idea being that without adequate minority "voices" or interests represented in legislative deliberations or educational admissions, representation in these forums would be incomplete. Second-generation voting rights, however, go beyond even this, reducing the American electorate to only a handful of "official minorities," all defined by race and ethnicity. Adopting a class-based analysis of contemporary society and an accompanying redistributive model of political power that is more akin to Marxism or deconstructionism than it is to pluralism or Madisonian republicanism, the VRA has devolved into consummate multicultural policy, reducing American politics to simple, binary racial categories.

Today's VRA challenges Madisonian republicanism in at least six distinct ways. First, it proposes that American republicanism take on the contours of a rent-seeking model of republicanism—that is, one in which representatives are expected to act on behalf of specific interests. In the case of the VRA, they are expected to act on behalf of specific racial interests. Social science studies of how "effectively" minorities are represented under the auspices of the act have framed the issue in precisely these terms: How exactly are minority "interests" to be measured, and how strenuously have members of Congress pursued these interests in legislative policy?[50] A cottage industry of sorts has developed in political science to evaluate electoral data and information, such as district voter makeup, voter preferences, candidate roll-call votes, constituency services, newsletters, press releases, and the like, to determine what types of representatives emerge from what types of districts and whether they help or hinder minority policy preferences. Such studies have enjoyed significant prominence in such Supreme Court cases as *Georgia v. Ashcroft* (2003).[51]

Like the Court's jurisprudence that relies on them, these studies presume that effective representation can be empirically measured, and that this measurement can be reliably translated into voting rights policy. Both VRA jurisprudence and the empirical studies on which it relies tend to reflect the credo of social science, assuming that political actors (such as voters and representatives) do not *act* freely but *behave* predictably.[52] They are also prone to adopt the view dominant in American political science that congressional policymaking consists of aggregating constituency and representative preferences through a variety of bargaining procedures such as logrolling, side payments, compromise, and other forms of interest exchange, with the purpose of benefiting specific constituencies and preferences.[53]

As George Carey has observed, "The currently fashionable interpretation of the American political process" explains it "in terms of a collision of interests where it is assumed that the outcome of the collision accords with the common good largely because of the degree of consensus behind it." But, as Carey emphasizes, absent "from this depiction are such considerations as [what Madison referred to as] 'the true interest' of the country, 'the permanent and aggregate interests of the community,' or the 'general good.'. . . Madison's theory, no matter how one chooses to read it, does not support the notion that the true interests of the country emerge through the resolution of interest conflict."[54]

The second way the VRA challenges Madisonian republicanism is in its preference for corporate or group rights over private or individual rights. Another way to put this point is to say that the VRA prefers "positive" rights over "negative" rights.[55] As Alexander Hamilton pointed out in *Federalist* 78, the original Constitution protected what we today would refer to as "negative," individual rights.[56] These are rights to noninterference from others and, most important, noninterference from government. Positive rights, by contrast, are group-oriented, prescriptive rights, entitlements for designated constituencies that require affirmative grants or dispensations from others, including dispensations from government. Negative rights can coexist without conflicting with the rights of others. Positive rights cannot.[57]

First-generation voting rights fit the model of negative rights because they are colorblind and protect the individual against governmental discrimination regardless of one's group status. Second-generation voting rights, by contrast, are group rights that are positive in nature, requiring an affirmative commitment from government of guarantees of office-holding for designated minority constituencies. With second-generation voting rights, the electoral process is viewed as a zero-sum game; every dispute involving vote-dilution claims, for instance, involves a conflict over which racial groups will get power at which other racial group's (or groups') expense. This becomes particularly acute when the groups competing under the VRA are both beneficiary groups, such as blacks and Hispanics. In such conflicts, what is at issue is clearly not a traditional, negative right of noninterference, but a positive right or entitlement that requires an affirmative governmental commitment. The difficulty in such cases is that the government is now committed to two positive rights that cannot coexist in harmony.

The third and fourth ways second generation voting rights challenge Madisonian republicanism are that they undermine, respectively, the separation of powers and the principles of federalism, immersing the judiciary in contentious political disputes while usurping state constitutional prerogatives over the most fundamental questions of electoral politics. In 1966, the Supreme Court ruled that the section 5 requirement that states covered by the VRA seek preclearance from the U.S. Department of Justice for electoral changes "may have been an uncommon exercise of congressional power," but that the "exceptional conditions" of the day—the conditions of the Jim Crow South—justified "legislative measures not otherwise appropriate."[58] What happened, however, once those "exceptional conditions" no longer prevailed—once Jim Crow was laid to rest? The Constitution charged the balancing of political interests to the political branches of government, not the judiciary. It is even less likely that the Constitution, properly understood, would tolerate any branch of government, political or judicial, attempting to balance racial interests throughout the entirety of the political process, as the VRA contemplates.

The fifth way the VRA challenges Madisonian republicanism is related to the first three: As an instrument of programmatic liberalism, second-generation voting rights threaten the limited government of the Founders' Constitution.[59] Second-generation voting rights are positive, welfare-state rights. They are intended to promote specific racial group interests. As one proponent of racial redistricting, David Canon, has put it: "It is possible to champion peanut subsidies or catfish sales to support the white farmers in one's district (as Sanford Bishop and Mike Espy have done), while at the same time pushing for money for a historically black college or minority enterprise program."[60] This "legislation as pork-barreling for designated clientele groups" approach to congressional lawmaking certainly captures much, perhaps even most, of the way congressional process unfolds today, but it is not Madisonian republicanism.

Independent of the important question of whether peanut subsidies, which presumably are available on a race-neutral basis (even if most beneficiaries of such policies happen to be white), and minority enterprise programs, which are restricted to designated racial and ethnic groups, are legally or constitutionally equivalent, we might ask whether we want to expand the institutionalization of what Gordon Tullock has referred to as "the rent-seeking society" through such enabling legislation as the VRA.[61] Canon's description of the representational process contemplated by the VRA comports with the rent-seeking nature of second-generation voting rights. "Ultimately," he writes,

> the question of how a House member represents constituents depends on how well that member serves the voters' needs. Standards should not be imposed by researchers, but should be set by the voters of each district. *What are the interests of African-American and white voters, and how do different types of representatives serve those interests?*[62]

Canon's democratic theory here is a paradigm of the republicanism of second-generation voting rights. Madison's republicanism would "refine and enlarge the public views, by passing them through the medium of a chosen body of citizens, whose wisdom may best discern the *true interest of their country*, and whose patriotism and love of justice will be least likely to sacrifice it to *temporary or partial considerations*."[63] For Canon, by contrast, acceding to the "temporary or partial considerations" of one's constituents is apparently the very essence of effective representation, particularly effective racial representation.

In the regime of positive rights, government is exposed to capture by specific interests because the objects of government are not public but private goods. This situation is as true for minority political interests, which may benefit from minority enterprise programs, as it is for any other particular special interests, which may benefit from such things as peanut subsidies. This notion is far, however, from Madison's theory of representation, which was intended for a regime of limited government, a government of limited objects and objects of common concern. The Madisonian system was not designed for the postprogressivist or post–New Deal era in which the original constitutional order was jettisoned in favor of a regime of programmatic liberalism, one in which government, and even the Constitution itself, is seen as a vehicle for potentially unlimited reform.

The unlimited form of government that defines modern American republicanism, in which representatives are expected to pursue virtually any object of public desire—and, in the case of the VRA, the particular interests of racial minorities—is not only marked by a transition from the natural rights of the original Constitution to the programmatic rights of the modern welfare state.[64] It is also marked by faction. By converting what were previously considered to be governmental dispensations into vested or positive rights,[65] the programmatic liberal state renders politics divisive because the positive rights granted designated beneficiaries are necessarily exclusive and discriminatory.

Once this change occurs on the scale of the economic and social regulatory state of the late twentieth century and today, where legislation is increasingly intended to benefit designated groups, members of the public find it virtually impossible not to take sides in partisan, heated, political controversies. Politics increasingly becomes precisely what the Court referred to, in *Georgia v. Ashcroft*, as a machination of political power in which interests and parties jockey with one another to maintain and enlarge winning coalitions.[66] In the case of the VRA, the polarization that takes place as a result of this process does so on the basis of that very spring of action Madison and the Constitution both suggested may be the most factious of all: race.[67]

The sixth and final way in which the VRA challenges Madisonian republicanism, then, is its propensity to incite not merely faction but racial faction.[68] The VRA divides the electorate into racial constituencies and freezes these racial divisions in law. In the next chapter I contend that the VRA undermines not only the nondiscrimination principles of individualism and colorblindness at the heart of the American constitutional order, but also the political science underlying the Constitution's distinctly commercial republicanism. As we will see in later chapters, the implementation of the VRA has subordinated markets to race, the Founders' commercial republicanism to identity politics.

2

Progressivism, Multiculturalism, and the Emergence of America's "Official Minorities"

In the 1970s a profound rift began to emerge in American law over the question of equality. The rift was particularly pronounced in affirmative action disputes before the Supreme Court, revealing a fundamental conflict between two visions of equality that have competed for America's constitutional soul for a generation now. On the one side was a colorblind, Madisonian vision that sought to uphold the individual rights of the Declaration of Independence and of the Constitution, and that would brook no compromise of these rights for group preferences. On the other side was a multiculturalist vision that was prepared to qualify individual rights in the name of group rights and racial group balancing. The multiculturalist understanding of equality, focusing as it did on results and proportional group representation, made one's individual rights conditional on the racial and ethnic group(s) to which one belonged. Although its objectives were admirable, seeking to hurry along the achievement of racial-group parity in a host of areas of American life, multiculturalism and its introduction into American law in the late 1960s represented a startling new approach to questions of equality.

Multiculturalism turned the original civil rights mission on its head, requiring a cognizance of race as a precondition for compensatory justice that the Civil Rights Act of 1964 and the VRA of 1965 were originally designed to overcome. James Ceaser has observed that American multiculturalism has "succeeded in joining together two terms—'race' and 'culture'—that many once labored to separate."[1] Whereas the civil rights and human rights policy that emerged in the wake of the genocidal atrocities of World War II sought to remove racial classifications from law, modern multicultural policy and civil rights laws have, by contrast, sought to reverse this process. Race has returned

> in a particular way—not as an obstacle to be removed or even as an important but secondary characteristic, but as the primary feature of social identity and the deepest source of authenticity. Race classifications have been reinstated as an ordinary part of the legal framework, and race is widely viewed as the most important element of social identity. If we are cultural beings and if race is a defining element of cultural identity, we cannot escape its importance. Race not only matters but is fundamental.[2]

The editors of a recent volume, *Multiculturalism and American Democracy*, remarked that whereas the countercultural or liberation movements of the 1960s focused on economic issues such as poverty, exploitation, imperialism, and the economic plight of women and minorities, multiculturalism would cast political warfare in terms of a different form of class struggle:

> The fundamental concern of the multicultural movement is no longer economics but esteem, not income but identity, and thus not Western capitalism but Western culture. . . . The main antagonists are understood not as economic classes, but ethnic and racial groups. There has been a shift, in a word, from political economy to identity politics.[3]

This description of a "shift" captures the transition from first-generation voting rights to second-generation voting rights. Perhaps more accurately, it captures the transition to *late* second-generation voting rights, in which the concern of those who had to apply the VRA—the courts and the U.S. Department of Justice—was no longer to remedy acts of invidious discrimination so much as to achieve racial balance in the political process. Once the Supreme Court decided in *Allen v. State Board of Elections* (1969)[4] that the VRA covered questions of vote dilution in addition to questions of ballot access—a legal mandate that *Allen* and later cases interpreted as a right to minority office-holding—it was only a small step to measuring electoral "fairness" by something approximating proportional racial representation.[5]

This requirement, which neither the language nor the legislative history of the VRA authorized, was nevertheless consistent with the multiculturalist ethos of other civil rights policy in the United States. As Thomas Sowell observed in 1984, federal civil rights policy by that time was shaped more by a vision than by facts. The "facts" had been shaped and reshaped to fit an orthodox "civil rights vision," an outlook that was "not only a moral vision of the way the world *should* be in the future, but also a cause-and-effect vision of the way the world *is* today."[6] The civil rights vision sought to replace equal-opportunity initiatives that might result in disparate racial-group outcomes with a legal regime in which precise symmetries of racial balancing would be pursued in all areas of civil rights policy. Failure to achieve proportional racial outcomes in such policy was seen as injustice and typically ascribed to "discrimination"—meaning, by this standard, any social or systemic forces that might produce unequal group outcomes.

Commenting in 1992 on Sowell's account of the new civil rights vision, Peter Brimelow noted that Sowell had captured the "neosocialism" that underlay the "racial spoils system" of current civil rights policy. The new civil rights vision sought to use government power "not to achieve economic efficiency, which traditional socialism can no longer promise, but ethnic equity—most importantly, the extirpation of 'discrimination.'"[7] Brimelow put the word discrimination in quotation marks because what the civil rights vision sought to eliminate was not so much discrimination as a lack of proportional representation based on race. Ironically, achieving that objective would require government to discriminate explicitly against nonminorities.

Progressivism and Historicism

The original VRA may have been the product of the discrete politics of race in America's South, but by the early 1970s it had begun to be driven by a broader ideological initiative of international dimensions, one that rejected the political science of the Founders' Constitution.

The most concerted effort to undermine that political science began much earlier in the twentieth century with progressivism, a political movement that originated in a widespread acceptance among its practitioners of German historicism. German historicism itself had originated in the philosophy of Friedrich Hegel, the German philosopher who tied truth to history and history to a definitive terminal point—the "end of history." History ended, according to Hegel, when Napoleon marched into Jena in 1806, thus giving practical expression to its completion. That is, Napoleon's march into Jena was historically and philosophically significant because it marked the practical victory of the universal principles of liberty, fraternity, and equality, even if that victory at the time was only partial. After 1806 all history would be "post-historical." It would simply be a repetition of what had gone before. As the Hegelian scholar Alexander Kojève would later remark, 1806 marked the beginning of the coming to be of the "universal and homogenous state."8

We need not concern ourselves with the niceties of Hegel's idea of the end of history or Kojève's idea of the universal and homogenous state; for our purposes, the important point is that by tying truth (particularly moral and political truth) to history, Hegel gave unprecedented coherence to philosophical relativism, the idea that individuals could not transcend their historical time to discover any universal or eternal truths.9 All truth was relative to time and place, dependent on history and on historical circumstances. By not only making truth relative but giving history a definitive purpose or coherent meaning, Hegel's philosophy also precipitated intellectual movements that saw a progress or evolution to history, such as Karl Marx's historical materialism and Charles Darwin's evolutionary understanding of social and political development ("social Darwinism").

Early twentieth-century American progressivism was another of these movements. Progressivism relied heavily on Hegel's historicism to show that the Founders' Constitution and political science were outdated; a more progressive political science that could better accommodate the historical conditions of the modern technological age was needed. Early twentieth-century progressivism gave rise to the postmodernism and deconstructionism of the late twentieth century, two movements that, like progressivism, saw truth as a function of history and thus of those powers that dominated or controlled history.

According to postmodernism and deconstructionism, understanding history required the deconstruction of power relations in American society, relations that both postmodernists and deconstructionists suggested were dependent on class structure, particularly racial and gender class structures. It was only a small step from this notion to the race-identity politics of today's multiculturalism, a vision of America that stresses the irreducible identities of designated racial classes. Postmodernism and deconstructionism captured the minds of America's most influential elites in the waning decades of the twentieth century, laying the groundwork for the race-identity politics of modern multiculturalism in American law, including the multiculturalism of the VRA. Multicultural orthodoxy also contributed, as we will see, to the emergence of America's "official minorities" in civil rights law.

Progressivism, Multiculturalism, and the Challenge to the Founders' Political Science

The politics of multiculturalism emerged in the late twentieth century as a response to traditional conceptions of equality and democratic process that originated in the classical liberal doctrine of natural rights—the doctrine expressed most succinctly in the Declaration of Independence "that all Men are created equal" and that all individuals have "unalienable Rights," among which "are Life, Liberty, and the Pursuit of Happiness." Like its progressive intellectual predecessors, multiculturalism sought to challenge and, ultimately, displace the doctrine of natural rights, which served as the animating philosophy for the Declaration and the Constitution. More particularly, multiculturalism sought to displace this tradition in American law with an ersatz theory of equality and positive rights based on racial-group identity.

Like progressivism, postmodernism, and deconstructionism, multiculturalism has its most discernable origins in nineteenth- and twentieth-century historicism. One of the most perspicacious critics of historicism was political philosopher Leo Strauss. In perhaps the most comprehensive indictment of that school of thought ever written, *Natural Right and History*, Strauss spoke in 1953 of the paradox of World War II: As much as the United States may have vanquished Germany on the battlefield and annihilated it as a political entity, the conquerors would be deprived of that most sublime fruit of victory by having the yoke of German thought imposed on them thereafter. American social science, in particular, would carry the torch of German historicism by denying the natural-rights teachings of the Declaration of Independence. According to modern social science, natural rights did not exist. All rights were positive rights—meaning here the product of human contrivance or positive law. The principles of natural rights were mere "ideals" or mysticism or ideology; they were certainly not true.[10]

Harry Jaffa has noted that, although Strauss was correct about the status of natural rights in the mid-twentieth century, the victory of historicism and relativism took place much earlier than Strauss said it did.[11] Historicism had its most definitive origins in the works of Friedrich Hegel, Karl Marx, Friedrich Nietzsche, and Max Weber.[12] In the American context, its most famous nineteenth-century proponent was John C. Calhoun, a constitutional critic who rejected the idea that there existed in America a general or common good that any institutions of representation could attain—an assumption that would become common currency in progressivist and multiculturalist thought.[13]

Carl Becker, perhaps the most influential scholar on the meaning of the Declaration of Independence, wrote as early as 1922 that the Declaration was "founded on a superficial knowledge of history" and "a naive faith in the instinctive virtues of human kind," a "faith that could not survive the harsh realities of the modern world."[14] According to Becker, "To ask whether the natural rights philosophy of the Declaration of Independence is true or false is essentially a meaningless question."[15] The natural rights of the Declaration were better understood as "historic rights," rights that might be founded in "nature," but nature as defined by the particular customs, traditions, and experiences of discrete historical times.[16]

Becker was not alone in his political thinking. An entire generation of progressivist thinkers who accepted the same assumptions emerged in the late nineteenth and early twentieth centuries. Woodrow Wilson, John W. Burgess, Westel H. Willoughby, J. Allen Smith, Charles Beard, Henry Jones Ford, and Ramond G. Gettell, among other progressive scholars, challenged, explicitly or implicitly, the assumptions of the Declaration and the original constitutional order based on those assumptions.[17] As Dennis Mahoney's study of American political science and its flagship professional organization, the American Political Science Association, has concluded, "Rejection of the Declaration of Independence, of its teachings, and of its applicability to our own times, was a necessary part of the foundation of a new American political science."[18] The rejection of the Founders' understanding of natural rights and limited government was also the basis for progressivism's critique of the original constitutional order.

Modern progressivist political science was instrumental in providing the intellectual foundations for the modern regulatory state of Franklin Roosevelt's New Deal and Lyndon Johnson's Great Society. As Theodore Lowi remarked in *The End of Liberalism*, "The tie between the modern liberal state and political science parallels the older tie between the capitalist system and laissez-faire economics."[19] Modern American political science was based largely on the assumptions of the historicist tradition, rejecting the natural rights theory and limited-government objectives of classical liberals such as John Locke, Adam Smith, Montesquieu, William Blackstone, and the American Founders. Following their historicist predecessors, America's progressives sought to replace the Founders' natural rights philosophy and its derivative Constitution of limited government with a new "rational state." This rational state merged the political and the social, the public and the private, in a novel American regime of programmatic liberalism that charged government with resolving all social, economic, and political problems for which there was a constituency.[20]

Similar to the German historicists, twentieth-century progressives accepted that there were no absolute, transhistorical, or transcultural political principles. All political systems were culturally and historically contingent, dependent on the social circumstances and prejudices of their day. This condition was as true of the Founders' political philosophy and its offspring, the Constitution, as it was of any other thinking or forms of government. Once the Founders' natural rights were viewed as mere historical contingencies that could be dispatched as simple anachronisms—all rights thereafter becoming mere "positive" rights, as the legal realists would later affirm—the limited government of the Constitution, which derived from the Founders' natural rights, could also be dispatched on grounds that it had been historically eclipsed. If constitutional law were not to be laden by the dead hand of history, the Constitution needed to become a "living" document, adjusting and adapting to the historical imperatives of the day—

an idea that became a doctrine of constitutional interpretation for those who wanted to use the Constitution for their own political purposes. It was also a critical ideological presupposition the progressives would have to adopt if the Founders' Constitution of limited government and separated powers were to be abandoned.[21]

The new discipline of political science was methodologically rigorous and value-neutral. It was intended to be divorced from the "subjective" speculations of political philosophy, including the political philosophy of the Founders. Under the guidance of the progressives, modern political science would be "applied science," social science in service to the ever augmenting administrative state.[22]

Value-neutral social science was designed to emulate the objectivity of the natural sciences by remaining free of value judgments. Yet this value neutrality was precisely the Achilles heel of modern social science; it rendered it vulnerable to allegations of indiscriminateness and relativism because it could not offer guidance concerning the most important question political science must answer: What ends should political action pursue?

In *Natural Right and History*, Strauss emphasized that modern social science was based on the "fact/value" distinction—the idea that from no "is" could one derive an "ought." The social scientific faith in the fact/value distinction was predicated on the idea that values were subjective, originating in social custom or personal preference. Facts, by contrast, were objective. If modern social science were to be scientific, then it would have to eschew values in favor of facts. But if it did this, how could it provide any guidance to politics? In fact, how could it even claim to be scientific? Strauss remarked that "a social science that cannot speak of tyranny with the same confidence with which medicine speaks, for example, of cancer, cannot understand social phenomena as what they are. It is therefore not scientific. Present-day social science finds itself in this condition."[23]

Ironically, then, consumed as it is with questions of "method," modern social science is unscientific and can offer guidance only on matters of secondary importance. It offers up, in Strauss's words, "retail sanity" at the expense of "wholesale madness,"[24] anchoring the truth about "values" (or, more precisely, political *principles*) in whatever preferences dominate at the time. It denies the possibility of any rational grounds for political action, identifying reason with history and right with whatever is historically successful.

Right, in a word, becomes identified with might, truth with the exercise of political will.[25] Politics comes to be about power, about getting one's way.

This reduction of politics to machinations of power, and the historical relativism that underlies this reduction, have had significant political repercussions both for the VRA and for American politics more generally. They have also had repercussions for those who shape American public opinion. The assumption that all political principles are indigenous to their historical times and cultures is dominant among the retailers of ideas in America: the media, the entertainment industry, political elites, and, perhaps most important, those in the universities.[26] As Strauss's student Allan Bloom remarked in his 1987 bestseller, *The Closing of the American Mind*, the fundamental faith of today's social science professoriate is the denial that there are any "absolutes." Their credo is that "we should not be ethnocentric . . . . We should not think our way is better than others . . . . Indiscriminateness [has become] a moral imperative because its opposite is [deemed to be] discrimination."[27] Because we have no criteria that allow us to stand beyond particular cultures to assess their goodness or badness, justice or injustice, sensibility or outright silliness, the attempt to impose a single view of justice through the Declaration's principles of natural right is understood by today's multiculturalists as a form of cultural imperialism.

The anti-imperialist mantra of multiculturalism turns out, as it happens, not to be that multi nor that cultural.[28] Multicultural theory may welcome "diversity" in areas such as education and employment, but it defines diversity strictly in racial and ethnic terms; "culture" generally refers only to one's race or ethnicity. It does not, for instance, refer to religion. Multiculturalism also tends to deny the notion of a common culture, common civilization, or common good. To impose such a universal notion of good or culture would be "imperialistic."

In the multiculturalist view, America is not a nation of one people defined by common principles and acceptance of a common political culture. Rather, it is comprised of a series of particularities, subcultures that are more or less distinct and independent from one another. These subcultures deserve recognition—and, in the case of the VRA, representation—not because they are superior in Matthew Arnold's sense of the word "culture," representing "the best which has been thought and said in the world," but because they belong to a constituency.[29] The principal emphasis of multicultural policy is equity, not substance. Those things contributing to a group's identity—its customs, traditions, mores, political preferences, and so on—are worthy of formal recognition regardless of what their specific content might be.

Bloom remarked how the rejection of the principles of the Declaration—the rejection of "absolutes"—led to the glorification of the particular, and of minorities, as well as the abandonment of the Founders' Constitution. We see here the hallmarks of multicultural theory:

> Much of the intellectual machinery of twentieth-century American political thought and social science was constructed for the purposes of making an assault on [America's] majority. It treated the founding principles as impediments and tried to overcome the other strand of our political heritage, majoritarianism, in favor of a nation of minorities and groups each following its own beliefs and inclinations . . . .
>
> This reversal of the founding intention with respect to minorities is most striking. For the Founders, minorities are in general bad things, mostly identical to factions, selfish groups who have no concern as such for the common good. . . . In twentieth-century social science . . . the common good disappears and along with it the negative view of minorities. The very idea of majority—now understood to be selfish interest—is done away with in order to protect the minorities.[30]

The minority-rights revolution that was at the heart of the growing interest-group liberalism of the late 1960s had significant intellectual roots in late–twentieth-century social science, as Lowi suggested in *The End of Liberalism*.[31] The early twentieth-century critiques of American constitutionalism and its undemocratic nature by progressive scholars were followed by more refined commentary later in the century by social scientists such as Robert Dahl. Questioning not just the fairness of American constitutional process and electoral politics, as the progressives had, Dahl expressed misgivings about the very existence and legitimacy of majoritarian rule itself.[32]

"Majority rule," Dahl wrote, was "mostly a myth."[33] Looking behind the constitutional forms of most governments, he said, including American government, we find they were ruled by a minority or minorities. The Madisonian ideal of promoting the public good through deliberation and the Constitution's complex institutional process was mostly a fiction.

Dahl's political science, like most modern political science, understood politics behaviorally: Political actors were portrayed largely as stimulus-response mechanisms set on maximizing their own particular preferences or interests. Legislative initiatives, accordingly, reflected little more than those preferences or interests of the political actors who passed them. The real question for mature democracies was not so much how to attain the public good, which no one could agree on anyway. It was, rather, an issue of fairness or of inclusiveness, of who was going to be allowed to participate in the bargaining process that gave rise to legislation. The great advantage of democracy or "polyarchy," Dahl's much-publicized term, was that it extended "the number, size, and diversity of the minorities whose preferences will influence the outcome of governmental decisions."[34]

The behaviorist critique of Madisonian republicanism by Dahl and other academics would create an auspicious intellectual climate for the reapportionment revolution and, later, the multiculturalist approach to American republicanism institutionalized in initiatives such as the VRA. Like so much other commentary of its genre, the analysis by Dahl and the behaviorists reduced legislative deliberation to bargaining about preferences among disparate minorities.[35]

Five years after Dahl's well-received *Preface to Democratic Theory*, the *American Political Science Review* would publish an article claiming that the Constitution itself was a product of political compromise. The idea "that the Framers divided their time between philosophical discussions of government and reading the classics in political theory" was denounced as a "common rumor."[36] Federalism was described as "an improvisation which was later promoted into a political theory."[37] The Electoral College "was merely a jerry-rigged improvisation which has subsequently been endowed with a high theoretical content."[38] The *Federalist* itself was "probative evidence for only one proposition: that Hamilton and Madison were inspired propagandists with a genius for retrospective symmetry."[39]

Essays such as this cut the Constitution and its framers down to size. The Constitution was merely a consequence of, and instrument for, mediating contesting interests. In response to the query Alexander Hamilton posed in *Federalist* 1, "whether societies of men are really capable or not of establishing good government from reflection and choice, or whether they are forever destined to depend for their political constitutions on accident and force,"[40] the behaviorist critique affirmed that political constitutions and legislative outcomes were invariably the products of accidents—accidents of negotiation.

Multiculturalism and the Emergence of America's "Official Minorities"

Multicultural theory created the intellectual backdrop for the group rights and results-oriented jurisprudence that came to define modern civil rights policy. That policy would, in turn, fortify the new ideology of multiculturalism, giving it real practical expression and impetus. The recognition of groups' rights in federal civil rights policy would lead to a transformation in the meaning of equality and democratic process in American constitutionalism, in the direction of the politics of multiculturalism and away from the Founders' republicanism.

In the case of the VRA, the shift of focus from first- to second-generation voting rights that took place following the *Allen* decision in 1969 entailed a shift from individual to group or collective rights, from a universally applicable nondiscrimination norm to a redistributionist program focused on alleviating the disadvantage of designated groups. As well-intentioned as this change was, it had important implications both for the rule of law and for the administration of the VRA. When equality is defined in group terms and civil rights are characterized as correctives for social, historical, and political disadvantage, respecting the rule of law becomes difficult because individual rights are not absolute but qualified, dependent on the groups to which one belongs rather than attached to all individuals equally. As Edward Erler has observed:

> There is no way to say that rights belong to classes without discarding the notion that the first object of civil society is the equal protection of equal rights. If rights belong to classes and not to individuals, then equal protection of the laws is impossible.

> Class considerations abstract from the individual and ascribe to him class characteristics that are different—and necessarily unequal—from those of individuals outside the class. Class claims are claims of inequality, not equality.[41]

The process of abstraction to which Erler refers is problematic because it treats individuals as parts of a class. In addition, the very process of abstracting to make classwide generalizations may itself be the product of orthodoxy rather than any concrete reality. In disputes over collective rights, not only is the rule of law undermined; the evidentiary aspects of judicial process also become much more complicated. Legal scholars have pointed out that group rights are much more difficult to vindicate than individual rights because they involve generalizations about social and political phenomena that usually involve thousands, sometimes even millions, of individuals presumed to belong to distinct classes.

Such controversies will center on what Donald Horowitz has referred to as "social facts" as opposed to "adjudicative facts." Adjudicative facts are those facts that courts and the rules of evidence were traditionally designed to address: events that have transpired between individual parties to litigation—who did what to whom, when, and where. As much as adjudicative facts are not always easy to establish in a court of law, they are much easier to establish than social facts, which involve assessing broad patterns of social and political behavior.[42] In cases involving social facts, the "rights" of claimants will generally depend more on approximation and imprecision than on fixed principles of law.[43]

Because courts do not have the institutional capacity to assess questions of social policy very accurately, they are vulnerable to deciding such matters more on the basis of fashionable or orthodox opinion than on the basis of hard evidence, especially if success in such litigation depends on the identification of individual status with group status and the establishment of group disadvantage independent of the legal classification being challenged. This latter stage is where the judicial process is particularly ripe for the introduction of the sort of multiculturalist orthodoxy that divides America into simple binary categories: oppressors and oppressed, victimizers and victimized, or, to use the arcane language of deconstructionist theory, Hegemon and Other (Hegemon here referring to majoritarian oppressors, usually white, Anglo males, and the Other referring to racial minorities and sometimes women).[44]

Multicultural orthodoxy has been at the center of the dispute over which groups should enjoy special dispensations in civil rights policy and which groups should not. Once the original civil rights vision of individual rights and equal opportunity was jettisoned in the late 1960s in favor of a new results-oriented approach devoted to collective rights and group-balancing, the question of which victim groups should enjoy special dispensations in civil rights policy became the next step in the process. In the case of the VRA, the legacy of slavery and black disfranchisement in the South—the latter remaining stark even into the 1960s—made the case for the original act easy to defend both as a matter of principle and of law. But the 1975 VRA, which recognized America's other "official minorities"— Hispanics, Asian Americans, and Native Americans—as protected language groups under the act was much more controversial (as we will see in chapter 4). The original VRA protected all individuals equally on a nondiscriminatory basis. By contrast, second-generation voting rights limited VRA protections to only a handful of ethnoracial groups.

Critics of the 1975 VRA asked what nonarbitrary criterion of demarcation was used to distinguish between those groups deserving special dispensations under the 1975 act and those groups that were not. Such questioning was standard fare with all race-preference affirmative action policy. Once such policy moved beyond providing special protections to blacks, the central question became which groups should count for those special dispensations. Yet even liberal Supreme Court justices, such as John Paul Stevens, had trouble identifying the conditions of Hispanics, Asian Americans, and Native Americans with the plight of black America in affirmative action policy. Stevens's opinion in *Fullilove v. Klutznick* (1980)[45] is instructive in this regard because it addressed the practical, legal, and moral issues involved with such policy.

In *Fullilove* the Court considered an equal protection challenge from nonminority construction contractors in New York who claimed that the 1977 federal Public Works Employment Act (PWEA) had unconstitutionally excluded them from government contracts. The act required that a set-aside of at least 10 percent of federal funds spent on local public works projects be granted to minority-owned businesses. These were defined as businesses owned by "citizens of the United States who are Negroes, Spanish-speaking, Orientals, Indians, Eskimos, and Aleuts."[46] A majority of the Court upheld the set-aside on grounds that Congress had the constitutional authority to impose such a program under article 1, the Fifth Amendment, or the Fourteenth Amendment. Justice Stevens disagreed with the Court's assessment and lodged a pointed dissent. His principal complaint was that insufficient congressional consideration had been given to the set-aside, as well as to the identity of the classes that were provided special protections under the act. "Racial classifications," he wrote,

> are simply too pernicious to permit any but the most exact connection between justification and classification. Quite obviously, the history of discrimination against black citizens in America cannot justify a grant of privileges to Eskimos or Indians.
>
> Even if we assume that each of the six racial subclasses has suffered its own special injury at some time in our history, surely it does not follow that each of those subclasses suffered harm of identical magnitude. Although "the Negro was dragged to this country in chains to be sold in slavery," the "Spanish-speaking" subclass came voluntarily, frequently without invitation, and the Indians, the Eskimos and the Aleuts had an opportunity to exploit America's resources before the ancestors of most American citizens arrived. There is no reason to assume, and nothing in the legislative history suggests, much less demonstrates, that each of the subclasses is equally entitled to reparations from the United States Government.[47]

Stevens's attempts at historiography and sociology may have seemed dilettantish, perhaps pointing up the unseemliness of federal judges acting as amateur sociologists in affirmative action disputes, but his point was nevertheless clear: Some sort of multicultural theory was at work with the PWEA, a race-centric theory that had deconstructed America into the binary world of racial oppressor and racially oppressed. Portraying American society in such simple dichotomous terms, the PWEA had indiscriminately drawn a parallel between the history of blacks and other ethnoracial groups who were provided a preference under the act. Stevens concluded: "Although I do not dispute the validity of the assumption that each of the subclasses identified in the Act has suffered a severe wrong at some time in the past, I cannot accept this slapdash statute as a legitimate method of providing classwide relief."[48] The difficult question here, of course, was whether any legislation attempting to provide class-wide relief, such as the PWEA or the VRA, could be applied in anything but a slapdash fashion.

The enormity of the evidentiary considerations tasked to courts that must assess collective rights leaves them exposed to the sort of multiculturalist orthodoxy alluded to by Justice Stevens in *Fullilove*. Courts simply cannot assess the claims of entire racial groups in American society on the basis of anything resembling evidentiary precision. Rather, speculation and guesswork will form the substance of what courts do in such cases.

Yet not just courts are prone to this multiculturalist orthodoxy. Civil rights scholars have pointed to a similar type of multiculturalist orthodoxy that has formed the basis for the recognition in federal law of those "official minorities" beyond blacks who have received special dispensations in affirmative action policy: Hispanics, Asian Americans, and Native Americans. In his extensive historical study of the evolution of Title VII of the Civil Rights Act of 1964, Herman Belz observed that

> blacks were *the* prototype for the proliferating assertions of group rights that in the 1970s and 1980s introduced a debilitating factionalism into American politics and government. As the original "discrete and insular minority," to use the language of constitutional law, blacks' claim to preferential treatment based on the collective victimization of slavery has become politically entrenched, making reform of contemporary minority group factionalism all the more difficult.[49]

Belz's analysis traced the emergence of race preferences in affirmative action policies, such as the VRA, to a multiculturalist civil rights orthodoxy similar to that alluded to by Justice Stevens in *Fullilove*. As the passage above indicates, Belz stressed the importance of theory and the emergence of the black "prototype" for other forms of group rights in American law. So, too, have such scholars as John Skrentny, Hugh Davis Graham, and Terry

Eastland.[50] In *The Minority Rights Revolution*, for instance, Skrentny emphasized that "After advocates for black Americans helped break the taboo on targeting policies at disadvantaged groups, government officials quickly categorized some groups as 'minorities'—a never defined term that basically meant 'analogous to blacks.' These classifications were *not* based on study, but on simple, unexamined prototypes of groups."[51]

The simple racial prototype, which the evidence in the historical studies above suggests was decisive for both the emergence of group rights and the limitation of these rights to only a handful of official minorities, is again consistent with multicultural theory and its propensity to generalize racial characteristics across a host of distinct groupings, many of which have little, if anything, to do with race.[52] This prototype is also consistent with the transposition of the progressivist class-conflict model of American politics that signified the transition from the economic regulatory state of the progressive and New Deal eras to the social and racial regulatory state of the Great Society and beyond.[53]

Today we continue to live in the era of multiculturalist orthodoxy. In the case of the VRA, that orthodoxy would be introduced with the *Allen* decision of 1969 and its recognition under the VRA of a right to effective racial representation. The epistemological foundations for that right, however, would first be asserted in the reapportionment cases, in which we would find most forcefully articulated the new rationalist ethos in judicial politics that assumed the judiciary could resolve complicated questions of representational "fairness." When this ethos was married to the politics of multiculturalism in second-generation voting rights, the stage would be set for a confrontation between Madisonian republicanism, with its defense of private rights and a constitutional theory devoted to limited government and the public good, and the politics of multiculturalism, which was prepared to qualify individual rights in the name of racial-group balancing and a legislative regime of virtually unlimited powers.

3

The Reapportionment Cases and the Origins of Judicial Rationalism

The Supreme Court's judicial rationalism received its single most significant boost in *Baker v. Carr* (1962),[1] where the Court held for the first time that a challenge to a state apportionment statute—here Tennessee's—was not a political question (best left to the political branches of government to decide), and was therefore appropriate for judicial review. Marking the Court's first foray into the politics of reapportionment, *Baker* would significantly expand the meaning of the equal protection clause of the Fourteenth Amendment by applying it to questions of representation. Equally important, *Baker* marked an unprecedented intellectual turn on the part of the Court, one that exhibited a bold new confidence on the part of its members that they could answer constitutional questions that earlier courts did not believe they had the legal authority or institutional capacity to answer.

The concern for fair and effective representation that was first raised in the reapportionment cases would lead to more exacting and contentious questions concerning race and representation under the VRA. As Robert Dixon has noted in his seminal study of the subject, the reapportionment cases invited fresh analyses of bicameralism; federalism; the separation of powers; systems of districting and alternative forms of voting; the geographic, institutional, and population bases of the American party system; and those conditions necessary to maintaining its two-party format. Above all, they invited scrutiny of those mechanisms used to temper majoritarian rule with deliberation and consensus through the use of nonmajoritarian principles of representation. The judicial reassessment of political power that the reapportionment cases entailed involved not merely legislative or even judicial acts, but also *constitutive* acts, restructuring American government at its core and setting the stage for many of the issues the Court would have to address in its interpretation of the VRA.[2]

Baker v. Carr and the Reapportionment Cases

Many legal and political commentators have observed that 1937 marked the beginning of a new era in Supreme Court jurisprudence. The Court halted its assault on Franklin Roosevelt's New Deal policies and turned its attention to political liberties and, later, civil rights.[3] The reapportionment cases were of a piece with this transformation in judicial policymaking, representing one-half of a two-pronged attack by the Court on state voting practices. The other half involved black voting rights.[4]

Following the Civil War, the Supreme Court had handicapped the federal government's efforts at securing and maintaining the black franchise in the South by restrictively interpreting the Privileges or Immunities Clause of the Fourteenth Amendment,[5] gutting the provisions of the federal Enforcement Act of 1870,[6] and later affirming the "state action" doctrine— the constitutional principle that civil rights protections guaranteed in the Fourteenth Amendment could not "be impaired by the wrongful acts of [private] individuals."[7] Strictly speaking, the state action doctrine was based on constitutional text and principles of limited government, but it impeded efforts to secure black voting rights because many of the obstacles to those rights, such as political parties, were deemed to be "private" entities.

Prospects for the black franchise had not improved much by the turn of the century. Literacy tests, which required voters to demonstrate they could read and had the political knowledge necessary to vote, were a primary obstacle to blacks' exercising the right to vote. Mississippi's literacy test was upheld in 1898,[8] as was Alabama's in 1903,[9] although in both cases the Supreme Court suggested that had the facts been different, demonstrating explicit, discriminatory application of the tests at issue, the results would have been different.[10]

In the mid-twentieth century the tide began to turn for black voters. The southern literacy test, which V. O. Key described in 1949 as "a fraud and nothing more,"[11] was upheld as late as 1959[12] but would eventually be laid to rest by the VRA.[13] The poll tax, levied as a requirement for voting and considered by many to affect minorities most adversely, had originally received the imprimatur of the Court in *Breedlove v. Suttles* (1937)[14] but would be overturned by the Twenty-fourth Amendment, which made poll taxes illegal in federal elections and primaries. *Harper v. Virginia State Board of Elections* (1966)[15] would make poll taxes illegal in state elections, thus further nationalizing election law standards.[16]

The most flagrant device used to keep blacks out of the electoral process in the twentieth century was the "white primary," the southern Democratic primary that was restricted to white voters. Although the white primary would survive an original challenge in 1921,[17] it would eventually be found to violate the Fifteenth Amendment in *Smith v. Allwright* (1944)[18] and *Terry v. Adams* (1953).[19] Seven years after *Terry*, in *Gomillion v. Lightfoot* (1960),[20] the Court would hold that a racial gerrymander in Tuskegee, Alabama, in which almost all of the city's four hundred black voters and no whites had been excluded from the city's redefined boundaries, similarly violated the provisions of the Fifteenth Amendment.

The black voting rights disputes provided an important impetus for the reapportionment cases. They also added legitimacy to the Court's role as an institution of national reconciliation. By the mid-1950s, southern intransigence to black constitutional rights had become increasingly notorious. Segregation and discrimination against blacks had become a national scandal and international embarrassment.[21] The South's largely unfavorable response to *Brown v. Board of Education* (1954),[22] along with mounting pressure from members of Congress, academics, and the civil rights community, helped lead to the passage of the Civil Rights Act in 1957, 1960, and 1964, as well as the VRA.

Carrying with it the momentum of national disaffection with voting inequality of all forms, the Court rendered its decision in *Baker v. Carr* in 1962 against a backdrop of remedial action taken to improve the condition of voting rights in the South. But the question then, as it remains, was how the representational inequality that the Court alleged was at issue in *Baker* could be identified with earlier voting inequality cases, particularly the black voting rights disputes of the previous decades. At issue in those disputes was the right to vote—the ability of black citizens to cast a ballot. What was involved in *Baker* was the qualitatively distinct question of what specific forms of representation the Constitution required.

Baker involved a dispute between Tennessee voters in three metropolitan areas (Memphis, Knoxville, and Nashville) and Joe Carr, Tennessee's secretary of state. The voters accused Carr of having failed to reapportion the Tennessee assembly districts in accordance with state and federal law since 1901. The most important part of the plaintiffs' pleadings would be the allegation that Tennessee's omission to act was a violation of the equal protection clause of the Fourteenth Amendment.

In *Baker* the Court challenged the proposition put forth by Justice Frankfurter sixteen years earlier in *Colgreve v. Green* that the federal judiciary should not get involved in congressional reapportionment disputes because they were political in nature.[23] Questions of reapportionment, the majority in *Baker* demurred, were not, in fact, political questions and could be readily addressed through judicial review.

The lengthiest part of the Court's opinion, written by Justice William Brennan, addressed the question of justiciability—of what the Court could do to remedy the problem raised by the plaintiffs. Brennan revisited *Luther v. Borden* (1849),[24] a key constitutional dispute in which the defendant had disputed the constitutional authority of the standing government in the state of Rhode Island, claiming that it was illegitimate because it had been established by a colonial charter dating back to 1663 and did not enjoy the support of the people. At issue in *Luther* was the meaning of article 4, section 4 of the Constitution (the guarantee clause), which provides that the "United States shall guarantee to every State in this Union a Republican Form of Government."

Writing for the Court in *Luther*, Chief Justice Roger Taney rejected the defendant's reasoning, arguing that what constituted a republican form of government was a political question that only Congress or the president could resolve. A court had no adequate criteria to determine whether a government was republican in form.[25] Brennan interpreted Taney's opinion to apply primarily to separation-of-powers issues—that is, to the inappropriate injection of the federal judiciary into disputes that were best resolved by the congressional or executive branches of the federal government. The doctrine did not apply to questions of federalism—that is, to disputes involving questions concerning "the consistency of state action with the Federal Constitution"—which was at issue in *Baker*.[26]

Although critics of *Baker* claimed the plaintiffs' action was just a guarantee clause claim masquerading as an equal protection action, Brennan insisted that the two provisions were distinct:

> Judicial standards under the Equal Protection Clause are well developed and familiar, and it has been open to courts since the enactment of the Fourteenth Amendment to determine, if on particular facts they must, that a discrimination reflects *no* policy, but simply arbitrary and capricious action.[27]

Justice Frankfurter, dissenting in *Baker*, contended that the majority had confused the issues. *Colgrove v. Green* had conclusively settled that reapportionment disputes were political questions that the judiciary had no business attempting to resolve.[28] To suggest, as the Court did in *Baker*, that such questions could be resolved under the pretext of the equal protection clause was simply to change the legal vehicle through which the Court sought to address the same intractable questions. The difficulty, regardless of which constitutional provision was used, was that no nonarbitrary standards existed that a court could use to measure a constitutional violation in a reapportionment dispute such as the one at issue in *Baker*. The plaintiffs in *Baker* had asserted that "representation ought to be proportionate to the population," and that this notion was the "standard by reference to which the reasonableness of apportionment plans may be judged." But Frankfurter objected:

> To find such a political conception legally enforceable in the broad and unspecific guarantee of equal protection is to rewrite the Constitution . . . . The notion that representation proportionate to the geographic spread of population is so universally accepted as a necessary element of equality between man and man that it must be taken to be the standard of a political equality preserved by the Fourteenth Amendment . . . is, to put it bluntly, not true. . . . It was not the English system, it was not the colonial system, it was not the system chosen for the national government by the Constitution, it was not the system exclusively or even predominantly practiced by the States at the

time of adoption of the Fourteenth Amendment, it is not predominantly practiced by the states today. Unless judges, the
judges of this Court, are to make their private views of political
wisdom the measure of the Constitution—views which in all
honesty cannot but give the appearance, if not reflect the reality,
of involvement with the business of partisan politics so
inescapably a part of apportionment controversies—the
Fourteenth Amendment . . . provides no guide for judicial oversight of the representation problem.[29]

To select a system of proportional representation, as the plaintiffs proposed
in *Baker*, would commit the Court to a political decision because it would
require it to decide without constitutional warrant which criteria should
count in redistricting disputes and which should not. Deciding which to
prefer over others was a question of democratic theory, Frankfurter proclaimed, not constitutional law.[30]

Dispute over the meaning of the Constitution and its relationship to
questions of redistricting would continue in *Wesberry v. Sanders* (1964).[31]
At issue was Georgia's Fifth Congressional District, which, it was claimed,
diluted the plaintiffs' votes. According to 1960 census figures, the Fifth
Congressional District was two times the size of the average congressional
district in Georgia. The plaintiffs, all of whom resided in the Fifth District,
claimed that the district violated various provisions of the Constitution, the
most important of which was article 1, section 2, which provides that "the
House of Representatives shall be composed of Members chosen every
second Year by the People of the several States."

Justice Hugo Black, writing for the majority in *Wesberry*, interpreted the
Constitution's words "by the People of the several States" to mean "that as
nearly as is practicable one man's vote in a congressional election is to
be worth as much as another's."[32] The Constitutional Convention, Black
argued, had made clear that, in Madison's words, congressional power
would have to be "immediately derived from the people, in proportion to
their numbers."[33] The Great Compromise, which created a bicameral
legislative body for the United States, had also "solemnly embodied" the
principle of "equal representation in the House for equal numbers of people."[34] In *Federalist* 57, Madison had highlighted that classifications of

citizens that unnecessarily abridged the right to vote would have no place under the new constitutional arrangement. He queried,

> Who are to be the electors of the Federal Representatives? Not the rich more than the poor; not the learned more than the ignorant; not the haughty heirs of distinguished names, more than the humble sons of obscure and unpropitious fortune. The electors are to be the great body of the people of the United States.[35]

According to Black, "Readers surely could have fairly taken this to mean, 'one person, one vote.'"[36]

Justice John Harlan begged to differ. Noting that the Court's decision impugned the validity of 398 congressional districts from thirty-seven states,[37] Harlan lampooned Black's opinion for its superficial and misleading interpretation of the Constitution and its history. Nothing in any of the comments referred to, wrote Harlan, suggested even remotely that the Constitution required a specific form of apportionment *within* the states, as the Court was suggesting. Discussion of the Great Compromise between large and small states at the Constitutional Convention, which centered on the representation of states in Congress, never suggested that what was at issue was *intra*state redistricting.[38] To the contrary, both the record of the convention and *The Federalist* made clear that the states enjoyed plenary power over the selection of congressmen once they had been apportioned among the states, save solely for the supervisory power of Congress itself.[39]

When one considered the text of article 1, Harlan contended, the case against the majority's proposition that "equal representation in the House for equal numbers of people" was "solemnly embodied" in the article was even more compelling. Article 1, section 2, for instance, provided that "each State shall have at Least one Representative." This provision alone implied unequally weighted votes because voters in sparsely populated states would have votes that were worth more than the votes cast by voters in more densely populated states. The "three-fifths compromise" similarly implied unequally weighted votes. Article 1 provided that members of Congress were to be apportioned among the states on the basis of free persons and three-fifths of the slave population. Because blacks had no right to vote in any of the slave states, clearly the basis of apportionment set out in the

Constitution would give voters in those states representation well beyond their voting populations. As Harlan surmised, when considering the provisions of the Constitution relevant to the plaintiffs' complaint—article 1, sections 2, 4, and 5—it was clear

1. that congressional Representatives are to be apportioned among the several states largely, but not entirely, according to population;

2. that the States have plenary power to select their allotted Representatives in accordance with any method of popular election they please, subject only to the supervisory power of Congress; and

3. that the supervisory power of Congress is exclusive.[40]

By arrogating to itself the right to determine issues of congressional reapportionment, Harlan concluded, the Court had contravened the constitutional separation of powers in addition to principles of federalism.[41]

The third and final case that would solidify the extent to which the Court was prepared to take the new rationalism of its reapportionment rulings was *Reynolds v. Sims* (1964).[42] *Reynolds* was the principal decision of six reapportionment cases released concurrently in June 1964 that would overturn legislative apportionment statutes in Alabama, New York, Maryland, Delaware, Virginia, and Colorado.[43] *Reynolds* itself involved an equal protection challenge to Alabama's legislative redistricting. At the time the litigation started, the state had not redistricted in more than sixty years. According to 1960 census figures, a majority of the state's senate seats consisted of a mere 25.1 percent of the state's total population. A majority of the state's house seats consisted of only 25.7 percent of the population. Population variance ratios were as high as 41 to 1 in the senate and 16 to 1 in the house. The Court further pointed out that no effective malapportionment remedy was available to the plaintiffs in *Reynolds* save for the litigation at hand.[44]

In an opinion written by Chief Justice Earl Warren, the Court held that the equal protection clause required seats in both houses of a bicameral state legislature to be apportioned on an equal-population basis.[45] The basic purpose of legislative apportionment, Warren wrote, was the "achieving of fair and effective representation for all citizens."[46] Every citizen had "an inalienable right to full and effective participation in the political processes of his State's legislative bodies," a right, in effect, to "an equally effective voice in the election of members of his state legislature."[47] Equally important, Warren rejected the "federal analogy" argument advanced by Alabama and other defendant jurisdictions. Since the federal Constitution provided representation in the Senate on the basis of geographic units of representation rather than population, states in the *Reynolds* cases had pleaded that they should be permitted the same freedom to structure their governments on the basis of similar countermajoritarian principles.

These pleas were to no avail. Relying on evidence that thirty-six state constitutions had originally provided that both houses of their legislatures would be based entirely or predominantly on population, Warren rejected the defendants' submissions. The reliance on the federal analogy was often just an "after-the-fact rationalization" for malapportionment.[48]

The *Reynolds* ruling rendered unconstitutional at least one legislative chamber in every state of the Union and in most states both.[49] Although in some states, such as Alabama, this decision effectively remedied some egregious cases of malapportionment, in other cases the outcome was quite different. In *Lucas v. Forty-Fourth General Assembly of the State of Colorado* (1964), one of *Reynolds's* companion cases, for instance, the Court would impose equally populated districts on both houses of Colorado's legislature despite a popular referendum supported by a majority of voters in every county of the state that had recently rejected such a plan.[50] The *Lucas* decision illustrated the categorical logic of equal protection law once the Court in *Reynolds* decided that the rights protected under the equal protection clause mandated equally populated electoral districts. Having committed itself to this formulation, the Court could not apply one equal protection principle to one house of the legislature and a different principle to the other.[51]

As he had done in *Baker* and *Wesberry*, Justice Harlan once again objected to the Court's textual and historical analysis in *Reynolds*. The equal protection clause, he contended, had nothing to do with the right to vote or questions of representation. The Court had confused the civil rights protected in section 1 of the Fourteenth Amendment (where the equal protection clause is located), with the political rights referred to in the second section of the Fourteenth Amendment and later the Fifteenth and Nineteenth Amendments. If the Thirty-ninth Congress—which drafted the Fourteenth Amendment—had intended to cover the right to vote, a political right, under any of the clauses of section 1 of the Fourteenth Amendment, it would have been redundant to specify this right in later amendments to the Constitution, as the Court had indicated almost ninety years earlier in *Minor v. Happersett* (1875).[52] Moreover, by virtue of the language of the second section of the Fourteenth Amendment, the states clearly retained an original control over electoral procedures and practices and were free to structure their governments on the basis of any republican forms they desired.[53]

Warren's opinion in *Reynolds*, however, as controversial as it was, won the day in the Court's subsequent jurisprudence and left Justice Harlan in virtual isolation on the reapportionment issue in every representational rights case to follow. What remained to be seen was how stringently the Court would apply the one person, one vote ruling and what electoral practices would be affected.

Rationalizing the Electoral Process after *Wesberry* and *Reynolds*

Finding a right to effective representation under the equal protection clause as the Court did in *Reynolds* would introduce a host of problems into equal protection litigation. Not the least of these was the apparent conflict between the individual rights guaranteed by the laws of equal protection and the group rights implied by the idea of effective representation.

In *Baker v. Carr*, Justice Frankfurter had refused to accept that the right claimed by the plaintiffs for a "proportionate share of political influence" was an individual right, a "private, less impersonal claim."[54] Such a share of political influence could only make sense in the context of political groups. Because the plaintiffs did not constitute members of a clearly identifiable political group, their claims were "hypothetical . . . resting on abstract assumptions." But the claims "foreshadow[ed] deeper and more pervasive difficulties,"[55] such as when more identifiable groups—racial groups, for instance—might make similar claims.[56]

Following *Reynolds*, the Court had to reconcile the twin and arguably contradictory requirements of one person, one vote with the principle of fair and effective representation, a principle that might require voters to be treated unequally if political balance were to be achieved in the political process. The Court also had to determine what burden of proof it would require in vote-dilution claims. Would it require evidence of invidious or intentional discrimination by public officials—the traditional standard in equal protection disputes—or would electoral schemes that inadvertently or unintentionally diluted citizens' votes also be subject to constitutional review? The Court addressed these issues in *Fortson v. Dorsey* (1965)[57] and *Burns v. Richardson* (1966),[58] two cases that followed closely on the heels of *Reynolds v. Sims*.

In *Fortson*, the Court was asked to review countywide voting in seven multimember districts containing twenty-one of Georgia's fifty-four senatorial seats. The plaintiffs had claimed that the Georgia senate plan created two classes of voters, those who resided in single-member districts and those who resided in multimember districts (districts in which voters voted for more than one representative). A three-judge federal district court had agreed with the plaintiffs' claim that electors in one area of a multimember district might defeat the preferred candidate of electors in another area, leaving the latter voters without a candidate of their choice—representation they might otherwise have enjoyed had their multimember district been divided into smaller, single-member districts. The Georgia plan amounted to "invidious discrimination."[59]

The Supreme Court, speaking through Justice Brennan, found otherwise. There was "no mathematical disparity" between the two classes of voters and thus no constitutional claim.[60] Although electors in multimember districts were not necessarily in the exact same position as electors in single-member districts, one could not say their votes were "not 'approximately equal in weight to that of any other citizen in the State.'"[61] As a result, no actionable discrimination occurred. But Justice Brennan immediately qualified:

> It might well be that designedly or otherwise, a multimember constituency apportionment scheme, under the circumstances of a particular case, would operate to minimize or cancel out

the voting strength of racial or political elements of the voting population.[62]

Multimember districts were not unconstitutional per se. But they might be. What exactly did Brennan mean by this statement?

If a multimember districting scheme might dilute votes "designedly *or otherwise*," were electoral practices that accidentally or unintentionally diluted citizens' votes now actionable under the equal protection clause just as those that intended to do so were? Justice Harlan filed a lone concurring opinion. He agreed with the Court's judgment but expressed concern about its language, which "might be taken to mean that the constitutionality of state legislative apportionments must, in the last analysis, always be judged in terms of simple arithmetic."[63] If intent did not have to be established in vote-dilution claims, as Brennan seemed to intimate, was he proposing a right to roughly proportional representation anywhere "racial or political elements of the voting population" might have their votes debased or diluted by multimember districts? When, precisely, were multimember districts discriminatory?

The Court returned to this issue in *Burns v. Richardson* (1966). In *Burns*, the plaintiffs challenged Hawaii's multimember senate districts, as well as its practice of using registered voters instead of population as the basis for districting. Acknowledging the *Reynolds* dictum that "legislative reapportionment is primarily a matter of legislative consideration and determination," not judicial prerogative,[64] Justice Brennan, again writing for the Court, upheld both Hawaii's multimember districts and its use of registered voters as the baseline for districting.[65]

Brennan's decision was a victory for advocates of judicial restraint in reapportionment, but, as in *Fortson*, the *Burns* ruling was again made with the proviso that if the *Fortson* test were met—a multimember apportionment scheme operating "to minimize or cancel out the voting strength of racial or political elements of the voting population"—single-member districts would likely be mandated.[66] Brennan also left the "intent" issue unclarified, suggesting in one instance that "invidious discrimination" would be actionable and in another place that "invidious effect" might, as well—that districting that had the effect of diluting a group's votes would not be immune to judicial oversight. Brennan further qualified that conjecture would be insufficient to establish a claim undermining a multi-member districting scheme: "Speculations do not supply evidence that the multi-member districting was designed to have *or had the invidious effect necessary to a judgment of the unconstitutionality of the districting.*"[67]

Again, what did Brennan's disjunctive language mean? Was he implying that invidious intent did not have to be proved to succeed in a vote-dilution claim, that proof of "invidious effect" or "invidious result" (as he also referred to it) was sufficient?[68] If mere "effects" or "results" were not a sufficient condition for a constitutional violation under the equal protection clause, why did the Court keep framing the vote-dilution problem in these alternatives? Under what specific circumstances would multimember districts contravene the provisions of equal protection? The Court never answered this question. And, as we will see in chapter 5, its failure to do so would generate confusion both in Congress and on the Court regarding what equal protection standards applied in the case of claims of vote dilution.

Initially, the Court refrained from applying the equal-population districting principle to local elections following the early reapportionment decisions. Later, however, it would require compliance with the rule by all local governments whose activity was sufficiently "legislative" in character.[69] Generally, the Court tended to take a more deferential posture toward both local and state redistricting than it would toward congressional redistricting. In a series of decisions beginning with *Kirkpatrick v. Preisler* (1969)[70] and *Wells v. Rockefeller* (1969),[71] the Court emphasized that under the provisions of article 1, section 2, the requirement that states create equipopulous congressional districts allowed for only those limited population variances that were "unavoidable despite a good-faith effort to achieve absolute equality, or for which justification is shown."[72]

In *Karcher v. Daggett* (1983), the Court reaffirmed this holding, emphasizing that there was no minimum threshold for avoidable population variances below which states would not have to meet the test established in *Kirkpatrick*.[73] In *Karcher*, the Court rejected the appellants' (defendants') theory that the inevitable statistical imprecisions of the census justified the population variances, in this case a disparity of 0.6984 percent between the largest and smallest congressional districts in New Jersey.[74] In 2001, a federal district court, relying on *Karcher*, threw out a redistricting map drawn by Pennsylvania's governing Republicans, in which the disparity between the largest and smallest congressional districts (exceeding 645,000 residents) was a mere 19 people. The court did this at the insistence of the Democrats, who had offered a plan in which the deviation had been reduced to a single person.[75]

Setting the Stage for the Voting Rights Act

The congressional redistricting cases, and in particular *Karcher v. Daggett*, symbolize, perhaps to the point of caricature, the Court's identification of equal population with equal representation. As Justice Byron White proclaimed in *Karcher*, one would have to "suspend credulity to believe that the Court's draconian response to a trifling 0.6984% maximum deviation promotes 'fair and effective representation' for the people of New Jersey."[76] Yet in a sense this inference was the necessary conclusion of the Court's one person, one vote decisions once geographic, economic, and political considerations were factored out of the reapportionment calculus. The Court's judicial rationalism had worked pure the reapportionment mandate. The Court had adopted the one person, one vote standard because it was justiciable—because it provided a simple, judicially measurable standard of "fair" representation. Yet *Karcher* revealed that even one person, one vote could not provide effective representation unless it was adhered to so strictly as to be absurd.

The reapportionment decisions epitomized a new era in American constitutional law, not merely because they conferred on courts judicial powers never before possessed, but also because their underlying presumption was that the judiciary had the intellectual wherewithal to rationally reconstruct America's republican institutions with a view to achieving greater political "fairness." By extending the meaning of vote discrimination from prohibitions on the franchise to prohibitions on electoral procedures that diluted or debased votes, *Baker v. Carr* marked the beginning of a judicial struggle to define the meaning of a vote that counted. In the wake of Justice Brennan's majority opinion in *Baker*, courts would have to answer all the hallmark questions that have come to define the voting rights debate: What exactly was a vote that counted? When did votes become diluted or debased? Could political influence be calculated, tallied up, and then evenly divided among all of a state's voters?[77] If mathematical exactitude were not required in redistricting plans, as Justice Douglas indicated in *Baker* and as the Court would later reaffirm in *Reynolds v. Sims*,[78] how much deviation from equipopulous districts would the Court tolerate? And what would be the nonarbitrary measure for such toleration? The intractability of the complex political questions that arose after *Baker* spoke to the enormity of the task the Court had taken on in 1962. As Robert Dixon noted in 1968, *Baker v. Carr* made Frankfurter's touchstone in *Colgrove v. Green* an epitaph: "Courts not only entered the [political] thicket, they proceeded to occupy it."[79]

Yet if the identification of "equal numbers of people" with "equal representation" in the reapportionment cases had smoothed over the complexities of America's republican form of government largely by ignoring them, it was equally true that the cases originated from a palpable concern for what was no doubt an unseemly aspect of American republicanism: grossly disproportionate electoral districts. Proponents of reapportionment reform saw judicial action as a vehicle of reckoning, the only effective means of throwing off the "rural strangle hold"[80] or "legislative straight jacket"[81] (to use the Court's terms) that had been imposed by derelict state legislatures.

Following the reapportionment decisions, it was hoped that state and federal legislators would no longer be able to ignore such pressing urban problems as the need for improved housing, increased employment, and education reform. Welfare-state programs were seen to be the great promise of these decisions, the means of addressing the neglected needs not only of America's urban minorities but of popular, predominantly urban, majorities as well. In the arena of political advocacy, those who favored the reapportionment cases tended to be urban advocates of modern programmatic liberalism who saw them as the precondition for the modern regulatory state.

On the other side, those who opposed the cases tended to be the more conservative rural constituencies who frequently loathed the potentially unlimited government that the new reformist vision of American liberalism sought to impose. The Kennedy administration epitomized the advocacy of the programmatic liberals. Its position in the reapportionment cases was succinctly summarized in its *Baker* brief: "Legislatures have, in very large part, failed to adapt themselves to modern problems, and majority needs and this failure has resulted in public cynicism, disillusionment and loss of confidence."[82] Seeking to displace such public cynicism and disillusionment, the Court in the reapportionment cases sought to clarify the lines of responsibility in state and local government to the point where failures to carry out legislative programs could be attributed more directly to defects in the *political* process rather than to *institutional* defects virtually guaranteed by grossly malapportioned electoral districts.[83]

The one person, one vote decisions may no longer occupy much of the Court's attention, enjoying widespread acceptance throughout the country despite an inauspicious beginning;[84] but the effects of the decisions can still be seen working their way through America's political institutions, if perhaps in ways unanticipated by those who initiated them. If the Court had stopped its judicial activism in the name of political "fairness" at the reapportionment decisions' "one person, one vote" mandate, much of the Founders' republicanism and its ideal of individual voting rights could likely have remained intact. Such an objective, however, was more to be hoped than expected from the Warren, Burger, or Rehnquist courts. The reapportionment cases marked the beginning, not the end, of a new adventure in judicial rationalism that today is still unfolding.

4

From the Founders' Republicanism to the Politics of Multiculturalism: The Voting Rights Act, 1965–80

When President Lyndon Johnson signed the Voting Rights Act on August 6, 1965, he referred to the legislation as "one of the most monumental laws in the entire history of American freedom."[1] Freedom was the appropriate focus of Johnson's remarks because the act represented an affirmation of political principle, of right over force, authority over power, an assertion of those fundamental prerogatives of self-governance that were prerequisite to free government. Passed to eliminate the barriers to exercise of the black franchise in the Jim Crow South, the VRA was a highly defensible and principled initiative. Its advocates could rightly argue that it represented a proper application of Congress's authority under section 2 of the Fifteenth Amendment to enforce that amendment "by appropriate legislation."

Shortly after passage of the act, however, in *Allen v. State Board of Elections* (1969),[2] the guiding objective of the VRA would change from a right to ballot access to a right to effective representation for legally recognized minorities. Eventually the antidiscrimination principle that underlay the original VRA and was directed against the invidious practices of intransigent southern governments would be transformed into an instrument of redistributive justice whose principal focus of concern was not so much the actions of governments as the actions of electors, and how certain electoral structures might produce electoral victory for statutorily protected minority groups. How did this change come about, and what did it portend for American politics?

Allen and the Birth of Second-Generation Voting Rights

Although the Supreme Court has been the principal source of innovations in VRA law throughout the history of the act, the original legislation was not designed to vindicate black voting rights through the vehicle of the courts. To the contrary, the most important remedial mechanisms of the act were designed to operate independently of any need for legal action. Congress recognized in 1965 that judicial remedies to voting rights violations imposed under the auspices of the civil rights acts of 1957, 1960, and 1964 had proved dilatory and costly and of only nominal effect in the face of southern resistance to the black vote.[3] The key to resolving these problems was, on the one hand, avoiding litigation and, on the other hand, preventing southern jurisdictions from circumventing federal protections of voting rights by replacing old means of disfranchisement with new ones.

The principal provisions designed to achieve these objectives were sections 4 and 5 of the VRA.[4] Section 4 set criteria calculated to identify ("cover") those states in the South with the most egregious history of black disfranchisement; the states had to have had voter turnout in the 1964 presidential election of less than 50 percent and to have used a literacy test. Section 4 also suspended for five years all literacy tests and other devices used as qualifications for voting in covered jurisdictions.

Section 5 required states covered by section 4 to submit any changes in electoral practices or procedures to the U.S. Department of Justice or the U.S. District Court for the District of Columbia for "preclearance." Because sections 4 and 5 represented a significant encroachment on state constitutional rights to control electoral practices, they were made temporary and set to expire in 1970. Their constitutionality was upheld in *South Carolina v. Katzenbach* (1966),[5] which justified the sections on grounds that the extraordinary circumstances of southern race politics in the 1960s warranted them.

Virtually every commentary on the VRA has noted that the act was very well-conceived and effective. Enjoying enormous nascent success, it reshaped both southern politics and American politics more generally. The original section 4 "trigger" provisions succeeded in covering the seven most notorious voting rights offenders—Alabama, Georgia, Louisiana, Mississippi, North Carolina, South Carolina, and Virginia. A number of jurisdictions without a history of black disfranchisement were also covered, and many of them successfully sued for exemption from the VRA; nevertheless, the act had a swift impact on black voting and registration. It also had a significant effect on black office-holding.[6]

In the wake of such success, one might expect the VRA's temporary provisions to have been allowed to lapse in 1970. Instead, however, Congress extended sections 4 and 5 for an additional five years. It would extend them another seven years in 1975, and, remarkably, for twenty-five more years in 1982. In 2006, Congress added yet another twenty-five years to their planned expiry in August 2007, thus confirming what was evident in 1982: that sections 4 and 5 were, in fact, permanent features of the VRA.

Although analysts have advanced differing interpretations of why Congress extended the VRA's temporary provisions in 1970, it was clear that by then the principal object of the act had changed from ballot-access questions to second-generation "political fairness" questions. The root of this change was *Allen v. State Board of Elections* (1969). Described as "the *Brown v. Board of Education* of voting rights,"[7] the *Allen* decision "marked a fundamental shift in the focal point of the Act."[8] Although not a constitutional decision, *Allen* nevertheless relied on a standard of electoral equality derived from the Court's reapportionment decisions following *Baker v. Carr.*

At issue in *Allen* were four proposed electoral changes—three in Mississippi and one in Virginia. The most important of these was a Mississippi statute that allowed the substitution of at-large elections for district elections in contests for county boards of supervisors. The apparent intent of this statute, like many others passed by the Mississippi legislature in the wake of passage of the VRA, was to dilute the black vote by submerging that vote in an at-large election rather than allowing blacks to vote for candidates in single-member districts, where they would be much more likely to elect a candidate of their preference. Critical to note, however, is that the Mississippi statute in dispute did not prohibit blacks from voting.

The principal issue the Court had to address in *Allen* was whether such attempts at minimizing the effects of the black vote were covered by section 5 of the VRA. Chief Justice Warren, writing for the Court, said they were: "The right to vote can be affected by a dilution of voting power as well as by an absolute prohibition on casting a ballot."[9] Warren added that the language of section 5 could not be construed narrowly because the VRA "was aimed at the subtle, as well as the obvious, state regulations that had the effect of denying citizens their right to vote because of their race."[10] The implication was that both major and minor changes to laws that might have an effect on the electoral process in covered jurisdictions would now be subject to preclearance. In the years following *Allen*, the Court would require preclearance for annexations,[11] legislative reapportionments,[12] and school board regulations requiring employees campaigning for elective office to take unpaid leaves of absence.[13]

Key to Warren's interpretation of section 5 was the section's broad language, covering any "voting qualification, or prerequisite to voting, or standard, practice, or procedure" different from what had been in force on November 1, 1964. Section 5 was distinct from section 2 of the VRA, the other key remedial provision of the act that served as a general preamble to the legislation and that mirrored the language of the Fifteenth Amendment. Unlike section 2, which made no reference to discriminatory results or effects, section 5 specifically provided that in applications for preclearance, states would have to prove that proposed voting changes would "not have the *purpose* and will not have the *effect* of denying or abridging the right to vote on account of race or color."[14] In addition to this distinction, the definition of "voting" in the VRA was also provided for in broad terms, covering "all action necessary to make a vote *effective* in any primary, special, or general election."[15] Warren concluded on the basis of this textual evidence that a narrow construction of section 5 had to be rejected.

The chief justice was properly suspicious of Mississippi's proposed changes. The tea leaves were not hard to read; the intent of the Mississippi legislature in 1966 pointed to the invidious purpose of limiting the effect of the VRA and the black vote, even if this goal had not been conclusively established at trial. As such, the Court understandably attempted to remedy the insolent behavior of Mississippi's legislature. The plaintiffs may have had constitutional remedies available to them, but the point of the decision in *Allen* was to vindicate the extraordinary remedies available under the VRA, failing which the force of the legislation would have been significantly diminished.[16] Yet, as understandable as Warren's decision was, it had its problems, as Justice Harlan pointed out in his dissent.

Harlan criticized the majority in *Allen* on grounds that its loose interpretation of isolated provisions of the act had worked to disregard the obvious purpose of the legislation. The purpose of the VRA was to guarantee the black vote. Nothing in the structure of the act, its language, or its legislative history suggested that questions concerning a vote's "effectiveness" were covered by it.[17] The effects of electoral changes on redistricting, annexations, school board regulations, and the like were outside the purview of what was contemplated when the VRA was drafted.

The central problem in *Allen*, Harlan contested, was that of statutory construction. By separating section 5 from its limited purpose of enforcing the section 4 proscription on bars against the black right to vote, the Court had unleashed the preclearance provisions from their limited purpose of ensuring the effectiveness of section 4. The majority in *Allen* had "construed § 5 to require a revolutionary innovation in American government," allowing for the imposition of "new substantive policies" on state governments—policies that would involve a broad range of electoral practices, because preclearance now extended beyond mere registration and ballot-access questions to encompass any law that might affect minority voting power.[18] In addition, by adopting the "expansive concept of voting" from the reapportionment cases, the majority had erroneously discovered a Fourteenth Amendment right in a statute based on the Fifteenth Amendment.[19]

The majority's opinion provided little guidance about what might constitute a violation of the VRA in the future and placed few restraints on judicial or administrative supervision of state electoral practices. Chief Justice Warren did, however, give some clues as to when vote-dilution claims might succeed. He had paraphrased, for instance, from *Reynolds v. Sims* when identifying the right guaranteed by the VRA that included "all action necessary to make a vote effective."[20] With reference to Mississippi's proposed change from district to at-large elections for county supervisors, Warren suggested that the measure of effective representation in such a scenario would be whether minority voters retained the ability to elect their preferred candidates to office. Switching from district to at-large elections could "nullify the ability [of minorities] to elect the candidate of their choice just as would prohibiting some of them from voting."[21] Warren further suggested that minority complainants did not have to establish intentional discrimination on the part of jurisdictions that had deprived minorities of effective representation. In *Allen*, no such intent had been established against the jurisdictions in dispute, but the plaintiffs were nevertheless entitled to relief.

By transforming the meaning of discrimination under the VRA in a manner consistent with other results-oriented civil rights policy, *Allen* effectively severed discriminatory intent from what constituted discriminatory treatment.[22] And by making this separation—by creating what amounted to a right to minority office-holding without proof of traditionally actionable discrimination—*Allen* would set the stage for the emergence of the politics of multiculturalism under the VRA. Already in 1969 it was apparent that if black voters were now considered a distinct political bloc entitled to their own representatives, it was only a small step to the idea that black Americans had a distinct political identity per se that needed to be preserved in representational policy. This identity presumably necessitated corollary rights to self-determination and, ultimately, self-governance— rights to set policy conducive to their own specific, racial interests. Both members of the Court and voting rights advocates would later make these very arguments.

As prudent as the Court's decision in *Allen* may have been in the face of the Mississippi legislature's evident intent to deprive blacks of the effects of their newly won franchise, Justice Harlan's dissent in *Allen* was nevertheless sound. *Allen* had unleashed a legal rule that could not be cabined to fact scenarios similar to *Allen*, where what was at issue was genuine discrimination. The ruling would create a legal mandate that would undermine the very objects of the original VRA, as well as the Constitution.

The conflict between second-generation voting rights and the Constitution would begin to play itself out in the 1970s. Once the ability of minorities to elect their candidates of choice to office became the measure of vote dilution, compliance with section 5 would require jurisdictions to predetermine to the greatest extent possible the outcomes of elections, focusing on race—which is, as noted earlier, a constitutionally suspect classification. The difficult question courts would face after *Allen* was this: If it was unconstitutional to carve blacks out of electoral success through racial gerrymanders, as the Court had held in *Gomillion v. Lightfoot* (1960),[23] on what basis could it be constitutional to carve them *into* electoral success through racial gerrymanders?[24] The Court would have to face this issue in *United Jewish Organizations of Williamsburgh, Inc. v. Carey* (1977).[25]

United Jewish Organizations and the
Racial Class–Warfare Vision of America

The transition from first- to second-generation questions in VRA law inaugurated by *Allen* marked the beginning of a move away from fundamental-rights questions of ballot access, on which there was virtually no disagreement, to contentious policy questions regarding "fair" electoral process, on which there was virtually no agreement. It also marked a move away from a republican to a democratic theory of representation, the preference for a descriptive model of representation that would increasingly identify race with political interest. With *Allen* the stage was set for the emerging conflict between Madisonian republicanism and the politics of multiculturalism, a conflict that would play out in *United Jewish Organizations Inc. v. Carey (UJO)*. There the Court would have to weigh the Constitution's laws of equal protection against the racial classifications that second-generation voting rights required as a matter of course.

By the early 1970s, when the dispute in *UJO* began to unfold, the initial scrutiny of the American representational process precipitated by the reapportionment cases had led to a doctrinal explosion in the area of representation law. This increase led, in turn, to the creation of new rights, as Nancy Maveety has observed, in the areas of occupational, partisan, administrative, and demographic representation.[26] The Burger Court's demographic theory of fair group representation that emerged in the wake of the reapportionment cases was intended to recognize the legitimacy of manipulating electoral district boundaries to achieve competitive balance among electoral groups,[27] but, like the one person, one vote requirement, it would eventually deteriorate into a simple quantitative measure of vote discrimination, this time measuring fairness on the basis of how electoral practices facilitated or did not facilitate minority office-holding.

In *White v. Regester* (1973) the Court declared that in constitutional cases it was prepared to entertain claims of multimember districts "being used invidiously to cancel out or minimize the voting strength of racial groups." The fact "that the racial group allegedly discriminated against [had] not had legislative seats in proportion to its voting potential" was not enough, however, to sustain such claims.[28] Contemporaneous with this decision was the emergence of a line of VRA cases conceding precisely the opposite: that minorities recognized under the act enjoyed a right to pro-portional representation, without any proof of invidious intent on the part of the offending jurisdictions.

UJO represented the most significant example of this latter trend in VRA law through the 1970s. Revealing the extent to which the adjudication and administration of the act had begun to collectivize people by race and ethnicity, *UJO* also exemplified the forces of interest-group liberalism that had been generated by second-generation voting rights. Second-generation issues had converted VRA disputes into partisan, political contests. Accordingly, they had helped facilitate the emergence of what voting rights scholars have referred to as a "voting rights bar"—what one such scholar described as a composite of "private attorneys, interest groups, attorneys for the federal government, expert witnesses, and consultants," most of whom have successfully pushed for an expanding mandate for the VRA.[29]

In the events leading to *UJO*, the U.S. Department of Justice (DOJ) had required that New York State create a 65 percent nonwhite voting quota proportionate to the black and Puerto Rican populations of Kings County and New York County. This meant creating seven assembly and three senate districts with majority-minority populations. The state's 1974 revised plan met the DOJ's threshold, but in the process it split a Hasidic Jewish com-munity in the Bedford-Stuyvesant area of Brooklyn (Kings County). The Hasidim had previously been part of a single assembly and a single senate district; now they were split into two assembly and two senate districts. The Hasidic community brought suit, alleging that New York's revised plan was unconstitutional because it split the community's votes "solely for the purpose of achieving a racial quota," contrary to the Fourteenth Amendment, and because the revised plan diluted the community's vote, contrary to the Fifteenth Amendment.[30]

Pitting Jewish petitioners against the attorneys general for the United States and the state of New York, *UJO* also arrayed a host of Jewish groups, such as the American Jewish Congress, against the National Association for the Advancement of Colored People (NAACP). It was the NAACP that suc-cessfully reopened a declaratory judgment consented to by the DOJ exempt-ing New York from the VRA's temporary provisions, compelling the state to seek preclearance for its 1972 redistricting plan (which it did not get). It was the NAACP that had apparently been the principal moving force behind the

DOJ's imposing the 65 percent nonwhite quota on the disputed districts.[31] It was the NAACP, along with the state of New York, that successfully moved to dismiss the petitioners' action summarily, propelling the case to the court of appeals and the U.S. Supreme Court. And it was the NAACP that urged that the real complaint of the Jewish appellants in *UJO* was "*qua Hasidim*, not *qua* white voter."[32] In other words, it was the NAACP that argued that race alone was what counted under the VRA, and that the Jewish appellants should fail in the litigation because they were advancing religious, not racial, interests.

The Supreme Court accepted these propositions. The crux of its decision in *UJO* was that there could be no discrimination against the Hasidic Jewish plaintiffs because they were part of a larger white majority. To the extent any discrimination against the petitioners existed, it was benign because New York's redistricting plan did not represent any kind of racial slur or stigma against whites or any other race.[33] What the state of New York had sought was simply "a fair allocation of political power between white and non-white voters in Kings County."[34] Because the VRA was not limited to remedying past discriminatory conduct,[35] and because the Hasidim enjoyed no constitutional right to separate community recognition, there was no cognizable harm for the Court to remedy.[36]

UJO was a case slightly ahead of its time. Although it would be almost twenty-five years after *Allen* before the Court in *Shaw v. Reno* (1993) would formally recognize the conflict between the race-conscious districting undertaken to comply with the VRA and the equal protection clause, *UJO* raised similar issues a generation earlier. At the height of the debate over race-conscious affirmative action in the years immediately following *Allen*, the Supreme Court had required the use of race as a precondition for compliance with the VRA in a number of cases.

In *City of Petersburg v. United States* (1973) the Court precleared a proposed annexation in Petersburg, Virginia, under section 5 on condition that the city switch to a ward system of election in order to "afford [blacks] representation reasonably equivalent to their political strength in the enlarged community."[37]

Two years later, in *City of Richmond v. United States* (1975), the Court reaffirmed that in annexation cases in which the percentages of blacks in a city were reduced, the annexing city could overcome section 5's proscribed "effects" by ensuring proportional representation of blacks after annexation.[38]

In *Beer v. United States* (1976) the Court ruled that the VRA prohibited the implementation of a redistricting plan that "would lead to a retrogression in the position of racial minorities with respect to their effective exercise of the electoral franchise."[39] If states failed to meet the retrogression test—that is, if they failed to provide minorities electoral districts at least equal to or greater than the number they enjoyed under earlier "benchmark" electoral plans used to measure retrogression—then the jurisdiction seeking preclearance would have to create sufficient majority-minority districts (MMDs) to comply with this mandate.[40] Failure to comply was tantamount to "retrogressing" the electoral power of protected minority groups.

Compliance with such a nonretrogression mandate was at issue one year later in *UJO*, where the Court interpreted *Beer* and *City of Richmond* to imply that "the Constitution does not prevent a State subject to the Voting Rights Act from deliberately creating or preserving black majorities in particular districts in order to ensure that its reapportionment plan complies with § 5."[41] The deliberate use of both race and racial quotas to create MMDs was a permissible exception to the constitutional prohibition on racial classifications.[42] Not only did it apply to jurisdictions in the South that had an egregious history of racial discrimination; now it applied to jurisdictions in the North with no such legacy.[43]

Critics of *UJO* were quick to point out that by consigning the Hasidic community's political interests to the status of race, the plurality had given undue salience to the very political consideration—race—that the VRA and the Constitution were intended to overcome. Chief Justice Warren Burger, dissenting, had objected that, by granting designated minorities their "deserved" representation through the vehicle of racial gerrymandering, the state had given its imprimatur to the use of race in the electoral process.[44] Signaling a "retreat from the ideal of the American 'melting pot'" that was "curiously out of step with recent political history,"[45] the use of mathematical quotas for the establishment of MMDs would have the propensity of sustaining "the existence of ghettos by promoting the notion that political clout is to be gained or maintained by marshaling particular racial, ethnic, or religious groups in enclaves."[46]

Judge Marvin Frankel, a federal district court judge sitting with the Second Circuit Court of Appeals in *UJO,* had similarly inquired into just what legal principle was at work with the DOJ's mandate of proportional racial representation. Although the majority of the court of appeals, like the plurality of the Supreme Court, had approved the DOJ's mandate as a remedy to retrogression, as prescribed by *Beer*, there were no data from New York's 1966 reapportionment plan against which any retrogression could be measured. Similarly, no court or any government agencies had found any past voting discrimination in New York warranting the type of corrective measures now being demanded by the DOJ.[47] Equally significant, once litigation started, the U.S. attorney general himself had disclaimed any approval of, or authority for, the 65 percent quota that the New York redistricting committee staff director had testified was what the DOJ had apparently demanded to secure preclearance.[48]

Judge Frankel observed that it was difficult to see where, in principle or in law, a minority's population in a county could be translated into a fixed percentage of districts that the minority was entitled to control, let alone control by some prescribed "effective" margin.[49] What precisely was the mandate of countywide proportional representation a remedy for? And on the basis of what constitutional doctrine could the explicit use of racial quotas be justified under the pretext of compliance with the VRA?

The substance of Justice Burger's and Judge Frankel's dissenting opinions in *UJO* was that the case was decided more by a multiculturalist orthodoxy than by the facts or law at issue. The first element of this orthodoxy consisted of the use of proportional racial representation as a panacea for compliance with the VRA, something neither the act nor any other law warranted.

The second element of this orthodoxy centered on the assumption that whites and blacks, respectively, thought alike and, accordingly, voted differently as racial groups. Chief Justice Burger had remarked that "it would make no sense to assure nonwhites a majority of 65% in a voting district unless it were assumed that nonwhites and whites vote in racial blocs, and that the blocs vote adversely to, or independently of, one another."[50] But, as Burger pointed out, not only was there no evidence of racial-bloc voting in Kings County; what evidence existed pointed in the opposite direction:

> Four out of the five "safe" (65%+) nonwhite districts established by the 1974 plan have since elected white representatives. . . .
> The assumption that "whites" and "nonwhites" in the county form homogenous entities for voting purposes is entirely

without foundation. The "whites" category consists of a verita-
ble galaxy of national origins, ethnic backgrounds, and religious
denominations. It simply cannot be assumed that the legislative
interests of all "whites" are even substantially identical. In similar fashion, those described as "nonwhites" include, in addition
to Negroes, a substantial portion of Puerto Ricans. . . . The
Puerto Rican population, for whose protection the Voting Rights
Act was "triggered" in Kings County . . . has expressly disavowed
any identity of interest with the Negroes, and, in fact, objected
to the 1974 redistricting scheme because it did not establish a
Puerto Rican controlled district in the county.[51]

The orthodoxy Chief Justice Burger described in *UJO* might be designated as the emerging racial class–warfare vision of multicultural theory, in
which racial groups were being deconstructed into the simple binary categories of victimizer and victimized, oppressor and oppressed, Hegemon
and Other. Blacks and Puerto Ricans in *UJO* had similar political interests
because, according to the plurality, they were defined in similar racial terms
under the VRA. In the language of multiculturalism, they were both part of
the statutory Other arrayed against Hegemonic whites. Because both blacks
and Puerto Ricans were minorities under the act, they could be lumped
together in MMDs. Conversely, Hasidic Jews were whites, and they could
therefore be lumped in with the white Hegemon, arrayed against blacks and
Puerto Ricans.

Chief Justice Burger's opinion had pointedly asked why, on the basis of
the limited facts in *UJO*, should the plurality assume an identity of political
interests along such starkly artificial and obviously racial lines as it did? The
answer lay in the multiculturalist ethos of second-generation voting rights.
If the DOJ and the decision in *UJO* seemed to have created artificial classifications utterly removed from the language of the VRA, as Burger contended, they had done so because vote-dilution jurisprudence required it.
The standard remedy in vote-dilution disputes was the creation of MMDs.
Affirming the court of appeal's decision, the plurality in *UJO* had emphasized that the "question whether a State could use racial considerations in
drawing lines in an effort to secure the Attorney General's approval under
the Voting Rights Act" had already been answered in the affirmative by

Allen. The lower court had reasoned that in the wake of *Allen* "the Act contemplated that the Attorney General and the state legislature would have 'to think in racial terms'; because the Act *'necessarily deals with race or color, corrective action under it must do the same.'"*[52]

This logic is what second-generation issues required the Court to affirm. VRA remedies had to be considered in racial terms because vote-dilution disputes centered on the appropriate balancing of political interests that were specifically defined as *racial interests*. That the VRA reduced the Hasidim's political interests to *racial interests* was a fact that even the petitioners' counsel apparently recognized: The plaintiffs did "not press any legal claim to a group voice as Hasidim."[53] Once the Hasidim's political interests had been reduced to white racial interests, the Court's conclusion automatically followed: "As long as whites in Kings County, as a group, were provided with fair representation," the plurality determined, "we cannot conclude that there was a cognizable discrimination against whites or an abridgment of their right to vote on the grounds of race."[54]

UJO was unseemly precisely because it classified the Hasidim's interests not as religious interests but as white racial interests. Indulging state action that condoned the idea that individuals could be defined solely on the basis of a single characteristic, here race, the Court made the dubious assumption that the Hasidim could be "virtually represented" in the state legislature by white gentiles from districts to which the Hasidim had no electoral connection. In addition, it assumed that the Hasidim were an undifferentiated group, indistinguishable from other whites in Brooklyn.[55] Yet the Hasidim were defined in their *very identity* by religion, not race; without their religious identity, they would have never filed the lawsuit.

Further Refining the Multiculturalist Vision: The 1975 Voting Rights Act and "Language Minorities"

UJO made clear that the purpose of the VRA as it applied to redistricting was to secure minority office-holding, a fact Congress had recognized in 1975.[56] Between 1970 and 1982, the powers of the federal government under the VRA grew both geographically and substantively. The 1970 extension and amendments to the act eliminated literacy tests nationwide for five years and extended coverage of the act's temporary provisions to states outside the South. The 1975 act permanently banned literacy tests nationwide and applied the act's protections to "language minorities," defined as "persons who are American Indian, Asian American, Alaskan Natives or of Spanish heritage."[57] The 1982 amendments to the VRA incorporated a "results" test into section 2, meaning that plaintiffs only had to establish that an electoral practice had the effect of reducing the power of the minority vote to succeed in litigation. The results test thus eliminated the requirement of proving discriminatory intent in section 2 actions.

The addition of the language minorities protections and the results test were the most significant changes made to the VRA during the 1970s and 1980s. For advocates of the inclusion of language minorities, extending the VRA to language groups was the logical extension of second-generation voting rights because it would increase political fairness by extending coverage to ethnic as well as racial groups. In 1975, the U.S. Civil Rights Commission had reported that "the most serious problem for minority voters now is practices which dilute the minority vote."[58] Recognizing that progress had been made in electing minorities to office in those jurisdictions covered by the VRA, the commission nevertheless qualified that "there is a very long way to go before minorities have gained an equitable share of political offices."[59] What, precisely, the commission meant by "an equitable share of political offices" would be settled in the future, but it was clear that the term "minorities" under the VRA was about to expand.

The U.S. Civil Rights Commission and the findings presented in *White v. Regester* (1973)[60] were two of the most important influences on Congress when it considered extending and amending the VRA in 1975.[61] In *Regester*, the Supreme Court found that Mexican Americans in Bexar County, Texas, had suffered from the lingering effects of invidious discrimination in such areas as education, employment, health, and politics. The cultural and language barriers Mexican Americans faced made participation in politics particularly difficult, a fact reflected in the low incidence of office-holding relative to the Mexican-American population in the county. "A cultural incompatibility," Justice White wrote for the Court, "conjoined with the poll tax and the most restrictive voter registration procedures in the nation, have operated to effectively deny Mexican-Americans access to the political processes in Texas even longer than the Blacks were formally denied access by the white primary."[62] Justice White believed that the facts in *Regester* warranted affirming the lower court's ruling disestablishing the Texas House of Representatives' multimember district in Bexar County in favor of single-member districts.

Congress, relying largely on the evidentiary findings in *Regester*, determined that Hispanics, along with Native Americans, Asian Americans, and Alaska Natives, warranted special minority language protections in voting rights under section 4 of the 1975 VRA. All states and political subdivisions subject to the minority language provisions were required to provide all election materials, including ballots, in the language of the applicable minority group as well as in English.[63] The minority language provisions were triggered when the director of the Census Bureau determined that more than 5 percent of the voting-age citizens residing in the jurisdiction at issue were members of a designated language minority.[64] Aside from the cost of the bilingual election materials, which would prove to be significant,[65] the provisions were important for the change in objectives they signified and for their long-term institutional implications.

Critics of the minority language provisions had argued that their inclusion in the VRA represented a host of significant changes. First, by expanding the act's coverage to ethnic as well as racial groups and further nationalizing it to regions outside the South, the 1975 VRA continued the blurring of the original purpose of the VRA that had begun in *Allen* six years earlier. Second, the new minority language provisions undermined American citizenship, confusing real discrimination with English-proficiency requirements that were not only a requirement for naturalization but, as the naturalization requirements themselves suggested, a necessary condition for participation in American politics, jury service, and other matters involving duties of citizenship.[66] Skeptics of the provisions pointed out that many, if not most, Hispanics in America were recent immigrants who suffered no measurable discrimination such as that contemplated by the 1975 VRA.

To the extent that Congress had relied on *White v. Regester* for evidence of discrimination against this group, critics further argued, *Regester* itself was misleading. Contrary to the Court's selective presentation of the evidence in the case, Mexican Americans had enjoyed significant political success in Bexar County and San Antonio long before the litigation. The

Court had failed to mention, for instance, that a Mexican American, Henry B. González, had represented Bexar County in Congress since 1961.[67] And even if one presumed evidence of discrimination against Hispanics in Texas politics, there appeared to be less evidence of electoral discrimination against the other groups covered by the VRA—certainly no more than existed for many other language minorities unprotected by the act.

Observations such as these led Civil Rights Commissioner Stephen Horn, in a surprising turn of events, to oppose the recommendations of other members of the Civil Rights Commission. In 1981, when the VRA's temporary provisions were set to expire, he urged Congress "not to extend the minority language provisions of the Voting Rights Act."[68]

Horn's concerns spoke to what was arguably the most significant political implication of the 1975 VRA: the public recognition that the preservation of ethnic identity was now a critical component of voting rights enforcement. Congressman Robert McClory expressed concerns similar to Horn's in the 1981 House report on extending the VRA:

> Many of those who favor the creation of bilingual ballots based on a reliance on a language other than English wish to permit the transfer of power without assimilation. . . . The 1975 amendments have the effect, whether intended or not, of encouraging minority language dependency and therefore self-imposed segregation, both politically and culturally. Indeed, if the language minorities now included under the administrative preclearance provisions of sections 4 and 5 are any accurate indication, federal law will continue to outlaw any state legislation which would have the effect, even if the purpose is benign, of reducing their group representation at any level of government.
>
> I believe such a federal policy, as contrasted to a localized state practice, is both misguided and inappropriate, and will have the counterproductive long-term effect of diminishing the homogenous character of our people. Large cultural constituencies whose concerns are more parochial than national ultimately threaten a move away from the precepts of republican democracy toward the uncertainties of coalition rule.[69]

Concerns that minorities might pursue their own "parochial" interests at the expense of the commonweal and move away from "republican democracy toward the uncertainties of coalition rule" have persisted since McClory's statement. Fifteen years after his remarks, when Congress revisited the question of whether the VRA's mandate for bilingual ballots should be repealed, Boston University president John Silber would similarly criticize the mandate as a "dangerous experiment in deconstructing our American identity."[70]

By defining the primary obstacles to the political advancement of groups such as Mexican Americans in racial terms, the 1975 VRA downplayed, if it did not entirely ignore, other demographic, political, and social factors that might have contributed to the condition of these groups.[71] Once the minority language amendments were translated into an entitlement to minority office-holding, the disregard of these factors would become even more significant. As one observer of Mexican-American politics has noted, the VRA, as an elite initiative of national magnitude, provided "the single strongest incentive for Mexican Americans and their leaders to define themselves as racial minority claimants."[72] The potentially incendiary repercussions of the minority language provisions afforded by the VRA would be further accentuated by the influx into the United States of millions of Mexican nationals in the waning decades of the twentieth century, a development that would act as a force multiplier, further eroding the coherence of affirmative action under the act and the concept of a uniform American citizenship.[73]

The Evolution of the Voting Rights Act through the 1970s

The 1975 VRA was testament to how skillfully civil rights advocates had created the appearance of continuity between the original intentions of the act and what it had become.[74] As Timothy O'Rourke has observed, although the number of minority voters and officeholders continued to grow dramatically following passage of the original act, with each extension Congress identified new obstacles to political equality that required increasing federal supervision over state and local electoral practices. Once the VRA shifted from legislation focused on suffrage to legislation concerned with representation, the conditions for the persistent expansion in the meaning of discrimination had been set.[75]

Establishing first- and second-generation voting rights as part of a single antidiscrimination continuum involved a rhetorical battle over the purposes of the VRA and what constituted "discrimination" under the act. The new war on discrimination has been described as "a war of words and a war about words" that is at the same time "an exercise in constructivist social technology."[76] By imputing "discrimination," a term connoting intention, to systemic or societal forces produced as a result of no discriminatory intent or conscious design, advocates of affirmative action and other constructivist models of equality have been able to use the popular disdain for discrimination to their advantage while applying it to activities most people do not consider to be inherently blameworthy.[77]

The extension of the VRA's provisions to nationwide constituencies in both the 1970 and 1975 legislation, as well as the addition of minority language protections in the 1975 act, complicated the question of just what precise "wrongs" the VRA was now intended to remedy. In *UJO*, Chief Justice Burger and Judge Frankel had asked a similar question regarding the mandate for proportional racial representation imposed on New York and approved by the Supreme Court. If the purpose of the VRA was now to promote racial balancing in politics for designated groups, as second-generation law by the late 1970s clearly seemed to indicate, what, precisely, was the endpoint of this new object in VRA law, and where in the actual language or legislative history of the act could such a requirement be found?

In 1975 the groups that would garner special language protections under the VRA were the same "official minorities" documented by scholars such as Herman Belz, John Skrentny, and Hugh Davis Graham as generally protected in all affirmative action legislation: Hispanics, Native Americans, and Asian Americans.[78] Objecting to the extension of the minority language provisions of the VRA in 1981, Civil Rights Commissioner Horn had proclaimed that providing aid to only a handful of the 387 language groups that the 1980 census had coded was not only discriminatory but "absurd."[79] In *Whose Votes Count?* Abigail Thernstrom similarly asked whether the limited number of recognized language minorities protected by the 1975 VRA was a "defensible list."[80]

The VRA's list of protected language minorities may have been indefensible—indeed, even absurd—in disregarding numerous other language groups who had suffered victimization at the hands of the statistical majority, but those who supported the amendments showed a great deal of political astuteness and foresight. On the one hand, by *expanding* the categories of VRA beneficiaries, as the 1975 act did, greater political impetus would be given to any future changes to the legislation, such as the 1982 amendments, since the number of groups that would benefit from such potential changes would be enlarged. On the other hand, by *limiting* the VRA's language protections to America's "official minorities," the 1975 act would be consistent with the orthodoxy of other civil rights initiatives whose affirmative action boilerplate recognized these same groups. More important, by limiting the VRA's protections to only a handful of ethnoracial constituencies—the same groups as other civil rights policy—the 1975 act would serve the critical strategic purpose of maintaining the multiculturalist vision of America, a racial class–warfare vision that depended on clear lines of demarcation between broadly defined ethnoracial constituencies. As Graham remarked, when it comes to affirmative action policy, federal officials are understandably reluctant to hold hearings on which groups should receive special dispensations, because "the number of groups seeking special advantage might escalate in problematical and embarrassing ways."[81]

By placing further emphasis on the racial class–warfare vision of American politics that became the signature feature of the politics of multiculturalism and one of its most enduring rhetorical levers, the 1975 inclusion of language-based beneficiaries under the VRA would further concentrate American republicanism on questions of race and ethnicity rather than on the genuine issues of politics and economics that the Framers of the Constitution, with their advocacy of commercial republicanism, had hoped would consume American government.

These latter issues were, as well, the focus of the progressive and New Deal eras of economic regulation. The beneficiaries of the "iron triangles" of the 1940s and 1950s that defined the economic regulatory state of that time—the congressional committees, executive agencies, and organized clientele groups who controlled policy development within the regulated fields—were agricultural, business, and other political and economic interests. The beneficiaries of the new social and racial regulatory state that emerged at the end of the twentieth century would be the litany of Great Society "victim" groups, comprising the recipient classes of the new redistributionist programs that followed on the heels of the original civil rights initiatives of the mid-1960s.[82] The *Allen* decision and second-generation voting rights more generally, including *UJO* and the 1975 VRA, would contribute to this new model of regulatory race politics. So, too, would changes made to the VRA in the 1980s.

5

The 1982 Amendments to the Voting Rights Act and Their Aftermath

In the wake of *Allen v. State Board of Elections*, the number of preclearance requests in jurisdictions covered by the VRA skyrocketed.[1] Between 1970 and 1975, preclearance submissions to the attorney general increased from 255 to 2,078.[2] Between 1975 and 1980, more than 30,000 changes were submitted.[3] The Department of Justice objected to only 22 preclearance requests between 1965 and 1969. This number rose to 251 between 1970 and 1974, and to 543 in 1975–80.[4] One consequence of the growth in preclearance submissions and objections was a rise in disputes over what burden of proof jurisdictions had to meet to satisfy the requirements of section 5. Although only a handful of these cases ever made it to the Supreme Court, those that did highlighted the ambiguous language of the section, as well as the equally elusive purposes of the evolving VRA.

Section 5 mirrored the language of the Fifteenth Amendment, providing that practices or procedures under review for preclearance "not have the purpose and . . . not have the effect of denying or abridging the right to vote on account of race or color." In *Miller v. Johnson* (1995), Justice Anthony Kennedy observed that "section 5 was directed at preventing a particular set of *invidious* practices which had the effect of 'undo[ing] or defeat[ing] the rights recently won by nonwhite voters.'"[5] Proof of invidious intent had been a well-entrenched element of equal protection[6] and Fifteenth Amendment[7] violations that alleged racial discrimination, but the precise relationship of intent or purpose to effects in section 5 following *Allen* remained ambiguous. So, too, did the relationship of section 5 to the Fifteenth Amendment, the original source of the VRA's constitutional authorization.

In *Allen* the Court failed to address the specific meaning of purpose and effect in section 5 because the lower courts had failed to determine whether the statutes at issue presented evidence of either.[8] The Supreme Court throughout the 1970s nevertheless made clear that the two prongs of the section were independent burdens of proof: Jurisdictions petitioning for preclearance had to establish that proposed electoral changes were devoid of both discriminatory intent *and* discriminatory effect. In *City of Rome v. United States* (1980) the Court affirmed that "by describing the elements of discriminatory purpose and effect in the conjunctive, Congress plainly intended that a voting practice not be precleared unless both discriminatory purpose and effect are absent."[9] Proof of discriminatory effect, in a word, was sufficient for a VRA violation and for a denial of preclearance.

Moreover, Congress had reaffirmed the conjunctive language of section 5 when it extended the VRA for an additional seven years in 1975.[10] In *Rome* the difficult question the Court had to confront was how an effects test that was independent of discriminatory purpose could be tied to the constitutional authority under which Congress had passed section 5. If jurisdictions proved lack of discriminatory intent as the basis for the electoral practice under challenge, as the city of Rome, Georgia, had before the district court, what precisely did the additional proof of nondiscriminatory effect amount to?[11]

Rome involved a constitutional challenge to Congress's power to prohibit state electoral practices after a locality had disproved the existence of any purposeful discrimination. The case raised two central issues: First, what specific wrong was being remedied once lack of intentional discrimination had been proved? Second, what did the Court's denial of preclearance imply for the purposes of the VRA's temporary provisions? What did adding the requirement of overcoming discriminatory effect or impact do to help realize the act's objectives? And just what did the Court think these objectives were? The Court held that

> Congress could rationally have concluded that, because electoral changes by jurisdictions with a demonstrable history of intentional racial discrimination in voting create the risk of purposeful discrimination, it was proper to prohibit changes that have a discriminatory impact.[12]

The problem with this argument was that the rationale the Court offered for section 5 no longer applied. The "risk of purposeful discrimination" could hardly persist where the city had proved lack of purposeful discrimination.

According to Justice William Rehnquist, joined by Justice Potter Stewart, dissenting, the majority's decision carried a number of implications. First, to the extent that the disparate impact of the electoral changes at issue was the result of racial-bloc voting, the Court was permitting Congress to redress *private*, not *governmental*, discrimination, which Congress could not do under either the Fourteenth or the Fifteenth Amendment.[13] Second, prohibiting all practices that had a disparate impact would not enhance Congress's attempt at prohibiting purposeful discrimination because there was no discriminatory conduct at issue, nor any future discriminatory conduct—such as the discriminatory application of literacy tests—that would be prevented by the Court's decision.[14] What, then, was the policy rationale for such a mandate if it was not a pure entitlement to representation on the basis of race?

Finally, the Court's requirement that the local government "structure its political system in a manner that most effectively enhances black political strength" was "premised on the assumption that white candidates will not represent black interests, and that States should devise a system encouraging blacks to vote in a bloc for black candidates."[15] The Court had proposed a dangerous ideological platform, one that not only identified race with political interest but also created an institutional incentive for minorities to continue to do so.

The questions raised by *Rome* and by other important cases, such as *City of Mobile v. Bolden* (1980),[16] would be extensively debated during the congressional hearings leading up to the 1982 amendments to section 2 of the VRA. The evidentiary issues involved were of a piece with other civil rights initiatives in which minority advocacy groups had lobbied for a results test as the measure of "discrimination." As the dissenters in *Rome* had suggested, the implications of these seemingly arcane disputes over burdens of proof stretched far beyond the world of litigation, indicating transformations in the very meaning of equality and representation in American law.

The Debate over the 1982 Section 2 Amendments

The 1982 amendments to section 2 of the VRA would change the statutory test for vote discrimination claims brought pursuant to the provision, codifying a results-based "totality of circumstances" test (explained in some detail below) originally developed by the Supreme Court in *White v. Regester* (1973)[17] and later elaborated by the Fifth Circuit Court of Appeals in *Zimmer v. McKeithen* (1973).[18] The purpose of the section 2 amendments, according to the House's *Report on the Voting Rights Act Extension*, was to "clarif[y] the ambiguities which have arisen in the wake of the [*City of Mobile v.*] *Bolden* decision" and to affirm "that proof of purpose or intent is not a prerequisite to establishing voting discrimination violations in Section 2 cases."[19]

In *Bolden* (1980), plaintiffs had challenged the three-member municipal commission in Mobile, Alabama, on grounds that requiring the commissioners to be elected at large unconstitutionally diluted black citizens' votes. The Supreme Court held that plaintiffs had to prove intentional discrimination in actions alleging vote discrimination under either the Fourteenth or Fifteenth Amendment or any derivative legislation such as the VRA.

The elimination of this requirement by the 1982 amendments would precipitate an unparalleled increase in section 2 litigation,[20] as well as an unprecedented rate of success for plaintiffs.[21] But the amendments had repercussions extending well beyond these effects. The House report's description of them as a "clarification" of ambiguities arising from *Bolden* belied the fact that what was being proposed was a radical change in the law as well as a turn away from longstanding precedents. As one astute observer characterized the proposed amendments, "It was not a stiff dose of medicine designed to restore a sick law to health but more like a sex-change operation intended to alter fundamentally the nature of the law itself."[22]

The implications of the section 2 amendments were examined in detail by the Senate Subcommittee on the Constitution, chaired by Utah Republican Orrin Hatch. The subcommittee summarized the implications in these terms:

> The debate over whether or not to overturn the Supreme Court's decision in *Mobile v. Bolden*, and establish a results test for identifying voting discrimination in place of the present intent test, is probably the single most important constitutional issue that will

be considered by the 97th Congress. Involved in this controversy are fundamental issues involving the nature of American representative democracy, federalism, the division of powers, and civil rights. By redefining the notion of "civil rights" and "discrimination" in the context of voting rights, the proposed "results" amendment would transform the objective of the Act from equal access to the ballot-box into equal results in the electoral process. A results test for discrimination can lead nowhere but to a standard of proportional representation by race.[23]

The warnings of Hatch's subcommittee would prove prophetic and provided an interesting contrast to the more sanguine prognosis of the House and Senate judiciary committees, the latter declaring that the section 2 amendments were "careful, sound, and necessary" and would "not result in the wholesale invalidation of electoral structures."[24] This conclusion, of course, would prove wrong.[25]

The ambiguity of the results test and its focus on racial outcomes led the Senate subcommittee to estimate that the proposed section 2 test would either be applied arbitrarily or, alternatively, would degenerate into a simple numerical calculus with proportional representation or quotas as its logical endpoint.[26] The consequences of such an approach, according to the subcommittee, would be twofold. First, "the rule of judges [would] effectively replace the rule of law," leaving communities to guess whether their electoral regimes were in compliance with the VRA. Second, the country would move increasingly away from the principle of colorblindness in law toward overt policies of race consciousness.[27] The original VRA was based on the presumption that minority interests were best served when narrow racial issues were subsumed within the broader political context where race did not define political interests.[28] The results test would reverse this process by requiring deliberations about public policy to take specific cognizance of racial interests.

The subcommittee then invoked a concept of republicanism similar to the Madisonian understanding we have discussed previously in this book: "The framers of our Federal Government rejected official recognition of interest groups as a basis for representation and instead chose the individual as the primary unit of government."[29] The original VRA was consistent with the Framers' objective, protecting the right of individuals, not groups, to cast a ballot. The amended section 2 threatened the Founders' republicanism by shifting emphasis from the individual citizen to the racial or ethnic group,[30] providing only the "members of a protected class" the newly codified right "to participate in the political process and to elect representatives of their choice."[31]

Proponents of the section 2 results test contested these arguments by the Senate subcommittee, denying that the test represented a substantive change in the law or a move in the direction of the politics of multiculturalism, as the subcommittee had suggested. They predicated their arguments largely on a critique of Mobile v. Bolden, which, they contended, seriously jeopardized minority voting rights. As the critics saw it, the problems with Bolden were fourfold:

First, the decision had the potential to negate the original intention of section 2, which, like section 5, was designed to bar discriminatory effects as well as discriminatory purpose.[32]

Second, Bolden was inconsistent with judicial precedents that had focused on the discriminatory results of electoral practices rather than on the intent or motivation of such practices. It was thus bad law.

Third, Bolden was also bad politics for the reasons outlined by the Senate Judiciary Committee: Searching for intent was "unnecessarily divisive because it involves charges of racism on the part of individual officials or entire communities."[33] By focusing on the consequences of actions rather than on the actions and intentions of legislators, this unsavory outcome could be avoided.

Finally, by requiring proof of discriminatory intent, Bolden rendered it virtually impossible for plaintiffs to succeed in section 2 actions. "Efforts to find a 'smoking gun' to establish racial discriminatory purpose or intent are not only futile," the House report contended, "but irrelevant to the consideration whether discrimination has resulted from such election practices."[34]

Battle was joined over all these issues during the House and Senate hearings of 1981–82. Typifying these battles were two divergent visions of America: what the VRA and other civil rights initiatives had wrought since the mid-1960s versus what was politically warranted in the early 1980s, given this legacy. Most commentators seeking to defend the section 2 changes to the act did accept the House report's historical account of the VRA and its none-too-sanguine prognostications about race and representation in the South. If the section 2 amendments were not approved and *Bolden* was left in place, the House report predicted, black voting rights in the South would be in serious jeopardy. "The *Bolden* decision," Frank Parker wrote in 1983, "evoked a storm of criticism in the legal community."[35] "The Supreme Court's decision in *Mobile*," Thomas Boyd and Stephen Markman agreed, "produced an avalanche of criticism, both in the media and the civil rights community."[36]

But why? Was *Bolden* really such an aberration of voting rights law? Did the plurality in *Bolden* get the legislative and judicial history of section 2 so wrong? Or was something else also at work? Perhaps what Senator John East, Congressman Henry Hyde, and others had suggested: a race-centric, liberal orthodoxy, or "zeitgeist," which had come to occupy the commanding heights of the legal, academic, and media worlds, and would brook no deviancy from the party line.[37]

The larger political and cultural context in which the 1982 VRA was situated was perhaps the most significant aspect of the 1982 legislation. Few issues in Congress throughout the 1980s pitted liberal Democrats against conservative Republicans and, more particularly, the orthodoxy of elite culture against its opponents, as did those involving the VRA. The debates preceding the 1982 act were the leading edge of a broader culture war that would consume much of American politics over the next three decades, as the hotly contested voting rights and affirmative action cases of the 1990s and 2000s would reveal.

The question of what America had become by the early 1980s and what it might become thereafter was the dominant underlying current of the debates over the arcana of the VRA, an act whose provisions many in the media and even in Congress did not seem to understand. James Blumstein has posited that what was being proposed with the section 2 amendments was a theoretical shift in the law, even if the subtlety and importance of this shift, often not identified or acknowledged in the political arena, were lost on many members of Congress.[38] The House report had implored that efforts "to establish racial discriminatory purpose or intent are not only futile, but *irrelevant* to the consideration whether discrimination has resulted from such electoral practices."[39]

The crux of the section 2 debate was, therefore, this: If discriminatory intent was not only difficult to prove but legally irrelevant, as the House report contended, then there had to be some underlying affirmative entitlement that could be abridged both inadvertently and intentionally under the section.[40] But this point in turn implied a racial entitlement to representation without proof of any racial animus or wrong in the governmental decision-making process, something that no one in Congress was prepared to admit. The House report on the VRA never made explicit the rejection of the long-established nondiscrimination principle in American law, nor could it. In Blumstein's words, "Explicit acknowledgment of a race-based entitlement to representation would have been the kiss of death."[41] But such an entitlement seemed to be a necessary implication of the section 2 results test—or was it?

The central issue that had been in dispute in Congress over the section 2 results test had also been at the center of contention in *Mobile v. Bolden*, the case that had precipitated the movement to amend section 2. The Court in *Bolden* had been concerned that a results test used in constitutional litigation or in disputes involving section 2 might introduce, for the first time in American law, an entitlement to racial representation. Was such a concern warranted? Not according to proponents of the section 2 results test. Nor was it warranted according to Justices Brennan and Thurgood Marshall, who had dissented in *Bolden*.

The Supreme Court and the Intent Test

Mobile v. Bolden generated great controversy within the civil rights community because it overturned the principal authority for the results test (also known as the "effects" or "impact" test) that had been relied on by both civil rights litigators and lower courts throughout the 1970s. That authority was *Zimmer v. McKeithen*, a 1973 ruling of the Fifth Circuit Court of Appeals. Although *Bolden* rejected the effects test proposed in *Zimmer*, the more general question of whether the High Court's decision represented a departure from previous Supreme Court jurisprudence, as the House report and many in the civil rights community had alleged, was a more dubious proposition. Critics of the section 2 results test claimed that many in the voting rights community disdained the ruling not on legal or constitutional grounds, but because it represented a setback for the new multiculturalist mission in civil rights advocacy—a mission, they said, that sought to drive American republicanism increasingly in the direction of race based, descriptive representation. The dispute between these competing visions of equality and representation crystallized in *Bolden*, where the meaning of *Zimmer* and whether it really was inconsistent with earlier vote-dilution law was at the center of contention.

Zimmer v. McKeithen was itself a controversial ruling that had provoked strong dissenting opinions from six members of the en banc (or full) court of the Fifth Circuit. The *Zimmer* majority overturned a lower court decision that had permitted at-large elections for school boards and police juries in a rural Louisiana parish. The central issue in the case was whether the majority's interpretation of *White v. Regester* (1973), decided only three months before, was sound.

Regester had referred to a number of factors that might be considered when determining whether electoral practices or procedures were discriminatory. The case had also established a test for discrimination which, as interpreted by the *Zimmer* majority, would permit successful vote-dilution claims on establishment of *either* discriminatory intent *or* discriminatory effects; proof of racial animus, in other words, was unnecessary to succeed in such an action.[42] To assess the constitutional issue, the court in *Zimmer* had provided a list of "primary" and "enhancing" factors—later known as the "*Zimmer* factors"—that might establish vote dilution, and then determined that the at-large electoral district in dispute might dilute the black vote.[43]

The Supreme Court in *Bolden* was concerned not only that *Zimmer* was wrong on the law, but also that its watered-down test for vote dilution in equal protection disputes would lead to a widespread assault on at-large districts in the name of proportional representation for designated racial groups. Writing for the plurality, Justice Stewart emphasized that the *Zimmer* court had misunderstood the burden of proof required in equal protection cases. A simple effects test was not enough. As the Court had stressed in a 1976 case, *Washington v. Davis*,[44] proof of purposeful discrimination was a necessary precondition for relief in equal protection disputes. Contrary to what the lower courts had held, *Davis* clearly applied to facts such as those in *Bolden*.[45]

Justice Stewart added that the history of section 2 made clear that it simply mirrored the terms of the Fifteenth Amendment.[46] The evidentiary standard applied to section 2 would, therefore, turn on the standard applied to Fifteenth Amendment cases. Stewart again was unequivocal here. A long line of decisions had established that proof of discriminatory purpose was requisite to succeeding in Fifteenth Amendment actions.[47] The same was true of equal protection actions under the Fourteenth Amendment.[48] The constitutional decisions dealing with multimember districts had established that such districts were not per se unconstitutional, and that to succeed in a constitutional challenge to such districts plaintiffs had to demonstrate an invidious purpose to minimize or cancel out the minority vote. *White v. Regester* and *Whitcomb v. Chavis* (1971) had also made clear that minority plaintiffs could not succeed in equal protection challenges to multimember districts simply by proving lack of proportional representation.

Only three justices out of nine in *Bolden* believed that an impact test rather than an intent test should apply in vote-dilution claims—liberal justices John Paul Stevens, William Brennan, and Thurgood Marshall. The question is what they understood this test to be and what its legal origin was. Proponents of the 1982 section 2 results test had largely adopted Marshall's position in *Bolden* when testifying in Congress. Understanding how Marshall arrived at his theory, therefore, went some distance toward understanding the rationale for the most important changes to the 1982 VRA.

The starting point of Marshall's opinion was that *Washington v. Davis* and its progeny did not apply to *Bolden* because *Bolden* involved an analytically distinct type of claim. What the plurality in *Bolden* had failed to appreciate, according to Marshall, was that voting rights, and specifically questions of vote dilution, involved a fundamental right protected by the Constitution. The *Bolden* plurality had characterized the plaintiffs' action as a race case, involving a suspect classification (what was at issue in *Davis*), rather than comprehending that at issue in *Bolden* was a different line of equal protection law altogether. This difference between the two strains of equal protection jurisprudence explained the critical distinction between *White v. Regester* and *Washington v. Davis*: "The former involved an infringement of a constitutionally protected right, while the latter dealt with a claim of racially discriminatory distribution of an interest to which no citizen has a constitutional entitlement."[49]

To flesh out this distinction, Marshall relied on many of the same cases as the plurality, but with a different gloss on their meaning. As noted in Chapter 3, for instance, in *Fortson v. Dorsey* the Court had affirmed that multimember reapportionments could dilute the minority vote "designedly or otherwise."[50] In this and other cases, the disjunctive language made clear that proof of discriminatory intent was not a necessary condition for success in vote-dilution claims.

Because the Court's vote-dilution jurisprudence was part of the "fundamental interest" strain of equal protection law rather than the "antidiscrimination" strain, the Court, according to Marshall, had recognized "a substantive constitutional right to participate on an equal basis in the electoral process that cannot be denied or diminished for any reason, racial or otherwise, lacking quite substantial justification."[51] The substantive right Marshall was asserting here was a collective or group right that only discrete racial or political groups could vindicate.

The plurality and Justice Stevens had expressed concern that such a substantive right, when combined with the results test Marshall was proposing, would amount to a right to race-based proportional representation. Attempting to rebut this allegation, Marshall responded that minorities could have access to or influence the political process in many different ways, not only by means of elections. The substantive right to participate in the electoral process could be realized only when other avenues to political participation had been closed off or locked up. Minorities in vote-dilution disputes would, therefore, have to do more than simply demonstrate that they were unable to elect candidates of their choice to office in numbers proportionate to their racial demographics. "Unconstitutional vote dilution," declared Marshall, "occurs only when a discrete political minority whose voting strength is diminished by a districting scheme proves that historical and social factors render it largely incapable of effectively utilizing alternative avenues of influencing public policy."[52] Accordingly, there was no automatic right to proportional representation with a results test for vote discrimination.

Justice Stewart and other members of the plurality were not convinced by Justice Marshall's reassurances. Marshall's refrain that the vote-dilution cases merely provided "a minimally intrusive guarantee of political survival" for minority groups, they suggested, belied the radical nature of what he was proposing. The "historical and social factors" he designated as touchstones for vote-dilution claims amounted to little more than "gauzy sociological considerations" with no foundation in constitutional law.[53] With such an amorphous and obviously subjective constitutional standard, what practical limitations would there be on the power of the judiciary to radically reconstruct American republicanism from the top down?

Further, if political influence were to be the measure of whether "equal access to the political process" existed, this measure would, as a legal rule, translate into a simple mathematical formula: "Every 'political group,' or at least every such group that is a minority," would have "a federal constitutional right to elect candidates in proportion to its numbers."[54] Because this rule would apply above all to racial groups, the transformation of American republicanism in the direction of descriptive representation would also be a transformation in the direction of a politics of racial identity.

The plurality believed that Justice Marshall had also misinterpreted the Court's vote-dilution and reapportionment cases. Those cases did not provide a collective or group right to representation, as Justice Marshall had asserted. *Whitcomb v. Chavis*, one of the principal decisions on which Marshall had relied, had explicitly denied the existence of group rights to representation and had pointed out how intractable such rights would be if conceded.[55] The reapportionment cases, like the Constitution, protected individual rights, not group rights. "It is, of course, true," Stewart emphasized, "that the right of a person to vote on an equal basis with other voters draws much of its significance from the political associations that its exercise reflects, but it is an altogether different matter to conclude that political groups themselves have an independent constitutional claim to representation." Independently of "the total absence of support for th[e] theory in the Constitution itself," the practical difficulties with the group representational rights Justice Marshall was proposing were significant:

> Indeed, certain preliminary practical questions immediately come to mind: Can only members of a minority of the voting population in a particular municipality be members of a "political group"? Can any "group" call itself a "political group"? If not, who is to say which "groups" are "political groups"? Can a qualified voter belong to more than one "political group"? Can there

be more than one "political group" among white voters (e.g., Irish-American, Italian-American, Polish-American, Jews, Catholics, Protestants)? Can there be more than one "political group" among nonwhite voters? Do the answers to any of these questions depend upon the particular demographic composition of a given city? Upon the total size of its voting population? Upon the size of its governing body? Upon its form of government? Upon its history? Its geographic location?[56]

These questions and related ones posed by Justice Stewart were both incisive and revealing. Recognition of group rights to representation would mark a radical transformation in American republicanism. The Founders' Constitution had recognized a form of geographic group rights anchored in notions of federalism, but this was something quite distinct from what Justice Marshall was proposing. Once group rights to representation moved beyond state or local jurisdictional issues and became based on race or some other ascriptive group characteristic, the meaning of American republicanism and citizenship would change forever. A host of irresolvable definitional and practical problems would also arise. Considered in this light, Justice Marshall's dissenting opinion in *Bolden* smacked of consummate judicial rationalism, presupposing that courts had not only the legal authority but also the institutional capability to answer questions that even the most astute democratic theorists had never been able to resolve.

Nevertheless, was Marshall's opinion really all that indefensible? Justice Stewart may have been correct to assert that a constitutional right to representation for discrete groups had never been formally recognized by the Court, but such cases as *Fortson v. Dorsey* and *Burns v. Richardson* had made it equally clear that questions of political equality could not be limited to simple notions of numerically equal districts. The pursuit of fair and effective representation might require other considerations and, specifically, the differential treatment of groups differently situated.

Even if such a line of reasoning were not to be imposed under the auspices of the Constitution, it had already been imposed under the auspices of the VRA. In *Allen*, for instance, Justice Harlan had taken pains to emphasize that the Court was embarking on a jurisprudential adventure that would visit on it all the conceptual and practical difficulties Justice

Stewart was now ascribing to Justice Marshall's constitutional theory in *Bolden*. In *City of Richmond* and *UJO* similar conceptual difficulties would arise. Chief Justice Burger's indictment of the Court's opinion in *UJO*, with which ruling Stewart had concurred, had raised the same catalogue of problems regarding the intractability, arbitrariness, and potential divisiveness of collective race-based representational rights Stewart was now raising in *Bolden*. On the same day *Bolden* was decided, *City of Rome v. United States* had granted racial-group entitlements to representation which, according to Justices Rehnquist and Stewart (who had dissented in the case), were based on a pure effects test divorced from any notion of invidious discrimination or evidence of wrongdoing on the part of the city of Rome.

All these cases made clear that as much as the Court may have preserved its innocence in *constitutional* rulings involving collective rights to racial representation, as Justice Stewart was proclaiming in *Bolden*, it had long ago lost that innocence in the case of the VRA and other affirmative action initiatives that had committed the Court to the sort of sociological jurisprudence against which Stewart was now admonishing in *Bolden*.

When viewed in this light, Justice Stewart's declarations in *Bolden* about the dangers of group rights to representation and of dividing the electorate into racial constituencies on the basis of dubious democratic and sociological theories had a decisively hollow, if not hypocritical, ring to them. Had the Court and Stewart himself not been indulging in such theories for years in the case of the VRA? Did it make any difference whether the Court was addressing the intractable problems of group rights to representation in the context of a statute as opposed to the Constitution? Was that statute, the VRA, not based on the very constitutional provisions in dispute in *Bolden*, in any event?

Observers could fairly ask in 1980 just where the Court's theories of racial-group representation were taking both it and the rest of the country that had to abide by its decisions. In *Allen*, the High Court had entered the political thicket of race-based representation without much guidance regarding just where, precisely, its vote-dilution jurisprudence was headed. As VRA cases through the 1970s as well as the debates in Congress over the 1982 VRA indicated, neither the courts nor Congress seemed to have come much closer to resolving the meaning of what constituted "effective" representation under the act than had Chief Justice Warren's musings in *Allen*.

Justice Stewart did seem to have the stronger argument when it came to the constitutional issues raised in *Bolden*. Indeed, if Justices Marshall and Brennan were the only two justices of nine in *Bolden* supporting the idea of a pure results test as the threshold to be met in vote dilution claims, and if this interpretation was unique in the pre-*Bolden* constitutional jurisprudence, as the plurality as well as concurring and dissenting justices in *Bolden* had all indicated, the 1981 House report's declaration that amending section 2 of the VRA to incorporate a results test would "restore the pre-*Bolden* understanding of the proper legal standard"[57] to be used in section 2 cases was misguided, if not disingenuous. The Senate subcommittee's conclusion would appear to have been sound: "There is no decision of the Court either prior to or since *Mobile* that has ever required anything other than an 'intent' standard for the 15th Amendment or section 2."[58]

Thornburg v. Gingles: Formalizing the Right to Proportional Racial Representation

In 1982, the Supreme Court and Congress stood at a crossroads as two antithetical theories of equality and representation vied for recognition before both. The movement away from an intent test to a results test that year was not an isolated event tied to the discrete politics of the VRA; it was just one aspect of a more general trend in the war against discrimination, both in the United States and elsewhere.[59]

As mentioned earlier, critics of the section 2 results test feared that if the burden of proof necessary to establish a violation of section 2 were changed from an intent standard to a results standard, the VRA might be interpreted to recognize, for the first time in American law, collective rights to racial representation, formally dividing the nation into a miscellany of racially differentiated groups for the purposes of representational politics.[60] Critics also feared that a section 2 results test might treat those not guilty of racial discrimination in voting rights disputes the same as those who were guilty, perhaps even making the very question of whether racial discrimination was at issue in such controversies legally irrelevant. Both of these fears would be confirmed in the Court's seminal interpretation of the amended section 2, *Thornburg v. Gingles* (1986).

Gingles involved a claim by black citizens in North Carolina that the state's 1982 senate and house redistricting plans had diluted their votes. The plaintiffs had successfully challenged one single-member district and six multimember districts before a federal district court. Although *Gingles* had commenced prior to 1982, by the time the case went to trial the section 2 amendments to the VRA had been passed. They were, therefore, in effect before the trial court that heard the case.

A critical component of the 1982 section 2 changes concerned the "totality of circumstances" test. This test, referred to in section 2(b) of the act, was to be the measure of whether a section 2 violation had occurred. The specifics of the totality of circumstances were never provided for in the VRA. Both Justice Brennan, who wrote the plurality opinion for the Court in *Gingles*, as well as the federal district court that heard *Gingles* in the original instance, relied on the Senate Judiciary Committee's report of 1982 when defining what the totality of circumstances consisted of. As quoted by Justice Brennan from the Senate report, the "typical factors" were

1. the extent of any history of official discrimination in the state or political subdivision that touched the right of the members of the minority group to register, to vote, or otherwise to participate in the democratic process;

2. the extent to which voting in the elections of the state or political subdivision is racially polarized;

3. the extent to which the state or political subdivision has used unusually large election districts, majority vote requirements, anti–single shot provisions [which prohibit voting for anything less than a full list of candidates in an at-large election], or other voting practices or procedures that may enhance the opportunity for discrimination against the minority group;

4. if there is a candidate slating process, whether the members of the minority group have been denied access to that process;

5. the extent to which members of the minority group in the state or political subdivision bear the effects of discrimination in

such areas as education, employment and health, which hinder their ability to participate effectively in the political process;

6. whether political campaigns have been characterized by overt or subtle racial appeals;

7. the extent to which members of the minority group have been elected to public office in the jurisdiction.[61]

Applying the "totality of circumstances" test, the district court had found that all seven of the legislative districts in dispute in *Gingles* were in violation of the amended section 2. The state of North Carolina appealed the court's judgment with respect to five of the multimember districts, contending that the lower court had misconstrued the meaning of "racially polarized voting" for the purposes of the section. The state also alleged that the district court had failed to account adequately for black electoral success when conducting its section 2 review.

Justice Brennan largely agreed with the district court's ruling, overturning its findings with respect only to one of the multimember districts. Although recognizing, like the district court, that the seven "typical factors" outlined in the Senate report's review of the totality of circumstances test were important, Brennan also emphasized they were "neither comprehensive nor exclusive." The Senate Judiciary Committee had stressed that determining whether the political processes were equally open to minorities under section 2 would depend on a searching evaluation of "past and present reality" as well as on a "functional" approach to the political process outlined in the Senate report.[62]

Brennan's emphasis that section 2 review should be wide-ranging and should consider the numerous circumstances outlined in the Senate report and by the Senate Judiciary Committee would be significantly narrowed in *Gingles*. Because North Carolina's appeal focused on the meaning of "racially polarized voting," and because he himself believed that this definition was the crux of a section 2 action, Brennan's opinion focused almost exclusively on the meaning of that term.

The dispute over how to define racially polarized voting turned largely on an abstruse technical question of social science methodology. According to Brennan,

North Carolina and the United States . . . argue that the term "racially polarized voting" must, as a matter of law, refer to voting patterns for which the *principal cause* is race. They contend that the District Court utilized a legally incorrect definition of racially polarized voting by relying on bivariate statistical analyses which merely demonstrated a *correlation* between the race of the voter and the level of voter support for certain candidates, but which did not prove that race was the primary determinant of voters' choices. According to appellants and the United States, only multiple regression analysis, which can take account of other variables which might also explain voters' choices, such as "party affiliation, age, religion, [and so forth]" . . . can prove that race was the primary determinant of voter behavior.[63]

Brennan rejected the argument that plaintiffs in section 2 cases had to demonstrate that race was the primary cause of racially polarized voting in order to succeed: "Under the 'results test' of § 2, only the *correlation* between race of voter and selection of certain candidates, not the *causes* of the correlation, matters." The "*reasons* black and white voters vote differently have *no* relevance to the central inquiry of § 2."[64] The very purpose of the 1982 section 2 amendments was to make such causes and questions of racial discrimination irrelevant to section 2 evidentiary dispositions, and this idea was the whole point of overruling *Bolden* and its holding that proof of discriminatory intent was required in section 2 actions.

In support of this interpretation, Justice Brennan cited the 1982 Senate report, which emphasized that proof of discriminatory intent had been repudiated by Congress because it was unnecessarily divisive, was too difficult to prove, and asked the wrong question. "The 'right' question, as the Report emphasizes repeatedly, is whether 'as a result of the challenged practice or structure plaintiffs do not have an equal opportunity to participate in the political processes and to elect candidates of their choice'";[65] and this question, said Brennan, was answered by looking at racial vote polarization in the jurisdictions in dispute.[66]

Justice Rehnquist had complained in the *Rome* decision that the attempt to regulate racial-bloc voting under the auspices of the VRA was an attempt to redress *private*, not *governmental*, discrimination, something Congress could not do under the Constitution. Where precisely Congress got the constitutional authority to regulate the voting behavior of the citizens of North Carolina, as Brennan seemed to suggest was authorized by section 2, was never explained. Still, this was not the issue in *Gingles*. Rather, the central question in dispute was what specific criteria minority groups would have to establish to challenge multimember districts in section 2 contests successfully. Brennan narrowed this issue to three conditions. First, minority groups would have to demonstrate that they were geographically widespread enough and sufficiently "compact to constitute a majority in a single-member district." Second, they would have to demonstrate that they were "politically cohesive," meaning that their members generally voted the same way. Third, they would have to prove that the white majority voted sufficiently as a bloc to defeat their preferred candidates most of the time.[67] Although Brennan clarified that these three prerequisites were necessary and not sufficient conditions for success in a section 2 action, in the future they would be the ones to dominate section 2 controversies.

Justice O'Connor, writing a concurring opinion on behalf of herself, Chief Justice Burger, Justice Lewis Powell, and Justice Rehnquist, agreed with Justice Brennan that the key language of section 2 was the latter part of section 2(b), providing that the "results" test was satisfied when minorities were shown to "have less opportunity than other members of the electorate to participate in the political process and to elect representatives of their choice." O'Connor objected, however, that Brennan had focused too much on the latter part of the section's test, the ability of minority voters "to elect representatives of their choice." By disregarding the earlier language of section 2(b) that emphasized minority opportunity to participate in the political process, Brennan had underemphasized the full "totality of circumstances" that the Senate report had outlined and that he himself had cited earlier in his opinion.[68] Brennan's construction of section 2, wrote O'Connor, gave rise to a singular racial entitlement divorced from any question of racial discrimination. His refusal to consider the reasoning behind racial voter preferences, Justice White wrote in a separate concurring opinion, was tantamount to "interest-group politics rather than a rule hedging against racial discrimination."[69]

White's description of *Gingles* as a ruling implicating interest-group politics was perhaps the most telling remark in the case, capturing the transformation in the purpose of the VRA that second-generation voting rights generally, and *Gingles* more particularly, had effected. Brennan's reduction of the section 2 totality of circumstances test to racially polarized voting and black electoral success, and his further abandonment of the notion that race needed to be the principal cause for racially polarized voting, confirmed what critics of the section 2 results test had feared: that the test would convert the VRA into an even starker instrument of race-based, interest-group liberalism than the act had been in the past. The *Gingles* holding created, in Justice O'Connor's words, "what amounts to a right to *usual, roughly* proportional representation on the part of sizable, compact, cohesive minority groups."[70] Political interests would now be identified with discrete racial groups, which would now have an entitlement to office-holding proportionate to their racial demographics. Even if this understanding was not formally or explicitly recognized in second-generation voting rights prior to *Gingles*, it would become the credo of section 2 litigation thereafter.

Setting the Stage for the 1990s

Gingles revealed that section 2, as it was amended in 1982, was a paradigm of Hayekian rationalism: The text of the section presumed that courts could assess the litany of historical, social, and political factors contemplated by the totality of circumstances test with sufficient precision to determine objectively whether the multifaceted political processes leading up to the election of representatives in federal, state, and local elections were equally open to all groups. This determination no court could possibly achieve.

Perhaps in recognition of the enormity of this task, Justice Brennan in *Gingles* had reduced the totality of circumstances test to two simple, quantifiable measures—racially polarized voting and black electoral success. Even if Brennan's opinion represented a misreading of section 2, having disregarded some of the most important provisions of the section while adopting a "functional" approach to its interpretation that was not located in the VRA but in a single footnote appended to the 1982 Senate report, it had the virtue of simplicity.[71] By contrast, Justice O'Connor's opinion may have been more consistent with the text of section 2, but it was precisely for this reason that it provided a less-cognizable legal rule for lower courts to follow than Brennan's simplified "mathematical principle."[72]

In truth, the language of section 2 was simply inchoate, explicitly establishing a results test as the measure of electoral opportunity under the section, thus implying a right to proportional racial representation, while also explicitly denying such a right in its concluding proviso, all the while suggesting that considerations other than discriminatory results might be taken into account when assessing electoral opportunity under the section.

Interestingly, in *Gingles* neither the United States nor North Carolina raised any constitutional challenge to the newly proposed section 2 results test. In the case of the United States the reaction was understandable. The Reagan administration could hardly oppose a statutory amendment that President Reagan himself had signed into law only a few years earlier. North Carolina, on the other hand, was under no such compulsion. Yet, like the United States, it raised no constitutional issue. Nor has any jurisdiction since *Gingles* brought such an issue before the Court. As three supporters of the 1982 VRA observed in 2001, the fact that "the Court has interpreted both the Fourteenth and the Fifteenth Amendments to prohibit only purposefully discriminatory actions" and yet "has never squarely addressed the question of the constitutionality of amended § 2's results test" is "striking."[73]

Congress in 1982 overturned a constitutional ruling in *Bolden* and got away with it. In *Gingles*, Justice Brennan emphasized that the "essence of a § 2 claim is that a certain electoral law, practice, or structure interacts with social and historical circumstances to cause an inequality in the opportunities enjoyed by black and white voters to elect their preferred representatives."[74] Brennan's reference to "social and historical circumstances" was virtually identical to those "historical and social factors" that he and Justice Marshall proclaimed in *Bolden* should be the measure of vote dilution. But in *Bolden*, Justices Brennan and Marshall lost; they were the dissenters in the case. The Court in *Bolden* had denounced their approach to vote dilution as dependent on "gauzy sociological considerations" that would produce arbitrary judicial outcomes and divide the country into an archipelago of racial confederations. In *Gingles* these same "gauzy sociological considerations" were now the test for vote dilution under section 2. All the questions Justice Stewart had warned about in *Bolden* that were corollaries to the recognition of racial-group representational rights—who was a member of what racial group, what racial and ethnic groups constituted "political groups," could there be more than one "political group" among those constituencies, and so on—were now matters that courts would have to take up following *Gingles*.

If nothing else, *Gingles* exemplified just how much the tables had turned in the six short years since the *Bolden* decision. Not only had the Court now explicitly endorsed racial-group rights to representation; few cases in Supreme Court history had attempted to reduce American republicanism to such precise, scientifically verifiable terms—what the plurality in *Bolden* had suggested no court could plausibly do. More than any other case in voting rights history, *Gingles* symbolized the Court's heightening judicial rationalism as well as its symbiotic relationship with the voting rights bar and the academic community, two critical forces driving the Court's augmenting rationalism and multiculturalist approach to voting rights.

Like so much other social science litigation, *Gingles* did not involve the pure adjudication of a dispute or the application of law to facts. Rather, the law itself had first to be defined, largely on the basis of social science and other third-party evidence. In *Gingles* the Court referred to seventeen articles written by prominent social scientists, the most important of which were used to define what constituted racially polarized voting. The very concept of "racially polarized voting" itself had originated in social science literature, and its very legal significance in *Gingles* would be defined by social scientists and legal academics.[75] The principal authority the Court would ultimately rely on for its three-part test for the concept of racially polarized voting was not the VRA, but a law review article by civil rights attorneys James Blacksher and Lawrence Menefee, the very lawyers who represented the losing parties in *Bolden*.[76]

The most serious constitutional question *Gingles* raised concerned its evident challenge to the Court's suspect classification doctrine—the doctrine that outlawed racial classifications in law save generally in circumstances where they were remedies to proven acts of racial discrimination. Requiring jurisdictions to create racially defined electoral districts, as *Gingles* did, and to do so without any proof that such districts were a remedy to proven acts of discrimination, placed the VRA in tension with the laws of equal protection.

In the late 1980s, the VRA's potential unconstitutionality was further aggravated by a 1987 Department of Justice regulation that required jurisdictions covered by section 4 of the VRA effectively to inoculate themselves against any potential *Gingles* lawsuits before section 5 preclearance would be granted.[77] This requirement would have the effect of transforming the section 5 preclearance test from one measuring retrogression to one calling for racial maximization, an imperative that would require states to create as many minority electoral districts as they could in order to protect against any potential preclearance objections. When this regulation was combined with the DOJ's aggressive enforcement of compliance with racial maximization as a precondition for preclearance of state redistricting plans following the 1990 census, the result would be bizarrely contoured congressional districts in states such as North Carolina, Texas, and Georgia that would be the subject of constitutional challenges making their way to the Supreme Court during the 1990s.

6

The 1990s: *Shaw v. Reno* and the Resurrection of the Founders' Republicanism?

In the years leading up to the constitutional litigation involving the VRA in the 1990s, voting rights scholars had expressed some surprise at how little notoriety affirmative action in minority voting rights had generated. Writing in 1987, for instance, Abigail Thernstrom observed that "minority voting rights is perhaps the most debatable, yet least debated, of all affirmative action issues."[1] Five years later, Hugh Davis Graham could still rightly claim that "[VRA] enforcement, unlike Civil Rights Act enforcement, has thus far navigated a relatively safe political passage through the shoals of public opinion."[2]

The low profile of the VRA would change dramatically in 1993. In the spring of that year, two events would bring the VRA into the limelight. The first was President Clinton's nomination of Lani Guinier to head the Civil Rights Division of the Department of Justice. Guinier was a law professor who had built her academic career on the basis of a controversial approach to voting rights that she claimed was an extension of the logic of *Allen v. State Board of Elections* (1969).[3]

The second event was *Shaw v. Reno*, a case that highlighted the extremes to which the racial political engineering under the VRA had been taken. *Shaw* involved a constitutional challenge to two bizarrely shaped North Carolina majority-minority districts, Congressional District 1 and Congressional District 12. Both had been drawn to comply with the pre-clearance demands of the Department of Justice following the 1990 census. Congressional District 1 resembled a Rorschach inkblot.[4] Congressional District 12 stretched 160 miles along the Interstate-85 corridor, for much of its length consisting of little more than the corridor itself. Incorporating rural, financial, and manufacturing centers, District 12 snaked through ten different counties until it swallowed up enough black neighborhoods from Durham to Charlotte to meet the preclearance demands of the DOJ.[5] As one expert witness would testify at the *Shaw* remand trial in 1994, a person driving west to east along I-85 would exit and reenter the district twenty-one times.[6] Two academics would later describe Congressional District 12 as the "worst district in the nation" in terms of dispersion and perimeter measures of congressional district shape.[7]

The *Shaw* litigation and Guinier's nomination generated significant public controversy largely for the same reason: Both seemed to reflect the new politics of racial identity that had become the animating vision of late–twentieth-century civil rights policy. In *Shaw*, Justice O'Connor observed on behalf of the majority that Congressional Districts 1 and 12 bore "an uncomfortable resemblance to political apartheid," reinforcing "the perception that members of the same racial group—regardless of their age, education, economic status, or the community in which they live— think alike, share the same political interests, and will prefer the same candidates at the polls."[8] For her critics, Guinier in her writings seemed to epitomize these very multiculturalist assumptions in voting rights scholarship, extolling the virtues of black descriptive representation and racial group identity.[9]

As Justice O'Connor's remarks indicate, faction, and specifically the racial and ethnic fragmentation of American society, was at the center of attention in the Supreme Court's voting rights cases in the 1990s. This very Madisonian theme pointed up the conflict between the two visions of equality and representation that were at war in voting rights law: Madisonian and multicultural republicanism. Justice O'Connor suggested in *Shaw* that this conflict was unique to the 1990s, due in particular to the aberrant way in which the Justice Department had enforced the VRA during that decade, demanding racial maximization in redistricting from states covered by sections 4 and 5 of the VRA.

Justices Thomas and Scalia begged to differ, however. Although they joined O'Connor in the majority opinion in *Shaw*, in subsequent cases they made clear that the conflict between the Constitution's laws of equal protection and the VRA was not isolated to the 1990s. In fact, it had existed for decades, ever since the Court's seminal decision in *Allen*. In *Holder v. Hall* (1994)[10] Thomas and Scalia would suggest that the only solution to the intractable problems the Court had created in its second-generation voting rights was to abandon this line of jurisprudence altogether. Only in this way could the Court extricate itself from the dubious democratic theories and unsavory racial classifications in which it had had to engage to give effect to vote-dilution law. In *Shaw*, the Court went some distance toward acknowledging and addressing this problem.

Reaffirming the Law of Equal Protection: *Shaw*, *Miller*, and the Repudiation of *United Jewish Organizations*

The *Shaw* cases discussed in this chapter consist of five rulings the Court delivered during the 1990s: *Shaw v. Reno* (1993), *Miller v. Johnson* (1995),[11] *United States v. Hays* (1995),[12] *Shaw v. Hunt* (*Shaw II*, 1996),[13] and *Bush v. Vera* (1996).[14] All five decisions were based on similar factual and legal scenarios involving constitutional challenges to racial redistricting.

In the 1990s, North Carolina, Georgia, Louisiana, and Texas had to seek section 5 preclearance from the Department of Justice for their congressional redistricting plans. The department imposed racial maximization policies on all four states, requiring congressional redistricting in which MMDs were created in rough proportion to the racial demographics of the states. These congressional plans were all challenged on grounds they consisted of unconstitutional racial gerrymanders. Although the politics leading up to the impugned redistricting plans were distinct in each of the states, the legal issues in the *Shaw* cases were fundamentally the same, driving the Court to revisit consistently its second-generation voting rights law and attempt to reconcile it with its equal protection jurisprudence. This task would prove increasingly difficult as the 1990s wore on.

In *Shaw*, the plaintiffs challenged North Carolina Congressional District 1 and Congressional District 12 (both MMDs created to comply with the DOJ's demands, as described above) as unconstitutional racial gerrymanders. The complainants asserted these districts were so irregular in their shape that they could only be understood as an effort by the state to segregate the races for purposes of voting. This the state could not do. The Supreme Court agreed, finding that the plaintiffs had, indeed, stated a legitimate equal protection claim. Accordingly, the Court remanded the case for further hearings consistent with its ruling.

Although forecasts immediately following *Shaw* speculated that the case would not lay "the foundation for a major attack on the Voting Rights Act"[15] or was "best read as an exceptional doctrine for aberrational contexts rather than as a prelude to a sweeping constitutional condemnation of race-conscious redistricting,"[16] subsequent rulings made clear that *Shaw* was, indeed, a bellwether in equal protection law, marking a significant turn away from earlier voting rights jurisprudence. In *Miller v. Johnson*, where plaintiffs challenged Georgia's congressional redistricting plan as an unconstitutional racial gerrymander, Justice Kennedy clarified on behalf of the Court that the *Shaw* holding was not limited to bizarrely shaped districts. Kennedy affirmed that any time race was the "predominant factor" motivating legislative districting, the districting would be constitutionally suspect.[17]

The *Shaw* and *Miller* rulings caused widespread consternation among minority advocacy groups and academics, and for good reason. By making the predominance of a racial motive the constitutional threshold for a challenge to legislative redistricting, the *Shaw* and *Miller* holdings jeopardized the very theory of racial representation on which second-generation voting rights had been based. As Justice Thomas would remark in *Bush v. Vera*, the Texas redistricting litigation: If predominance of racial motive was now the touchstone for constitutional actions in redistricting disputes, it was hard to see how the remedy of choice in vote-dilution law—MMDs—could survive the *Miller* test. How could race not be the predominant factor in the creation of an MMD when the very measure of such a district consisted of the intentional placement of a predetermined number of minorities within its boundaries, sufficient to elect a minority-preferred candidate?[18]

Much of the disagreement in *Shaw* centered on the 1977 case, *United Jewish Organizations Inc. v. Carey*, discussed at length in chapter 4. The *Shaw* dissenters argued that *UJO* was directly on point since it made those racial classifications necessary to comply with the VRA constitutionally acceptable and thus barred the plaintiffs' action. The *Shaw* majority disagreed. In 1977 the Supreme Court had been dominated by liberals sympathetic to race-preference affirmative action. By 1993 that was no longer the case.

This personnel change on the Court accounted for not only a change in the Court's perspective toward affirmative action, but also a deep appreciation among at least some of its members that the political circumstances in the United States had changed dramatically since the 1970s. If *UJO* reflected a climate in which a majority on the Court was concerned about redressing the recent legacy of racial discrimination in the Jim Crow South, *Shaw*, by contrast, reflected a different era, in which a majority of the Court was now concerned about the racial balkanization of the country precipitated by federal initiatives such as the VRA.

The context for the dispute in *Shaw* over *UJO* was set by recent affirmative action rulings, the most important of which was *City of Richmond v. J. A. Croson Co.* (1989).[19] *Croson* marked a critical turning point because it was the first decision in which a clear majority of the Court applied strict scrutiny to state and local affirmative action programs, regardless of which racial group was burdened by or benefited from the racial classification in dispute.[20] *Croson* was consistent with earlier equal protection rulings, but the manner in which it qualified earlier equal protection law would set the backdrop to the *Shaw* litigation and the dispute over *UJO*.

At issue in *Croson* was a business set-aside program in Richmond, Virginia, that required all prime contractors awarded city construction contracts to subcontract 30 percent or more of the dollar amount of each contract to minority business enterprises. Under the terms of the set-aside, the J. A. Croson Company had been denied a waiver from the plan's provisions and had lost a plumbing fixtures contract on which it had been the sole bidder. The company sued the city, alleging the minority business set-aside violated the equal protection clause of the Fourteenth Amendment. The Supreme Court agreed.

Examining the record, Justice O'Connor, on behalf of the Court, could find no legitimate purpose for the Richmond plan. In particular, the Court found no evidence that the plan was a remedy for past discrimination against the intended beneficiaries—black, Spanish-speaking, Oriental, Indian, Eskimo, and Aleut contractors. There was a serious question whether some of the set-aside's beneficiaries had ever even lived in Richmond.[21] O'Connor also pointed out that the city did not know how many minority business enterprises in the relevant market were qualified to provide prime or subcontracting work, nor did it know what percentage of money minority subcontractors were currently receiving from prime contracts let in the city.[22] Five of the nine Richmond City Council members who approved the minority set-aside were black, leading O'Connor to suggest that the set-aside program may have been an act of self-dealing, intended not so much to help disadvantaged groups as to assist the majority in Richmond itself.[23]

Although *Croson* has been explained as having presented a fact scenario ripe for judicial attack, a characterization that is accurate enough, the case was also consistent both with recent civil rights rulings[24] and constitutional holdings in which the Court had signaled a less auspicious approach toward race-preference affirmative action. In *Croson*, for instance, Justice O'Connor made clear that the "benign purpose" doctrine of equal protection review, championed by some of the justices on the Court, would not be tolerated.

The "benign purpose" approach made its first appearance in *University of California Regents v. Bakke*,[25] a sharply divided 1978 decision involving affirmative action in education. At issue in *Bakke* was a constitutional challenge to a set-aside for minority applicants at the UC Davis medical school. Justices Brennan, White, Marshall, and Harry Blackmun had proposed that race-conscious programs that were aimed at alleviating the condition of "disadvantaged" groups should be subjected to a standard of constitutional review less exacting than the strict-scrutiny test—the usual standard applied in cases involving fundamental rights or suspect classifications.[26] Justice Powell's opinion for the Court in *Bakke* rejected this proposal, pointing out that the "intermediate" standard of equal protection review that it engendered was unprincipled and intractable, creating what would amount to an evolving racial caste system where some groups would be treated differently depending on what the Court perceived their social and political status to be at any given time.[27]

In *Croson*, Justice O'Connor rejected yet another plea from Justices Marshall, Brennan, and Blackmun to apply a more relaxed level of constitutional scrutiny to the set-aside at issue. The Fourteenth Amendment, she emphasized, was intended to make race irrelevant in American politics, and thus focused attention on the individual, not the group—and certainly not racial groups. To the extent that racial-group classifications were made, they needed to be closely scrutinized to be sure that the goal pursued by the legislative body was important enough to warrant indulgence in a suspect classification.[28]

Whether *Croson* clarified earlier jurisprudence or simply abandoned it, the decision obviously did not augur well for the defendants in *Shaw*. Applying *Croson* to the VRA, however, would not be an easy task. Cases prior to *Shaw* clearly indicated that racial considerations pertaining to redistricting legislation were not per se unconstitutional. Justice O'Connor emphasized that *Shaw* was not a vote-dilution decision but, rather, a race classification case.[29] Insofar as it was, it was consistent with longstanding equal protection doctrine that had applied the race discrimination norm to other areas of public life, such as education, public parks, beaches, and golf courses.[30] Nevertheless, O'Connor qualified that "redistricting differs from other kinds of state decisionmaking in that the legislature always is *aware* of race when it draws district lines. . . . That sort of race consciousness does not lead inevitably to impermissible race discrimination."[31] If it did not, what type of race consciousness did? What was the constitutional cutoff point?

O'Connor never answered this question, and perhaps for good reason. To the extent the VRA guarantees minorities the right to an undiluted vote, it provides for group rights that require racial classifications to be complied with. This was Justice Thomas's point in *Vera*. It is impossible to create MMDs, for instance, or in fact provide for any other kind of racial representation without engaging in those very classifications the Constitution generally proscribes.

Yet the constitutionality of race classifications engaged to comply with the VRA seemed to be squarely addressed in *UJO*, where a plurality suggested that racial classifications and even racial quotas undertaken to comply with the act were perfectly constitutional. Recall that in *UJO* Justice White, writing for the plurality, had accepted the Second Circuit Court of Appeal's reasoning that the VRA "contemplated that the Attorney General and the state legislature would have 'to think in racial terms'; because the Act '*necessarily deals with race or color, corrective action under it must do the same.*'"[32] A few pages later, White emphasized that implicit in the Court's section 5 case law was "the proposition that the Constitution does not prevent a State subject to the Voting Rights Act from *deliberately* creating or preserving black majorities in particular districts in order to ensure that its reapportionment plan complies with § 5."[33] Unless the Court had "adopted an unconstitutional construction of § 5 in *Beer* and *City of Richmond*, a reapportionment cannot violate the Fourteenth and Fifteenth Amendment merely because a State uses specific numerical quotas in establishing a certain number of black majority districts."[34] As Justice White again argued in his dissenting opinion in *Shaw*, the entirety of the Court's section 5 vote-dilution law seemed to be arrayed against the majority's holding in the North Carolina case.

Justice O'Connor disputed White's interpretation, asserting that *Shaw* involved a claim that was "analytically distinct" from the constitutional claims advanced in *UJO*.[35] Yet O'Connor's argument was not very compelling. She emphasized that three justices in *UJO* had qualified that remedying minority electoral ineffectiveness was permissible only in cases in which compact electoral districts could be drawn[36]—a qualifier suggesting district shape was indeed an important consideration when providing relief in vote-dilution cases, as Justice O'Connor asserted.

But this argument missed the more fundamental point: Whatever restrictions may have been placed on the forms or shapes MMDs could assume as a *remedy* to a constitutional or statutory violation, the very *cause of action* pleaded by the plaintiffs in *Shaw* seemed to be extinguished by *UJO*. Justice O'Connor's assertion that the *Shaw* claim was "analytically distinct" from the claims advanced in *UJO* was untenable in the face of the Hasidic plaintiffs' explicit allegation that New York had "violated the Fourteenth and Fifteenth Amendments by *deliberately revising its reapportionment plan along racial lines*"[37] and that "there could be—and in fact was—*no reason other than race* to divide the community at this time."[38] *UJO* not only appeared to provide little support for the plaintiffs' claims in *Shaw*; it seemed positively to eliminate them, as the dissenters in *Shaw* were quick to point out.

The majorities in *Shaw* and *Miller* never fully confronted the obvious incompatibility of the *UJO* and *Shaw* holdings. As Justice White had emphasized in *UJO*, the VRA, and in particular second-generation voting rights, required judges and legislators to "think in racial terms." Vote-dilution law was impossible without regulating and allocating on the basis of race. Now such regulations were apparently unconstitutional, even though three members of the Court majority in the *Shaw* cases could not quite bring themselves to say so. The new equal protection ruling established in *Shaw* and *Miller*—finally taking seriously the application of the Constitution to the VRA a quarter-century after *Allen*—was at odds with the standard remedies of the VRA, mandating as they did the intentional creation of racial districts.

Although the *Shaw* cases attempted to reaffirm the laws of equal protection in the face of those racial classifications undertaken to comply with the administration of the VRA in the 1990s, they nevertheless accentuated, perhaps paradoxically, that vote-dilution law was inconceivable without legislatures and members of the judiciary dividing the electorate into racial classes in order to balance the power of these constituencies throughout the entire political process. "In construing the [VRA] to cover claims of vote dilution," Justice Thomas remarked in *Holder*, "we have converted the Act into a device for regulating, rationing, and apportioning political power among racial and ethnic groups."[39]

The dissenters in the *Shaw* cases would have agreed with this assessment. What they would have disputed (and what Justices Stevens, Blackmun, David Souter, and Ruth Bader Ginsburg did dispute in *Holder*) were Thomas's additional remarks that second-generation voting rights were a judicial concoction, the contrivance of an activist federal judiciary that had granted itself authority "to develop theories on basic principles of representative government," "highly political judgments" involving questions of political theory "that courts [were] inherently ill-equipped to make."[40]

Justice Thomas's comments in *Holder* were provocative and were joined only by Justice Scalia. Yet even though other members of the *Holder* court did not join Thomas's concurring opinion, the racial class analyses and related assumptions that had been standard fare in vote-dilution law for more than a generation were clearly in serious jeopardy following *Shaw* and *Miller*. Both the multiculturalism of second-generation voting rights, which assumed racial class conflict in politics on the basis of thin, if nonexistent, evidentiary thresholds, and the rationalism of such law, which assumed that the judiciary could construct coherent, nonarbitrary theories of "fair" or "effective" racial representation, were under assault in the 1990s.

As we will see, Justice Thomas's concurring opinion in *Holder* was by far the most comprehensive and cogent critique of vote-dilution law in this regard. There Thomas made the case for why second-generation issues were not, and should not be, covered by the VRA, a position that provoked the four dissenting justices in the case to author a separate dissenting opinion directed solely at his interpretation of the act, a rarity in Supreme Court jurisprudence.

The Counterassault on the Rationalism and Multiculturalism of the Voting Rights Act

Holder v. Hall (1994) involved a section 2 lawsuit brought by the National Association for the Advancement of Colored People and black residents of Bleckley County, Georgia, who alleged that the county's longstanding single-commissioner form of government diluted black citizens' votes. The plaintiffs contended that if the county adopted a hypothetical five-member commission, black voters in the county could elect a candidate of their choice. The Supreme Court dismissed the plaintiffs' claims because, among other things, there was no baseline or objective benchmark against which any vote dilution could be measured.

Holder addressed whether the size of a governing body constituted a "standard, practice, or procedure" covered by the VRA. A plurality of the Court answered this question in the negative, including Justice Thomas. Thomas, however, took the occasion to elaborate that not only did the VRA not cover the size of a governing body, it did not cover questions of vote dilution per se. This position shocked the dissenters in *Holder*, as well as many voting rights academics.

In *Holder*, Thomas declared that a systematic reassessment of the Court's vote-dilution law was necessary. He was specifically critical of the "sort of statutory construction through divination" that continued to lead members of the Court to assert that "Congress 'really meant' to enact a statute about vote dilution even though Congress did not do so explicitly."[41] Thomas noted that at no point in the history of the VRA had the language of the act ever made any direct reference to the concept of "vote dilution"; yet the Court had perennially read vote dilution into the legislation. Perhaps most important, it did so in *Allen*, misconstruing the meaning of section 5, and again in *Gingles*, misinterpreting the meaning of section 2.

The result of these misinterpretations was the conversion of the VRA's individual rights into group-based entitlements. Thomas highlighted that the most obvious problem with vote-dilution analyses, as the facts in *Holder* demonstrated, concerned the point of comparison that was to be used to measure undiluted voting power. Without warrant in the language of the VRA, the Court had surreptitiously settled on a simple, quantifiable yardstick: control of seats by racial minorities. The next question the Court had to answer—the "proper" number of seats minorities should control—was also answered without reference to the text, and in a predictably mathematical manner: Minorities should control seats proportionate to their racial demographics.[42] The consequence of the Court's misconstruction of the VRA was that federal judges were now "engaged in methodically carving the country into racially designated electoral districts,"[43] precisely the opposite of what one would have thought the VRA was intended to achieve.

Throughout his opinion, Justice Thomas sounded a decisively Hayekian tone, criticizing the judicial orthodoxy in vote-dilution law that had presumed the Court could know what theory of "fair" racial representation should be imposed on jurisdictions throughout the country. It was the imposition of such "correct" theories of representation that had become the hallmark of the Court's vote-dilution law since the late 1960s.[44] Although single-member districts had been used by federal courts both as the benchmark for measuring vote dilution as well as the principal remedial mechanism for guaranteeing minority voting power, nothing in the VRA or in America's constitutional system or history warranted mandating single-member districting as the proper mechanism for electing government officials, or even for remedying alleged problems of "vote dilution."[45] Thomas suggested that this element of the Court's rationalism had been combined with an equally brazen multiculturalism that could not have been better calculated to fragment the nation into racial constituencies, inviting the very race factionalism that the original Constitution and the Civil War amendments were designed to avoid.

Perhaps the most pernicious aspect of the Court's vote-dilution law was its members' willingness to assume that "the group asserting dilution is not merely a racial or ethnic group, but a group having distinct political interests as well."[46] *Gingles* had promoted race-identity politics by suggesting that any time black-preferred candidates lost to white-preferred candidates, it was due to racism (how else were section 2 remedies to be justified?), while at the same time prohibiting any inquiry into whether race was, in fact, the cause for such differences. As Justice Thomas emphasized, the *Gingles* section 2 inquiry was specifically "not designed to provide a test" for whether race was what defined "a distinctive political community of interest."[47]

Justice Thomas also declared that the assumptions on which the Court's vote-dilution jurisprudence had been based "should be repugnant to any nation that strives for the ideal of a color-blind Constitution."[48] Thomas was certainly aware that the Court's equal protection law did not require colorblindness in law, but he was also aware that the only time the Court had tolerated racial classifications by state governments was when they were necessary to compensate for past discrimination or to provide for national security.[49] How could equal protection of the laws be maintained in the face of a section 2 results test and a section 5 preclearance mandate that required racial classifications, even where no proof existed that these requirements were remedies for proven acts of discrimination?

The Court, Thomas suggested, had failed through the 1990s to answer this most significant question. By then, section 5 had virtually nothing to do with redressing invidious discrimination and was almost entirely a race-entitlement initiative. The same was true of section 2. The *Gingles* test precluded judges faced with potential vote-dilution claims from even inquiring into whether intentional discrimination was the reason for the legislative action at issue or the racial-bloc voting in dispute—the critical evidentiary threshold that usually triggered relief in post-*Gingles* section 2 litigation.

Another affirmative action decision of the same ilk as Justice Thomas's opinion in *Holder* was *Adarand Constructors, Inc. v. Pena* (1995).[50] *Adarand* involved an equal protection challenge to a federal highway set-aside in Colorado. Finding for the plaintiff, the Court in *Adarand* ruled that strict scrutiny applied to federal affirmative action programs as well as to state affirmative action programs. This decision would prove to be a watershed in equal protection law, consolidating the Court's affirmative action jurisprudence by making clear that any time a state *or the federal government* classified citizens by race, whites as well as blacks could sue, demanding the imposition of strict scrutiny on the jurisdiction at issue.[51] *Adarand* overruled *Metro Broadcasting, Inc. v. FCC* (1990),[52] a decision which held that the federal government was subject to a lesser standard of constitutional scrutiny with respect to its affirmative action programs than were state governments.

Like Justice Thomas's remarks in *Holder*, *Adarand*, along with *Croson*, represented a new antirationalism and antimulticulturalism strain of equal protection law. Writing for the Court in *Adarand*, Justice O'Connor summarized the Court's equal protection decisions through to *Croson*. Those decisions consisted of three general propositions: first, that all racial classifications were subject to *skepticism* or to the most searching judicial examination; second, that all such classifications required *consistency*—that is, the standard of review in equal protection law did not vary depending on the race of the individuals benefited or burdened by a particular race classification; and third, that equal protection law required *congruence*, the application of the same equal protection scrutiny to both state and federal law.[53]

Adarand's "skepticism" principle was the analogue of antirationalism because it signified that the Court would no longer tolerate racial classifications by any level of government without detailed proof that such classifications were necessary, either to compensate for past discrimination or to provide for national security. In *Shaw v. Hunt* (*Shaw II*), the second instance of the North Carolina redistricting litigation before the High Court, Chief Justice Rehnquist, speaking on behalf of the Court, paraphrased from earlier equal protection rulings, declaring that the discrimination purported to be remedied by any racial classification "must be 'identified discrimination'" and "must have had a 'strong basis in evidence . . . *before* [a government] embarks on an affirmative-action program.'"[54] A mere generalized assertion that an affirmative action program was intended to remedy past discrimination would be insufficient.

This requirement was as true of racial redistricting engaged in under the auspices of the VRA as it was of any other federal affirmative action initiative. In *Miller v. Johnson,* the Court reiterated this theme. The "presumptive skepticism of all racial classifications" set out in *Adarand*, Justice Kennedy declared, prohibited the Court

> from accepting on its face the Justice Department's conclusion that racial districting is necessary under the Voting Rights Act. . . . Were we to accept the Justice Department's objection itself as a compelling interest adequate to insulate racial districting from

constitutional review, we would be surrendering to the Executive Branch our role in enforcing the constitutional limits on race-based official action.[55]

As much as *UJO* may have reflected deference by the Supreme Court toward the DOJ's preclearance authority under the VRA, in *Miller* that deference evaporated, largely due to the intensification of judicial scrutiny of all race classifications set out in *Croson, Adarand,* and *Shaw.*

The Court's antirationalism complemented its antimulticulturalism, which was evident in its reassertion of the primacy of the Constitution's individual rights in *Croson, Adarand, Shaw, Miller, Shaw II,* and *Vera.* In *Adarand,* Justice O'Connor had declared that the three propositions applicable to race classifications—skepticism, consistency, and congruence—"all derive from the basic principle that the Fifth and Fourteenth Amendments to the Constitution protect *persons,* not *groups.* It follows from that principle that all government action based on race—a *group* classification long recognized as 'in most circumstances irrelevant and therefore prohibited' . . . —should be subjected to detailed judicial inquiry to ensure that the *personal* right to equal protection of the laws has not been infringed."[56] O'Connor's repeated stress on the individual-versus-group dimensions to equal protection disputes involving affirmative action highlighted the tension between the Madisonian and the multiculturalist understandings of equality at war in these controversies throughout the 1980s and 1990s.

In the latter decade, the central question in the redistricting disputes before the Court was whether the equal protection principles set out in *Croson* and *Adarand* could be reconciled with VRA law, as that law had been judicially interpreted and administered through the 1990s. *Croson* and *Adarand* had followed longstanding equal protection rulings that required proof of invidious discrimination as a precondition for race-based classifications. *Shaw* and the *Shaw*-legacy cases purported to respect these same principles, placing renewed emphasis on the individual rights of equal protection. In *Miller,* Justice Kennedy had emphasized that states could not use race as a proxy for the political views and preferences of voters. The Constitution prohibited governments from treating individuals as mere "components of a racial, religious, sexual or national class."[57] This emphasis on class seemed to constitute an illiberal, anti-Madisonian element of affirmative action policy in voting rights, at least as that policy had been implemented by the DOJ in its southern congressional preclearance activity in the 1990s.

Yet as much as the Court in the *Shaw* cases purported to take the same position it had taken in *Croson* and *Adarand*, the justices could not respect the individual rights of the Constitution because they remained committed to the doctrine of vote dilution under the VRA. The problem was that vote-dilution law was inconceivable without the use of race as a proxy. Justices Thomas and Scalia recognized this. So, too, did the dissenters in the *Shaw* cases. All would argue that racial classifications and the use of race as a proxy constituted the very essence of second-generation voting rights.

The Dissenters Respond

Justice Ginsburg observed, in response to Justice Kennedy's assertion in *Miller* that "government must treat citizens 'as individuals, not "as simply components of a racial, religious, sexual or national class,""[58] that when adopting districting plans, "States do not treat people as individuals. Apportionment schemes, by their very nature, assemble people in groups."[59] As soon as the Court committed to protecting against racial vote dilution in *Allen*, it necessarily committed to protecting group rights to representation based on race. The fact that ethnicity defined many of the groups that legislators classified for purposes of redistricting was a "political reality" that had been acted on in the past, Ginsburg argued:

> If Chinese-Americans and Russian-Americans may seek and secure group recognition in the delineation of voting districts, then African-Americans should not be dissimilarly treated. Otherwise, in the name of equal protection, we would shut out 'the very minority group whose history in the United States gave birth to the Equal Protection Clause.'"[60]

"Special circumstances," she concluded, "justify vigilant judicial inspection to protect minority voters—circumstances that do not apply to majority voters."[61]

Like Justices Stevens, Stephen Breyer, and Souter, who joined her opinion in *Miller*, Justice Ginsburg accepted the position of the judicial rationalists—that race classifications could be "contextualized" and that the Court could distinguish good from bad uses of race in public policy when conducting equal protection review. This rationalist ethos was central to the notion of the "two-class theory" of equal protection review proposed in the 1970s, whereby whites and minorities would be treated differently under the Constitution because some groups would be recognized as "special wards entitled to a degree of protection greater than that accorded to others."[62] Ginsburg's suggestion that minority voters required more vigilant judicial supervision than majority voters indicated that the dissenters in *Miller* had effectively adopted this "two-class" approach. Critical to the dissenting opinions throughout the *Shaw* cases was the assumption, as Justice Souter declared in *Vera*, that "contexts are crucial in determining how we define 'equal opportunity.'"[63]

In *UJO* a plurality of the Court had indicated that race classifications were legally indistinguishable from political, social, or economic classifications when it came to redistricting to comply with the VRA. Justice Ginsburg's point in *Miller* was the same. Second-generation voting rights required the use of racial classifications and race as a proxy because they dealt with racial balancing in the political process. How could such racial balancing be achieved without thinking in such racial terms? The Court in *UJO* had stated that the only constitutional cause of action that could challenge a state's compliance with the VRA was a vote-dilution claim. In the absence of this claim, plaintiffs had no cause of action, which is why in the dissenters' view the plaintiffs' complaints in the *Shaw* cases should have been dismissed.

This view also explains why, for the dissenters, the critical issue in voting rights disputes was not whether states engaged in racial classifications—which inevitably they must. Rather, it concerned the "contextualization" question, that is, the *nature* of the racial classifications in which the state has engaged. As Justice Stevens pointed out in *Miller*, the majority's attempt to describe the redistricting at issue in the *Shaw* cases as a form of "political apartheid" was a misnomer that failed to grasp the fundamental difference between a true "gerrymander"—a term that referred to a dominant group's attempt to enhance its political power by using grotesque district lines to carve a minority out of power—and what was going on in the *Shaw* disputes, which involved those same dominant groups attempting to enhance the political power of minorities.[64]

The most significant objection the dissenters raised in the *Shaw* cases was that the new constitutional claim in *Shaw* could not be reconciled with second-generation voting rights. How could vote-dilution law conform with the new *Shaw* holding that precluded race from being the predominant consideration in the drafting of electoral districts? As the dissenters indicated, such application was impossible. Moreover, according to the dissenters, the *Shaw* cases were problematic because the representational harms outlined in them violated traditional rules of standing.

On the standing question, the central issue raised by the dissenters focused on what had to be established to proceed with a *Shaw* claim. The majority in the cases had sent mixed signals in this regard. In *United States v. Hays* (1995), for instance, Justice O'Connor, speaking on behalf of the Court, had dismissed the complaints of the plaintiffs because they did not live in the MMDs they were challenging. Citing precedents that made it imperative that plaintiffs suffer "individualized harm" as a prerequisite for standing in constitutional claims, O'Connor declared that there was no exception for the rule against "generalized grievances" in equal protection law generally, or with respect to *Shaw*-based claims more particularly.[65] Voters in racially gerrymandered districts "may suffer the special representational harms racial classifications can cause in the voting context. On the other hand, where a plaintiff does not live in such a district, he or she does not."[66] The representational harms O'Connor had outlined in *Hays* consisted of the stigmatization individuals might experience by virtue of their membership in a racial group, the incitation of racial hostility, and the fact that officeholders in the impugned MMDs might represent only the majority racial group in the district.[67] In other words, the harms O'Connor outlined consisted of the *effects* of racial classifications rather than their *inherently* wrong nature.

Responding to O'Connor, Justice Stevens pointed out that the *Shaw* harms, as revisited in *Hays*, were based on speculation rather than fact. There was no empirical evidence in *Shaw* itself or any of the other *Shaw* cases that representatives elected from MMDs would necessarily consider the dominant minority group to be their primary constituency. Assuming that minority-preferred candidates from MMDs would conduct themselves in this way was to indulge the very sort of racial stereotypes of which the majority in *Shaw* was so critical.[68] In addition, how were members of MMDs stamped with a badge of inferiority or any other incidence of stigmatization, as O'Connor had suggested in both *Shaw* and *Hays*? Was this not something that had to be proved and not merely presumed? The black plaintiffs in the famous school desegregation case, *Brown v. Board of Education* (1954),[69] for instance, had empirically demonstrated through psychological evidence that, despite formally equal treatment under the law, they had suffered stigmatization and feelings of inferiority by virtue of their segregation from white students. No such evidence existed in any of the *Shaw* cases.[70]

What was in dispute in the *Shaw* cases was a longstanding conflict over the constitutional threshold that had to be met to have standing in a challenge to race classifications in law. Much of the confusion originated from *Brown v. Board of Education* itself, where the Court's reliance on "modern authority," specifically psychological studies that demonstrated the adverse effects of segregated schools on black schoolchildren, had suggested that the separate but equal doctrine from the notorious *Plessy v. Ferguson* (1896)[71] decision had not, in fact, been overruled—that the plaintiffs had simply met the *Plessy* standard by having demonstrated that despite equal treatment in terms of "tangible" factors, the adverse psychological effects of segregated schools meant that black students were, in fact, unequally treated at the level of "intangible" factors.[72] In the paragraph in *Brown* immediately following the Court's reference to "modern authority," however, Chief Justice Warren had written that "separate education facilities are inherently unequal,"[73] suggesting that the deprivation of equal protection in *Brown* was not based on psychological evidence or any adverse *effects*. Rather, the harm *inhered* in the race classification itself; race classifications *in and of themselves* were inequitable. No independent proof of demonstrated harm needed to be adduced once a racial classification had been established.

Both the majority in *Hays* and the dissenters in the *Shaw* cases appeared to adopt the *Plessy* reasoning of separate but equal, taking the position, as Justices White, Blackmun, and Stevens did in *Shaw*, that mere demonstration of discriminatory intent was insufficient to succeed in an equal protection challenge to racial redistricting.[74]

In *Miller*, Justice Kennedy would clarify what the Court (including himself) had left vague in *Hays*. The "injury in fact" suffered by *Shaw* claimants, Kennedy indicated, was simply the denial of equal treatment, not the inability to obtain a benefit. It consisted, in other words, of the mere fact that the government had classified voters on the basis of race.[75] If "race was the predominant factor motivating the legislature's decision to place a significant number of voters within or without a particular district," that was sufficient.[76] There was no need to establish a discriminatory *effect* in addition to discriminatory intent, as the dissenters in *Shaw* and *Miller* had demanded.

Although Justice Kennedy's description of the representational harm in *Miller* may have been difficult to square with Justice O'Connor's remarks in *Hays*, it was consistent with a long line of per curiam decisions that immediately followed *Brown v. Board of Education*. Kennedy had cited these cases in *Miller* as the basis for the *Shaw/Miller* line of constitutional jurisprudence.[77] They were compelling authorities to rely on. As William Van Alstyne has pointed out, in all the per curiam decisions over the two years that followed *Brown v. Board of Education*, the Court made no attempt to inquire who was being disadvantaged by the race classifications at issue; whether any groups, whites or blacks, were being stigmatized more than others; or whether the laws at issue had been consented to by whites and opposed by blacks, or enacted by some of each group, while opposed by others. Nor had the Court made any other related inquiry.[78] This colorblind approach to racial classifications had held constant before the Court for roughly twenty years until it ran up against the race-preference affirmative action initiatives of the 1970s. According to Van Alstyne, race-preference affirmative action threatened a return to the *Plessy* era of "genuflect[ing] to the wisdom of legislative bodies to sort out good from bad uses of race."[79]

Plessy was based on a rationalist principle, whereas *Brown* and the cases that followed immediately thereafter were based on an antirationalist principle: The Court could not be trusted to "contextualize" racial classifications, determining which were good and which were bad. This view had been the message of the Supreme Court from the mid-1950s through the mid-1970s, as well as of Justice John Marshall Harlan's dissenting opinion in *Plessy* in defense of the colorblind Constitution. Such a constitution was not only principled, Harlan contended; it was also the only *prudent* course of constitutional action. Attempting to assess the "reasonableness" of racial classifications made by government had been an unmitigated disaster, leading in the worst case to civil war.[80]

The proposition by the dissenters in the *Shaw* cases that whites should be allowed to succeed or be permitted standing in racial redistricting cases only if they could demonstrate "particularized harm" (that is, vote dilution), which the dissenters denied whites could do, was tantamount to advocating the resurrection of the notorious separate but equal doctrine from *Plessy v. Ferguson*. The dissenters in essence contended that jurisdictions should be free to segregate the races into racially defined districts so long as voters are treated "equally," that is, so long as there is no demonstration of "harm," in this case harm to whites. Understandably, the majority in *Miller* rejected this line of reasoning and adopted a more principled approach to equal protection review, one consistent with longstanding precedent that required plaintiffs to demonstrate discriminatory intent, the usual test applied in equal protection law.[81]

Questions Left Unanswered

In *Bush v. Vera*, Justice Souter acknowledged that only Justices Thomas and Scalia had gone on record to declare that strict scrutiny always applied to the intentional creation of MMDs—what VRA law typically required. In *Shaw* and later cases, the Court had explicitly refused to address this point. Justice Thomas pointed out in *Vera*, however, that if any ambiguity in the law existed at the time of *Shaw*, cases such as *Adarand* had "effectively resolved it." Whether strict scrutiny applied to racial districting "was never a close question."[82] It most certainly did.

This apparently obvious conclusion from the Court's equal protection jurisprudence was not so obvious to the Court's other members, most of whom sought to make an exception for racial classifications engaged under the pretenses of the VRA. In *Vera*, for instance, Justice O'Connor had asserted that compliance with the section 2 results test was a "compelling state interest" for purposes of meeting the first prong of the strict-scrutiny test.[83] This statement (which no one else on the Court joined) astonished many Court observers because it seemed to signal a repudiation of O'Connor's own earlier opinions for the Court in *Croson* and *Adarand*—the latter decided only a year before *Vera*. In her affirmative action cases, O'Connor had argued that all racial classifications required the most searching judicial inquiry to determine whether they were legitimate responses to proven acts of racial discrimination. Now O'Connor seemed to be making an exception for the VRA. But her reason may have been quite simple. O'Connor may well have recognized in 1996 (if not before) that applying strict scrutiny to all intentionally created MMDs would spell the end to vote-dilution law under the VRA.

Justice Souter concluded in *Vera* that because only Justices Thomas and Scalia supported the applicability of strict scrutiny to all intentionally created MMDs, "a radical transformation of the political selection process in the name of colorblindness is out of the question."[84] Yet eight years into the first decade of the twenty-first century we might ask ourselves whether such an approach is not merely what is constitutionally required, but also what is most principled and prudent. The unseemliness of attempting to reconcile the principles of equal protection with the requirements of second-generation voting rights has been on display now for more than three decades. How long does the American public have to wait for the Supreme Court to do the right thing?

7

The Supreme Court and the Voting Rights Act after 2000: Deconstructing the Republic for Now and Forever

Justice O'Connor's separate concurring opinion in *Bush v. Vera*, contending that compliance with the section 2 results test was a compelling state interest for the purposes of equal protection review, was apparently a signal of things to come.[1] *Easley v. Cromartie* (2001)[2] was the last installment of North Carolina's redistricting woes to make it to the High Court. In it, O'Connor would join the Court's more liberal members, who had dissented throughout the *Shaw* cases, in reversing a lower court's ruling. The reversal did not overturn the central holding from the *Shaw* cases, but it did effectively gut it.

Easley involved an appeal from a lower court decision that North Carolina's 1997 version of Congressional District 12, which the state had been compelled to redraw as a result of the Court's holding in *Shaw v. Hunt* (*Shaw II*, 1996),[3] was unconstitutional. The state argued that the newly drafted Congressional District 12 was the product of political, not racial, considerations. Specifically, it was the result of a desire on the part of the North Carolina legislature to create a safe Democratic seat. A three-judge district court disagreed, finding that District 12 was drawn predominantly for racial, not political, reasons. The snakelike contours of the district, which continued to split towns and counties in order to draft high numbers of black-voting populations into the district, as well as other documentary evidence and testimony, indicated that it was predominantly racial considerations that had driven the district's contours. The court ruled that these considerations could not be justified on constitutionally compelling grounds.[4]

In a decision written by Justice Breyer, a majority of the Supreme Court took the rare step of overturning the district court's factual findings. Contesting everything from the lower court's method of assessing voting data, to its preference of expert witnesses, to even the meaning of e-mail communications between key players in North Carolina's redistricting, Justice Breyer held that District 12 was, indeed, a political, rather than a racial, gerrymander. The district court's ruling, accordingly, had to be overturned. The principal finding of the majority in *Easley* was that North Carolina's reliance on heavily black precincts in designing District 12 could be construed as a political gerrymander because black voters registered as Democrats were more reliably Democratic than white voters registered as Democrats. Many of these latter voters crossed over to vote Republican during elections in a way that black registered Democrats did not.

Justice Thomas, dissenting on behalf of himself, Chief Justice Rehnquist, Justice Scalia, and Justice Kennedy, accused the majority of having ignored its own standard of appellate review: that lower courts were only to be overturned where their factual findings were "clearly erroneous." According to Thomas, the majority had simply substituted its own factual determinations for those of the district court—precisely what the authorities prohibited.[5]

Easley signaled a retreat from the Court's earlier attempts at reining in race-conscious affirmative action. In *Shaw II*, Chief Justice Rehnquist, writing for the Court, had found that race was the predominant factor motivating the drawing of North Carolina's Twelfth District because it was the only criterion that could not be compromised: "Respecting communities of interest and protecting Democratic incumbents came into play only *after* the race-based decision had been made."[6] It was hard to see how this was not the case in *Easley* as well. District 12 remained the most geographically scattered district in the state, with bizarre contours that still hugged the I-85 corridor through six counties, incorporating black communities along the way.[7] Black Democrats might indeed be more loyal Democrats than white Democrats, but using this rationale to justify race classifications opened the door to just about any rationalization for such classifications in the future. The question following *Easley* was whether plaintiffs could ever meet the exceedingly high evidentiary threshold *Easley* seemed to set for success in *Shaw* claims.

One consequence of *Easley* was the confusion it introduced into the administration of section 5 of the VRA following the 2000 census. In *Miller v. Johnson*, the Court had criticized the U.S. Department of Justice for imposing on the state of Georgia a "max-black" congressional redistricting plan (which sought to maximize black representation) conceived and advocated by the American Civil Liberties Union.[8] The majority had also raised the specter of a potential constitutional conflict between the VRA as administered by the DOJ and the Fourteenth Amendment.[9] Speculation following *Miller* that the Court's stern words for the department might temper its administration of the VRA in the decade to follow was further fueled by *Reno v. Bossier Parish School Board* (*Bossier II*, 2000), where the Court once again took the department to the woodshed for its expansive interpretation of the section 5 "purpose" prong[10]—the DOJ having construed "purpose" under section 5 to mean any failure to maximize minority representation.

Miller and *Bossier II* signaled to jurisdictions covered by section 5 that the Supreme Court would closely police the Justice Department's adminis tration of the VRA. Public officials charged with complying with section 5 might not, therefore, have to worry as much in the future about the imposition of legal irregularities or racial maximization policies by the department under the auspices of preclearance, a problem that had caused them so much trouble and cost in the 1990s. *Easley*, however, worked at cross-purposes with *Miller* and *Bossier II*, suggesting, contrary to those earlier cases, that the Court would turn a blind eye to the department's administrative activities. Although the Justice Department would probably not pursue racial maximization policies following the 2000 census, what federal courts would let the department do short of that was left opaque.

A few months before the Court delivered its decision in *Easley*, the DOJ released its 2001 guidance on redistricting, in response to the confusion generated by the effects of *Shaw* and subsequent cases on VRA enforcement.[11] It confirmed that the "nonretrogression" rule established in *Beer v. United States* (1976)[12] still governed section 5 preclearance applications, and that the DOJ would respect the Court's holding in *Bossier II*.[13] Yet the guidance also made clear that even though the Justice Department might preclear section 5 applications and follow *Bossier II*, jurisdictions were not immunized from subsequent legal challenges by the department on the basis of section 2 or the Constitution.[14]

Given the ambiguities of the 2001 redistricting guidance and the conflicting messages of recent case law, jurisdictions compelled to seek section 5 preclearance for their redistricting plans following the 2000 census were left largely in the dark as to what to do. Because compliance with the DOJ's directives in the 1990s had exposed jurisdictions to constitutional challenges that, in at least one case, lasted the better part of a decade, states throughout the country understandably approached the post-2000 redistricting with skepticism. Predictably, there was litigation. Alaska, North Carolina, Louisiana, Florida, and Texas were all involved in disputes over the meaning of section 5. In the case of Louisiana, the state challenged the 2001 redistricting guidance itself.[15]

The most important of the post-2000 section 5 contests to arise out of the confusion over preclearance standards involved the state of Georgia. In 2001–2, Georgia's Democrats controlled the state legislature. Tasked with redistricting federal and state electoral districts, the party's leadership sought to maximize minority and Democratic representation in the state senate without violating the provisions of section 5. Ironically, the VRA may have stood in the way of black members of the Georgia Assembly and their Democratic allies by requiring the Democrats to create senate districts that contained more minority Democratic voters than were necessary to reelect Democratic incumbents. This was a problem for Democrats because they needed additional voters in other districts to secure victory in those districts. The Democrats sought to overcome this problem by "unpacking" minority voters from MMDs required by the VRA and placing them in minority "influence" or "coalition" districts, in which less than 50 percent of the voting-age population was black, but it was presumed that black-preferred candidates would be elected. Georgia's Democrats realized they were proposing a novel interpretation of section 5 that was likely not going to sit very well with the Justice Department, let alone one controlled by a Republican administration.

Accordingly, they sought preclearance from the U.S. District Court for the District of Columbia, the only other alternative, but one that was more dilatory and expensive. Predictably enough, the Bush DOJ did object to the Georgia senate redistricting plan, claiming that the Georgia legislature had failed to create a sufficient number of MMDs for compliance with the *Beer* retrogression test. *Georgia v. Ashcroft* (2003)[16] was the case that arose out of this conflict.

Georgia v. Ashcroft and the New Section 5 Test

Although it would be overturned by the 2006 VRA,[17] *Georgia v. Ashcroft* was nevertheless the most important section 5 case since *Beer v. United States* (1976) for a variety of reasons. First, it not only significantly modified section 5 law (if only temporarily); it was also the first case in which the Court recognized the limits of its own multiculturalist rationalism in VRA law. Despite that recognition, *Ashcroft*, ironically, would serve to perpetuate the very rationalism and multiculturalism under the VRA of which it seemed so critical.

Second, although *Ashcroft* was not a constitutional case, like so many other VRA decisions, it invited yet further speculation on whether the principal provisions of the VRA remained constitutional. Third, and perhaps most important, was *Ashcroft's* defense of minority coalition districts as a means to comply with section 5. The use of coalition districts as potential remedies to section 2 actions would be embraced by six justices in *League of United Latin American Citizens v. Perry* (2006)[18]—an ominous development which, with the 2006 VRA, should not leave us very sanguine about any future reduction in the multiculturalist rationalism of the VRA.

In raising its objections to Georgia's senate redistricting plan, the Bush administration may have been acting purely as a matter of legal principle, but it was just as likely applying the same brazen utilitarian calculations as had the Democrats in creating the plan. The consequences of not acting would have been stark: A victory for the state meant that black and Hispanic Democrats in the South would be able to hold Republican-dominated states hostage to increased Democratic capture of electoral seats in future redistricting. Republican legislatures that failed to provide these seats would be immediately branded as racist. Democrats had already been swift to accuse Texas Republicans of having engaged in precisely such tactics during the redistricting debacle of 2003, when Democratic senators fled the state twice to avoid voting on redistricting plans proposed by the Republicans.[19]

By holding Democrats in Georgia to the more rigid test of retrogression the DOJ was proposing, such unsavory political outcomes for Republicans might be reduced in the future. Moreover, by aggressively enforcing the status quo under the *Beer* retrogression test—which required states to meet or exceed the black population figures in benchmark electoral districts— Republicans could continue to capture seats in the South by "packing" minority voters, who were overwhelmingly Democratic, into MMDs, thus "bleaching" the surrounding districts for Republican capture. Just how many congressional seats the Republicans gained in the South during the 1990s as a result of VRA enforcement has been a subject of a great deal of academic controversy, but virtually no one contests that they benefited significantly as a result of the DOJ's administration of the act during that decade. Many academics believe the Republicans recaptured Congress in 1994 precisely because of the VRA.[20]

In 2002, the Georgia Democrats knew that if they complied with the standard *Beer* retrogression test, black representatives would most likely get elected to office, but they would do so at the expense of the party to which all black representatives belonged: the Democrats. To avoid this eventuality, Georgia's Democrats, as noted earlier, reduced the number of black voters in senate MMDs that had been designated benchmarks for the purpose of assessing retrogression under section 5. Black voters taken out of these MMDs would be placed in coalition or minority influence districts (MIDs), where they would have an increased opportunity of electing their candidates of choice.[21]

As had been the case in the 1990s, black politicians were influential in the districting process in Georgia in 2002. All of the state's thirty-four black representatives and eleven black senators were part of the governing Democratic majority.[22] Of these, only one representative and one senator opposed the Democrats' house and senate redistricting plans.[23] Blacks were well represented on the Senate Reapportionment Committee (comprising six of twenty-four members) as well as on the House Reapportionment Committee (comprising six of twenty-nine members). In addition, Robert Brown, a black senator from District 26, one of the districts in dispute in *Ashcroft*, was both the vice chairman of the Senate Reapportionment Committee and chair of the subcommittee that drafted the senate plan itself. The majority leader of the senate was black, as was the chair of the rules committee.[24]

A key issue in *Ashcroft* was whether the trial court should take into account the obvious overwhelming support of these black legislators for the redistricting plan in dispute when considering whether the plan had the purpose or effect of "denying or abridging the right to vote on account of race or color" (the section 5 test). The district court responded in the negative. In an opinion written by Judge Emmet Sullivan, the majority adhered to the traditional meaning of "retrogression," accepting the U.S. Justice Department's submission that retrogression occurred when there was any diminution of minority voting strength relative to the benchmark senate districts at issue—here districts 2, 12, and 26. Judge Louis Oberdorfer dissented on this score. Oberdorfer accepted the State of Georgia's contention that retrogression occurred only where there was less electoral opportunity for minorities vis-à-vis benchmark districts—that is, the state could reduce minority populations in benchmark districts relative to earlier benchmark numbers as long as minorities retained an equal opportunity to elect their candidates of choice. In this way, minorities could be "unpacked" from MMDs where their votes had been "wasted" in earlier elections and reallocated to districts where they could help elect additional candidates of the minority's choice.[25]

Besides illustrating the arcana and guesswork involved in section 5 evidentiary disputes,[26] *Ashcroft* highlighted the problem of how to measure retrogression. Should jurisdictions be held to a fixed benchmark, ensuring that black voting population percentages would not be reduced from what they were prior to the electoral changes proposed? Or should a broader analysis be permitted, like that proposed by Georgia and Judge Oberdorfer, in which a wide variety of electoral and political phenomena could be considered to assess the overall political opportunities blacks might enjoy?

The answer to the measurement question reflected a further question at the heart of *Ashcroft*, one that occupied both the lower court and the Supreme Court: If the judiciary abandoned the more simplistic, purely mathematical approach to retrogression analyses proposed by the Justice Department, what would be the effect on the administration of section 5 and the rule of law? Would a more complex analysis of the effective representation of black political interests allow for the administration of the section in a manner that was predictable and consistent? Or might it result in rulings that were an utter mash of arbitrary and subjective opinions?

This issue was key when *Ashcroft* reached the Supreme Court. Justice O'Connor, on behalf of the majority, made clear that the more comprehensive approach to section 5 proposed by Georgia would now be permitted, allowing for either the *descriptive* or *substantive* representation of minorities.[27]

O'Connor then proceeded to dispatch the district court's interpretation of retrogression. When "assessing the totality of circumstances," she declared, "a court should not focus solely on the comparative ability of a minority group to elect a candidate of choice."[28] Rather, section 5 analyses should incorporate all potentially "relevant circumstances."[29] In other words, the retrogression test was not to be limited to a simple focus on minority *electoral* opportunity, but rather on the overall *political* opportunities available to minorities.

By including in section 5 analyses the kaleidoscope of considerations that might contribute to minority political opportunities and no longer limiting retrogression evaluations to mere assessments of minority electoral opportunities (the old retrogression test), *Ashcroft* marked a significant expansion of what could be considered in section 5 preclearance applications. O'Connor had effectively incorporated into section 5 assessments the broad "totality of circumstances" test from section 2. Factors such as what legislative leadership positions, political influence, and power minority candidates might enjoy after election could be considered in section 5 evaluations, as could the opinions of minority incumbents elected from those districts created by the VRA.[30]

O'Connor's opinion also made clear that section 5 review following *Ashcroft* would require increasing reliance on social science evidence. This change had to do with the introduction of coalition districts or MIDs as potential substitutes for MMDs when assessing section 5 preclearance. The introduction of such districts would complicate, rather than simplify, evidentiary submissions in section 5 disputes. As Justice Souter highlighted in dissent:

> Before a State shifts from majority-minority to coalition districts . . . the State bears the burden of proving that nonminority voters will reliably vote along with the minority. . . . It must show not merely that minority voters in new districts may have some influence, but that minority voters will have effective influence translatable into probable election results comparable to what they enjoyed under the existing district scheme. And to demonstrate this, a State must do more than produce reports of minority voting age percentages; it must show that the probable voting behavior of nonminority voters will make coalitions with minorities a real prospect.[31]

The potential for increased multiculturalist rationalism on the part of courts and administrators was now more of a threat than it had ever been.

Justice Souter was joined in his *Ashcroft* dissent by Justices Stevens, Ginsburg, and Breyer, all of whom agreed that the Court's opinion was an aberration that ignored the history of section 5 and longstanding precedents. Perhaps the most damning criticism the dissent raised was that the majority had unmoored section 5 from any kind of practical or administrable concept of minority influence in retrogression analyses.[32] Once a jurisdiction moved from MMDs to minority influence or coalition districts, Souter asked, what guarantee was there that nonminority voters would vote along with protected minorities, thus preserving the latter's effective representation?

There was also no guarantee that basing the measurement of retrogression on minority incumbents' approval of a redistricting plan, as had occurred in *Ashcroft*, would necessarily benefit minority voters, as opposed to minority incumbents. Retrogression analyses following *Ashcroft* would involve assessing everything from what committee assignments minorities might get after election, to which incumbents might be reelected, to what sort of preelection promises had been made to minority political groups. Numerous other considerations would also have to be accounted for. Where in any of the Court's decision was there any intelligible standard of retrogression to apply?

The majority's decision was particularly problematic when considering the burden of proof in preclearance applications. The "unquantifiable standard" that the Court had now made the measure of retrogression analyses meant that the outcomes of preclearance applications would be arbitrary. If a "serious burden of persuasion" remained on states, their reliance on the novel theory of influence now being propounded by the majority would likely guarantee that they would lose such applications because minority influence would be "too amorphous for objective comparison" to allow conclusive findings of nonretrogression. Placing an onerous burden on states, however, was the least likely scenario in the future, according to Justice Souter. The more likely outcome would be deference to states, allowing them to satisfy their burden through an "unquantifiable influence" that could "be equated with majority-minority power." If that occurred, section 5 would "simply drop out as a safeguard against the 'unremitting and ingenious defiance of the Constitution' that required the procedure of preclearance in the first place."[33] For this last point, Justice Souter quoted *South Carolina v. Katzenbach* (1966),[34] the Court's original decision upholding the constitutionality of section 5 as an extraordinary measure for extraordinary times.

Ashcroft and Its Implications

Justice Souter's dissent in *Ashcroft* raised a host of questions that would have to be dealt with in the future. He correctly noted that the majority's new retrogression test was ambiguous. It would be difficult, if not impossible, to apply, and would virtually guarantee arbitrary outcomes and unnecessary litigation. What factors would count toward enhancing potential minority political power in the future was anyone's guess. In addition, little assurance was provided that respecting the wishes of minority incumbents would guarantee that minority voter interests would also be respected, however one might calculate these. Indeed, some believe that protecting incumbent interests of any sort—minority or otherwise—is inconsistent with sound democratic practice.

The more important point, however, was whether sections 4 and 5 of the VRA still had any relevance to twenty-first–century American politics. Souter's contention that the old standards of retrogression needed to be retained because minority "influence" in the political process could not otherwise be measured seemed merely to concede the narrowness of the Court's multiculturalist rationalism in voting rights. In other words, Souter's argument showed just how impossible it was to calculate "effective" racial representation and how arbitrary and oversimplified the Court's past measures of effective representation under the VRA had actually been. As Justice O'Connor's opinion indicated, this oversimplification applied not only to section 5, but also to Justice Brennan's interpretation of section 2 in *Gingles*.

Souter's invocation of *South Carolina v. Katzenbach* and his suggestion that the state of Georgia or any other jurisdiction covered by section 5 was today engaged in "unremitting and ingenious defiance of the Constitution" was equally hollow. No one in the case was even remotely suggesting the existence of invidious discrimination against blacks by the Georgia

Democrats. To the contrary, the Georgia legislature had made every reasonable attempt to accommodate black politicians, and the Georgia Black Caucus had been intimately involved in the state's post-2000 redistricting negotiations. Critics might say this involvement had occurred precisely because the legislature had to comply with the VRA, but even in the absence of the act, could anyone seriously suggest, as Souter seemed to, that the political circumstances of twenty-first–century Georgia were in any way similar to those of South Carolina in the mid-1960s, or that the state of Georgia was today engaged in "unremitting and ingenious defiance of the Constitution"? Could *any* jurisdiction covered by section 5 in 2003 be accused of "unremitting and ingenious defiance of the Constitution"? If not, what did this absence imply about the relevance of section 5 to present-day American politics? Ironically, it was the VRA, not the Georgia Democrats, or even the state's Republicans, that stood in the way of black Democratic political prospects after 2000, a fact that the majority in *Ashcroft* appeared to recognize but refused to acknowledge explicitly.

In the context of the *Beer* retrogression test and the VRA more generally, *Ashcroft* is important because it represents the first time the Court recognized the narrow multiculturalist rationalism of VRA law, of both section 5 as construed in *Beer* and section 2 as construed in *Gingles*. Up until 2003 the Court had calculated "effective exercise of the electoral franchise" for minorities (the last part of the *Beer* test) in purely descriptive, racial terms. Following *Ashcroft*, that calculation would no longer apply. Descriptive or substantive racial representation could be promoted to avoid retrogression.

Yet as much as *Ashcroft* might have been intended to recognize the limitations of the multiculturalist rationalism of section 5 preclearance law, as Justice Souter emphasized, the decision would nevertheless require ever more refined calculations of the descriptive or substantive representation of minority groups. Because virtually any evidence might count in assessing the political opportunities available to minority politicians, *Ashcroft* would likely eviscerate any coherent legal standards that might apply to section 5 preclearance. In addition, because section 5 applications would now involve comprehensive questions concerning the descriptive and substantive representation of minority groups, the evidence that jurisdictions would have to marshal to secure preclearance would likely have to be correspondingly complex. Ironically, as much as *Ashcroft* may have been intended to reduce the role of the courts in the preclearance process, its effect—to the extent it is used in future VRA disputes—will likely be the opposite, further rationalizing and formalizing the representational process through the invitation of even more comprehensive judicial and administrative supervision of racial balancing in the political process.

Nor will *Ashcroft* eliminate the need for legislators, judges, and administrators to continue thinking and classifying in racial terms to comply with the VRA. Justice Kennedy and Justice Thomas joined the majority's opinion in *Ashcroft* because no constitutional issue had been raised in the case. Both made clear, however, in separate concurring opinions that the administration of the VRA remained constitutionally suspect. According to Kennedy, it was "evident from the Court's accurate description of the facts in this case [that] race was a predominant factor in drawing the lines of Georgia's State Senate redistricting map." Yet, Kennedy continued,

> race cannot be the predominant factor in redistricting under our decision in *Miller v. Johnson*. . . .
>
> There is a fundamental flaw, I should think, in any scheme in which the Department of Justice is permitted or directed to encourage or ratify a course of unconstitutional conduct in order to find compliance with a statutory directive.[35]

Justice Thomas was equally skeptical, remarking in his brief concurrence that he continued "to adhere to" his opinion in *Holder v. Hall* (1994).[36] Thomas's reference to *Holder* suggested that any extension of section 5 beyond ballot-access questions was a derogation from the text of the VRA that would involve the Court in all the usual unsavory questions of political theory and race-identity politics with which the Court inevitably got caught up any time it tried to assess "effective" racial representation—precisely what it was doing once again in *Ashcroft*. *Ashcroft* may have attempted to soften the hard racial classifications required by traditional vote-dilution law, with the latter's emphasis on descriptive racial representation; but even if states could now promote substantive racial representation in addition to, or instead of, descriptive racial representation, the mandate following *Ashcroft* would remain what it had always been with the VRA: a racial calculus intended to benefit specific racial groups.

The Persisting Constitutional Questions

As Justice Thomas's remarks in *Ashcroft* and *Holder* indicated, the constitutionality of the VRA's vote-dilution law hangs tenuously on a number of presuppositions, all of which have been crucial to supporting second-generation voting rights. The constitutional questions that persist concern not merely the race classifications that second-generation issues require as a matter of course, but also whether Congress still has the constitutional authority to regulate state electoral practices under sections 4 and 5 of the act, and whether the section 2 results test has ever been constitutional. In all these cases, I suggest, the VRA cannot pass constitutional muster.

Sections 4 and 5 of the VRA were originally justified as emergency measures necessary to deal with the problem of black disfranchisement in the Jim Crow South. That situation is how Congress justified sections 4 and 5 in 1965 and how the Supreme Court rationalized their extraordinary constitutional impositions in *South Carolina v. Katzenbach* in 1966. The question now is whether the exceptional conditions the Court said existed in the mid-1960s still exist today. I suggest not.

In *City of Boerne v. Flores* (1997), the Court clarified that Congress's powers under the Fourteenth Amendment are remedial, not substantive.[37] Congress cannot create new constitutional provisions; it can only enforce those that exist under the authorizing provision of the Fourteenth Amendment (section 5). The Court added that where there was "a lack of proportionality or congruence between the means adopted [by remedial legislation] and the legitimate end to be achieved,"[38] legislation was constitutionally infirm. Congressional action cannot be "so out of proportion to a supposed remedial or preventive object that it cannot be understood as responsive to, or designed to prevent, unconstitutional behavior."[39] The rule from *City of Boerne* applied not only to the Fourteenth Amendment but to the Fifteenth Amendment as well.[40]

Because sections 4 and 5 of the VRA rely on both of these amendments for their constitutional authority, we might ask what "unconstitutional behavior" Congress intended to remedy by extending these sections for twenty-five years beyond their expiration in August 2007. In editorials and in hearings before Congress leading up to the extension in July of 2006, critics of the proposed congressional action pointed out that there was no evidentiary basis on which Congress could have extended the VRA's temporary provisions, let alone for twenty-five years.

The critics emphasized that, by any measure, blacks and Hispanics in the South have become integral and powerful components of the political process. Whether this participation is measured by minority voter registration rates, minority electoral turnout rates, minority office-holding, crossover support from whites for minority candidates, or racial polarization levels, minorities are no longer outsiders in southern electoral politics. To the contrary, in states covered by the VRA's temporary provisions, minorities today frequently participate in politics at rates higher than those of their white neighbors.[41] The *Shaw* cases and *Ashcroft* all illustrated the extent to which black voters and their representatives had become important and powerful components of southern politics. The *Shaw* decisions in particular emerged not because of the exclusion of blacks from the political process, but rather because of the opposite—the overzealous solicitation of minority political claims.[42]

The original VRA was undoubtedly instrumental to securing this new reality in American politics. Without the original act, southern politics would have been arrested by the legacy of Jim Crow for years, perhaps even decades. Just as obvious, however, the *Shaw* cases and *Ashcroft* illustrate that today's VRA impedes as much as facilitates those very biracial coalitions that would have been seen as the promised land of racial politics by those who passed the original VRA.

Even longstanding supporters of second-generation voting rights have begun to wonder whether section 5 is not now working at cross-purposes with black political interests. As one such supporter, Samuel Issacharoff, recently remarked, those who seek the continuance of section 5 enforcement but who recognize (as the Democrats did in *Ashcroft*) that section 5 compliance should be permitted to promote the substantive representation of black interests or black and white political coalitions are caught in a logistical quandary. As Issacharoff highlights, "It is difficult to argue for the congruence of a statutory response to the extreme isolation of blacks in the political process at the constitutional plane, while at the same time arguing for the importance of coalitional politics as the basis for statutory implementation."[43]

Sections 4 and 5 are draconian provisions that have effectively put states into "administrative receivership," undermining constitutional

principles of federalism at their most fundamental level.[44] The only constitutional foundation on which they could have been extended in 2006 is if
it could have been established that blacks were still systematically excluded
from the political process in the South in some way similar to the way they
were in the mid-1960s. The evidence, however, shows overwhelmingly that
this is not the case.

It would seem, then, that sections 4 and 5 of the VRA are ripe for a *City
of Boerne* challenge,[45] as is section 2's results test. In *Bush v. Vera* (1996)
Justice O'Connor reminded her readers that the constitutionality of the
amended section 2 had never been tested.[46] As the next section should
make clear, now would be an ideal time for such a test.

The 2006 Voting Rights Act, *Perry*, and the
Future Deconstruction of American Republicanism

When Congress extended sections 4 and 5 of the VRA for twenty-five years
beyond their planned expiry in 2007, it did so by overwhelming numbers:
390–33 in the House and 98–0 in the Senate. Shortly thereafter, President
Bush signed the extended legislation into effect with much fanfare and little apparent concern for the racial entitlement regime that the VRA had created. For skeptics of the multiculturalist rationalism that second-generation
voting rights have perpetuated, neither the 2006 VRA nor the Court's decision in *League of United Latin American Citizens v. Perry*,[47] decided one
month before the 2006 legislation was signed into law, was very reassuring.

Section 5 of the 2006 act requires that jurisdictions covered by section 4 not diminish the opportunity of minorities "to elect their preferred
candidates of choice."[48] This is legal code that will have the effect of overruling the *Ashcroft* decision, requiring states once again to provide minorities descriptive representation—the ability to elect as many, if not more,
minority representatives as they were able to elect under previous redistricting schemes. Pursuit of substantive representation or the provision of
coalition districts as was proposed by *Ashcroft* will not be tolerated under
the new section 5. The 2006 VRA thus assures that descriptive representation—racial representatives representing their racial groups—will remain
the credo of section 5 law for at least another quarter-century.

Section 5 also defines "purpose" under the section as including "*any* discriminatory purpose."[49] This wording will have the effect of overruling *Bossier II*, which had limited the meaning of discriminatory purpose under section 5 to only those acts where jurisdictions evinced a discriminatory intent to reduce minority voting power. Whereas the repeal of *Ashcroft* by the new section 5 will mean that jurisdictions covered by section 4 will now have to resort once again to the stark racial bean-counting of descriptive representation, by overruling *Bossier II* the 2006 VRA will, in addition, invite the Department of Justice once again to pursue racial maximization policies of the sort it pursued in the 1990s. The combination of overruling *Ashcroft* and *Bossier II* thus constitutes one of the most serious attacks on the Founders' republicanism ever conducted through the vehicle of the VRA.

Perhaps the greatest significance of *Ashcroft* was that its defense of minority coalition districts as a means to comply with section 5 would be embraced by six justices in *League of United Latin American Citizens v. Perry* (2006)[50] as potential remedies to section 2 actions. *Perry* was the section 2 case instigated by minority activist groups and Democrats to challenge the Texas Republicans' congressional redistricting plan of 2003. In it, the Court ruled that partisan gerrymandering was permissible unless it adversely affected the ability of minorities legally recognized under the VRA to elect their preferred candidates of choice.

Distilled to its simplest meaning, *Perry* held that although political gerrymandering—the drawing of electoral districts for the benefit of specific political parties—was permissible, a state must nevertheless guarantee political office-holding to designated racial groups. In addition, the VRA protected not only candidates elected from districts in which minorities were a majority of the voting-age population, but, in certain situations, also those elected from districts where minorities were only a small percentage of the voting-age population.

The *Perry* decision offered up for the first time in American history the possibility of having white Democrats elected in minority influence districts protected from political competition by federal legislation. Critics of the theme of this book who think it is overblown or that the provisions of the VRA are of little significance to American republicanism because they affect so few electoral districts overlook two critical facts. First, section 2 of the VRA has the potential to affect every single electoral district, federal, state, or local, anywhere in the country there is a minority population. Second, six justices in *Perry* appeared willing to consider white Democrats elected with minority support from influence districts to constitute minority representatives of choice for purposes of section 2. Thus, the *Perry* decision offered up the prospect that once white Democrats were elected from MIDs, they would enjoy incumbency protection indefinitely from the VRA.

The *Shaw* cases and *Ashcroft* demonstrated the extent to which the VRA converts partisan, political contests into incendiary racial disputes. The backdrop to the *Perry* case provides yet further evidence of the incendiary effects of second-generation voting rights. In 2003 and 2004, for instance, Texas Republicans were accused of being racist and antiminority for failing to create a sufficient number of black and Hispanic congressional districts under the VRA. These allegations, made by Democrats and minority groups, were widely reported over the period of a year in the national news media. Yet the federal court that heard these groups' complaints dismissed them all, pointing out what was obvious to everyone, including the Democrats: that what was at issue was not race prejudice, but partisan politics.[51]

Yet it was the VRA that provided the vehicle for the inflammatory allegations of racism—the playing of the "race card"—that defenders of racial redistricting claim the act does not facilitate. As the federal district court noted in *Session v. Perry*—the *Perry* case in the original instance—the purely partisan nature of the Texas Republicans' congressional redistricting plan was agreed to not only by the Democrats' own expert witness, but by the Texas House Democratic Caucus and congressional Democrats John Lewis, Chris Bell, Sheila Jackson Lee, Martin Frost, and Nick Lampson, all of whom filed a brief in *Vieth v. Jubelirer*[52] conceding that "the newly dominant Republicans . . . decided to redraw the state's congressional districts *solely* for the purpose of seizing between five and seven seats from Democratic incumbents."[53]

When *Perry* got to the Supreme Court, the majority agreed with this latter assertion: that the Republicans gerrymandered the state's congressional districts for the purpose of partisan advantage, not because of any racial animus toward blacks or Hispanics. The Court in *Perry* nevertheless reversed the lower court's decision with respect to one of the VRA districts in dispute, Congressional District 23. Although the district court had found that District 23 was a partisan gerrymander that did not violate section 2 of the VRA, the Supreme Court disagreed.

In an opinion by Justice Kennedy, which will virtually guarantee that political contests such as those that took place in Texas after 2000 will continue to be redacted into inflammatory racial contests, the Court conceded that the reason for the Republicans' gerrymandering of Congressional District 23 was political, not racial: to preserve the seat of Republican incumbent Henry Bonilla, an Hispanic—a perfectly legitimate, constitutionally permissible course of action by a political party. According to Justice Kennedy, however, Bonilla was apparently an Hispanic affiliated with the wrong party. The Republicans' redesigning of District 23 was illegal because, although they were free to engage in partisan gerrymandering, they could not do so where that reduced the possibility of electing the preferred candidate of a group protected by the VRA. The evidence in *Perry* suggested that the Latinos' preferred candidate of choice in District 23 would have been a Democrat rather than Bonilla had the district's boundaries not been redrawn by the Republicans the way they were. To act as the Republicans did, Justice Kennedy proclaimed, bore "the mark of intentional discrimination."[54]

Partisan gerrymandering, then, was apparently constitutionally permissible as long as it did not result in the wrong racial outcomes. Failure to create the correct racial outcomes was tantamount to "intentional discrimination." Equal electoral opportunity was once again defined in terms of statewide proportional representation for America's "official minorities"—an outcome that the Court in *Perry* came dangerously close to saying was now required by section 2. As Chief Justice John Roberts demurred: "It is a sordid business, this divvying us up by race."[55]

Yet *Perry*, and Roberts's own position in the case, virtually guaranteed that such divvying up by race would continue indefinitely into the future. Roberts, along with Justice Alito, joined Justice Kennedy in part IV of his decision, in which Kennedy agreed that "it is possible to state a § 2 claim for a racial group that makes up less than 50% of the population."[56] Relying on the *Ashcroft* decision's recognition of MIDs as districts protected by section 5 of the VRA, the plaintiffs in *Perry* had sought to apply *Ashcroft's* reasoning to section 2. Specifically, they had claimed that Congressman Martin Frost, a white Democrat from District 24, was a black representative of choice protected by section 2 because blacks, who made up 25.7 percent of the voting population of Frost's old district, had consistently voted for him. Moreover, blacks also made up 64 percent of the voters in the Democratic primary that selected Frost, the district's eventual representative.

Justice Kennedy disagreed with the plaintiffs' contentions, but he left the door open to such an argument in the future. Contrary to the plaintiffs' allegations, Kennedy held that since the district court had found Frost was never challenged in a Democratic primary, he was not necessarily black voters' representative of choice. It was insufficient that blacks merely exercise some control over the outcome in District 24. As Kennedy observed:

> The opportunity "to elect representatives of their choice" . . . requires more than the ability to influence the outcome between some candidates, none of whom is their candidate of choice . . . while the presence of districts "where minority voters may not be able to elect a candidate of choice but can play a substantial, if not decisive, role in the electoral process" is relevant to the § 5 analysis, . . . the lack of such districts cannot establish a § 2 violation.[57]

But what if minorities *did* play a decisive role in the election of a white or Anglo candidate in an MID? What if it was clear that blacks *did* control the Democratic primary, and that a white representative like Frost was *indeed* a black representative of choice in a contested primary? Kennedy never answered this question but, as noted above, seemed to suggest that such a scenario would indeed be covered by section 2. If he, Roberts, and Alito were not prepared to consider such a possibility, why else even consider the issue and elaborate the distinctions they did instead of foreclosing such claims outright?

Justices Souter and Ginsburg left no room for doubt where they stood on this issue. In an opinion by Souter, both he and Ginsburg made clear that they would have acceded to the plaintiffs' request and remanded the case to the trial court to reconsider the section 2 claim. Souter believed that *Ashcroft* made recognition of MIDs of universal significance for the VRA. Despite *Ashcroft*'s limited application to section 5, there was "reason to think that the integrity of the minority voting population in a coalition district should be protected much as a majority-minority bloc would be."[58] Because preclearance, with which protection should begin, is determined only by states and the DOJ—and in some cases by the U.S. District Court for the District of Columbia—minority plaintiffs unhappy with preclearance decisions are without remedy in section 5 disputes. Souter argued, "Unless a minority voter is to be left with no recourse whatsoever . . . relief under § 2 must be possible."[59]

Although Justice Stevens did not address whether a vote-dilution claim under section 2 could succeed where the minority voting population in a district was less than 50 percent, he made clear where he stood on this question: "I am in substantial agreement with Justice Souter's discussion of this issue. . . . Specifically, I agree with Justice Souter that the '50% rule,' which finds no support in the text, history, or purposes of § 2, is not a proper part of the statutory vote dilution inquiry."[60] Stevens did not consider the section 2 issue in *Perry* because he believed that the Republicans' "cracking" of the black vote in District 24 and the spreading of that vote to other districts for purely partisan reasons constituted an unconstitutional gerrymander. He thus did not have to consider the statutory section 2 question.[61]

Stevens's opinion nevertheless made clear that at least six justices on today's Court are prepared to accept MIDs as electoral districts protected by section 2. The only question that remains in contention is under what conditions such districts are protected. The dispute between Justices Kennedy, Roberts, and Alito, on the one hand, and Justices Souter, Ginsburg, and Stevens, on the other, turned on whether Martin Frost was a black representative of choice. Justice Kennedy did not think he was. Justice Souter did. The central point here, however, is not the dispute between Kennedy and Souter, but rather the fact that a majority on the Court is now prepared to accept that white Democrats such as Martin Frost may, indeed, be able to have their districts preserved in perpetuity by the VRA, if in the future they can conclusively establish that they are, in fact, a minority group's preferred representative of choice in an influence or coalition district.

Such an entitlement to electoral office would be a first in American politics. It would constitute an unparalleled partisan lockup of the political process expressed in inflammatory racial terms and hold out the promise of even more factious racial politics in the future. If such a rule guaranteeing nonminority Democrats office under the VRA were established, the Democrats would only have to secure political power once in a state. Having done so, they could then redesign electoral districts, designating as many

MMDs or MIDs as possible as protected by the VRA. The only way Republicans could then regain political power would be either to create uniform white hostility to the minority community's preferred candidates or to focus the entirety of their attention on the votes of the minority community to the exclusion of all other voters. In either case, the racial factionalism facilitated by today's VRA would seem tame compared to what we might expect if Justice Kennedy's or Justice Souter's opinion in *Perry* were ever to become law.

The only hope, then, for recapturing the Founders' republicanism in the face of the rationalist and multiculturalist assault on it constituted by today's VRA may be for the Court to find sections 2, 4, and 5 of the act unconstitutional. The likelihood of that happening with today's Court, however, is virtually nil.

Perhaps the most surprising—and disappointing—opinion in *Perry* was Justice Scalia's concurring and dissenting opinion, joined by Justice Thomas. Scalia was prepared to dismiss the plaintiffs' partisan gerrymandering claims as nonjusticiable and to reject their section 2 claims on the grounds he and Justice Thomas had outlined in *Holder v. Hall*—namely, that section 2 did not permit vote-dilution claims. These aspects of Scalia's opinion were predictable and consistent with earlier positions he had staked out in previous cases. But part III of Scalia's opinion was not.

In *Bush v. Vera*, Scalia had joined an opinion by Justice Thomas which suggested that any time MMDs or other race classifications were created to comply with the VRA, strict scrutiny necessarily applied. Thus, states engaging in race classifications for the purpose of meeting the requirements of the VRA would have to show a compelling state interest for the racial classifications at issue, as well as demonstrate that such classifications were narrowly tailored to meet those state interests. As Thomas concluded in *Vera*: "Strict scrutiny applies to all governmental classifications based on race, and we have expressly held that there is *no exception* for race-based redistricting."[62] That opinion was given in 1996. Ten years later in *Perry*, Scalia and Thomas seemed willing to compromise their position in *Vera*:

> We have in the past left undecided whether compliance with federal antidiscrimination laws can be a compelling state interest. . . . I would hold that compliance with § 5 of the Voting Rights Act can be such an interest. We long ago upheld the

constitutionality of § 5 as a proper exercise of Congress's authority under § 2 of the Fifteenth Amendment to enforce that Amendment's prohibition on the denial or abridgment of the right to vote. See *South Carolina v. Katzenbach*. . . . If compliance with § 5 were not a compelling state interest, then a State could be placed in the impossible position of having to choose between compliance with § 5 and compliance with the Equal Protection Clause.[63]

Not only did this statement seem to be a repudiation of Scalia and Thomas's position in *Vera*, where they held that a compelling state interest had to be proved and not merely assumed when a state engaged in race-based redistricting, but Scalia's declaration seemed to be an express admission of the incompatibility of the VRA with the laws of equal protection. Why else concede that without recognizing section 5 as a compelling state interest, states might fail to comply with the equal protection clause?

But was Scalia not giving away the farm here to the multiculturalists, who continue to maintain that the race classifications demanded by the VRA are as necessary today as they were in the 1960s? Scalia's reliance on *South Carolina v. Katzenbach* (1966) as a warrant for section 5 today was just as uncompelling as was Justice Souter's reliance on this same authority in *Ashcroft*. Was Scalia suggesting, in a vein similar to Souter's, that the bald racial classifications required by section 5 in 2006 could be excused on the basis of an authority that was forty years old? Or was he suggesting that the politics of Texas in the twenty-first century were somehow similar to or identifiable with the politics of South Carolina in the mid-1960s? Could a reasonable or fair-minded person subscribe to such a position? The admission in his *Perry* opinion that the redistricting in dispute was the product of partisan, not racial, considerations formed the basis for his dismissal of the plaintiffs' constitutional vote-dilution claim. "The District Court's conclusion that the [Texas] legislature was not racially motivated when it drew the plan . . . dooms appellants' intentional-vote-dilution claim," he wrote.[64] How could Scalia justify his position regarding the constitutionality of section 5 as a remedy for "identified past discrimination" when he had already acknowledged that no such discrimination was at issue in *Perry*?[65]

Perhaps as disappointing as Justice Scalia's opinion was the fact that newly appointed Chief Justice Roberts and Justice Alito signed onto part III of

Scalia's opinion providing this constitutional exception for section 5. For Court observers hoping Roberts and Alito might bring a more principled perspective to questions of race and representation, *Perry* was certainly a disappointment.

Perry and the 2006 VRA promise greater entrenchment of racial divisions in American law, the further formalization of the view that American republicanism should be used as a partisan tool for unlimited welfare-state liberalism, judicial intervention into core political decisions that may now extend all the way to racial bean-counting in primaries, and the further fracturing of American citizenship. Voters are now being invited to an even greater extent to identify not with the high ideals of American republicanism, but with those base and inflammatory identities anchored in race and ethnicity. In the conclusion to this book I will recount that the highest objectives of the Founders' republicanism consisted of their desire to promote individual, political, and martial excellence through a commercial republicanism of limited government and rational and durable liberty.[66] The predicate for the attainment of these objectives was union. This precondition was required for American greatness, the theme *The Federalist* reminds us of time and again.

It is perhaps then this—American greatness—that is most jeopardized by the rationalist and multicultural challenge to the Founders' republicanism that the VRA has institutionalized over the last four decades. Having eroded the very idea of a uniform understanding of American citizenship— a citizenship that remains the principal intangible source for the American exceptionalism that only appropriate instruments of state can foster— Congress has now promised us more of the same for decades to come. Can anyone expect that once this multiculturalist ethos has become entrenched in federal law for yet another generation, we will possibly be able to extricate American republicanism from its grasp? The 2006 VRA and decisions such as *Perry* virtually guarantee that the rationalist and multiculturalist deconstruction of American republicanism will persist indefinitely.

In the 1990s the Supreme Court had the opportunity to expunge the politics of race and racial identity from the VRA. It missed the opportunity. As a result, American republicanism continues to be deconstructed along rationalist and multiculturalist lines. And a statute that once stood as much as any other to fulfill the promise of American republicanism continues today to operate as much as any other to undermine it.

Conclusion:
American Greatness and
a Founders' Voting Rights Act

The authors of *The Federalist* did not accept what today has become standard academic orthodoxy about classical liberalism: that classical liberalism's promotion of the rights of property and of commerce was intended to reduce the aims of modern politics to the "low but solid" objectives of providing for security and comfortable well-being. Although the liberalism of such classical liberals as John Locke, Montesquieu, Adam Smith, and David Hume was certainly intended to provide for stability, security, and the betterment of the human condition, the most astute of the Framers did not see classical liberalism as limited to these objectives alone. For example, they saw the promotion of security, in particular national defense, as a function of high politics, of that martial virtue that was best cultivated in free regimes and that required the sturdiest of human character.

Moreover, they saw the pursuit of commerce and the economic dynamism that the new constitutional union of 1787 would facilitate as the precondition for American greatness. Jean-Jacques Rousseau, perhaps the most famous eighteenth-century critic of Europe's nascent commercial society, viewed the cultivation of commerce as synonymous with the promotion of inequality, avarice, vanity, and an enervating consumption with luxury.[1] Many Anti-Federalists and even some supporters of the Constitution expressed similar reservations about the relationship between commerce and America's fledgling republicanism. Nevertheless, almost none of these skeptics took the position that commercial development should be abandoned. To the contrary, both skeptics and advocates of commercial expansion were consumed with the singular question of how to promote private and public virtue in a new constitutional union that would be determinately commercial. The key questions dealt with means, not ends: How far should commercial development be taken? What types of commercial activities should be promoted? How might individual and political character best be shaped through commercial instruments of greater or lesser variety?[2]

The obvious questions here as we conclude this book are: Why is the Founders' commercial republicanism relevant to the reapportionment cases and second-generation voting rights? And how precisely does this republicanism relate to the themes of this book and to a critical assessment of the sort of multicultural representation that has developed under the auspices of the VRA since 1969? In chapter 1, I provided a preliminary answer to these questions. In the following conclusion, I will supply more in-depth responses and provide a more explicit context from which we might flesh out the features of a Founders' VRA that can be used as a barometer for assessing the historical VRA discussed in chapters 3 through 7.

The Founders' Commercial Republicanism: A Blueprint for the Promotion of Liberty, Union, and Individual, Political, and Martial Excellence

In 1781 Alexander Hamilton sent a letter to Robert Morris, then the confederation's superintendent of finance, promoting the establishment of a national bank. In it Hamilton acknowledged that the commercialization of a society may indeed "lead to insolence, an inordinate ambition, a vicious luxury, licentiousness of morals, and all those vices which corrupt government, enslave the people and precipitate the ruin of a nation." But Hamilton quickly responded to this restrictive interpretation of commerce by stating that "no wise statesman will reject the good from an apprehension of the ill. The truth is in human affairs, there is no good, pure and unmixed; every advantage has two sides, and wisdom consists in availing ourselves of the good, and guarding as much as possible against the bad."[3]

The critics of commercial republicanism focused almost exclusively on the disadvantages associated with commercial development. The supporters of vigorous commerce, however, argued that the advantages far outweighed any negative consequences that might arise. For them, commercial development was the necessary precondition for the generation of wealth, which made civilization itself possible. It promoted equality of opportunity and provided all, including the poor, the chance to rise up socially and economically. It facilitated industry and induced everyone to work and to avoid sloth. Those who possessed superior talents and who might contribute most to the public weal might be especially enticed to perfect their faculties in a commercial republican regime in which (as Madison emphasized in *Federalist* 10) the first object of government was the protection of those faculties. Developing American commerce would enhance the division of labor as well as the division of knowledge, thus increasing productivity while developing understanding in the arts and sciences. An energetic commercial republic would also provide the technological wherewithal necessary to wage modern war, and it held out the promise, with the appropriate institutional changes the Constitution would bring about, of creating a new civic dynamism and martial spirit that might reinvigorate public morale.[4]

When combined with the security of property that was the cornerstone of liberal constitutional regimes such as the United States, an advanced division of labor in such a dynamic commercial republic as America offered up for the first time in history the possibility of perfecting those very intellectual, political, and martial virtues that had never flourished together in any single regime. The question was what types of political institutions or constitutional structures might best allow for this development.

The answer was to be the Constitution. In *Federalist* 1 Hamilton referred to the United States as "an empire in many respects the most interesting in the world."[5] In *Federalist* 9 he reminded his readers that those "petty republics of Greece and Italy" that had been exemplars of premodern republicanism and the models of approbation for so many of the Anti-Federalists had also been plagued by those "vices of government" that served to "pervert the direction and tarnish the luster of those bright talents and exalted endowments for which the favored soils that produced them have been so justly celebrated."[6] The Platos, Aristotles, and Ciceros of Greek and Roman antiquity had flourished not *because of* but *in spite of* the regimes of which they were a part.

America's new constitutional order would correct this premodern defect. It would avoid the vices of government by creating the conditions in which the talented and the highly endowed could flourish. It would combine patriotism, unparalleled military power, and a civic spirit with rational and durable liberty to produce that "fabric of American empire"[7] that was the necessary concomitant to combating the world empires of the day. Unlike the empires of Britain, France, and Spain, *The Federalist* emphasized, America's republican empire would "flow immediately from that pure, original fountain of all legitimate authority," the consent of the people.[8] The nationalism facilitated by the new Constitution would not be the irrational sort originating in an ethnic, religious, or martial chauvinism. Rather, it would be anchored in the universally legitimate principles of liberty and consent.

In *Federalist* 15, Hamilton had inveighed that the Articles of Confederation had reduced the United States to "almost the last stage of national humiliation."[9] The Constitution would change this situation, paving the way to potential American greatness by providing those energetic institutions of state and facilitating that commercial dynamism that were the preconditions to securing America's martial prowess, civic militarism, and politics of high principle.

This successful regime depended, however, on union and its corollary of a uniform concept of American citizenship. Madison and Hamilton had defended the opening of the channels of commerce that the Constitution's extended republic would promote because such commerce would help fight faction. The Founders' commercial republic would integrate the American economy and sow the seeds for a more perfect union, raising citizenship above the vain and factious particularities of region, race, creed, and any class divisions based on disparities of wealth.

As imperfect as the realization of this objective may have been prior to the Civil War, the concept of America as it would develop under the Constitution was based on the twin principles of liberty and equality. These architectonic principles of American citizenship, originally expressed most succinctly in the Declaration of Independence, rendered that citizenship a function of high politics, transcending those base political and national identifications that had typified premodern republics, to say nothing of earlier regimes that were nonrepublican.

Today's VRA, unfortunately, seeks to institutionalize legally those very political identities based on notions of racial and ethnic distinction that the Constitution's commercial republicanism was designed to transcend. Second-generation voting rights have effectively removed the public good from the calculus of representation by indicating that members of Congress should be rent-seekers or spokesmen for the particular interests of their racial constituencies. Today's VRA has also displaced the Constitution's individual rights in favor of corporate or group rights. It has enervated the separation of powers and principles of federalism by granting the federal judiciary extraordinary powers of political surveillance, presuming an almost omniscient capability on the part of the judiciary to balance not merely political interests but also racial interests throughout the entirety of the political process. The natural rights of the Founders' Constitution have been jettisoned in favor of the programmatic, welfare-state rights of racial constituencies, a development that has promoted not only faction but, worse, racial faction.

Today's VRA denigrates the high objects of the Founders' republicanism, undermining that republicanism's singular understanding of citizenship. In the process it has jeopardized the Founders' hopes for that individual, political, and martial excellence that might arise as a concomitant to the Constitution's promotion of a more perfect union anchored in rational and durable liberty. Today's VRA, in this most fundamental way, is decisively un-American.

A Founders' Voting Rights Act

What, then, would a Founders' VRA look like? What sort of rights would it protect, and what sort of republicanism would it promote? How would it have addressed those tangible problems of race politics in the Jim Crow South in the 1960s that were the impetus for the original VRA?

In chapters 1 and 2, I noted that the new republican order the Constitution institutionalized was intended to promote a deliberative republicanism that would protect private rights and promote the public good in a regime of limited government. Obviously enough, a Founders' VRA would emulate these same objectives.

As a preliminary matter, we might say that a Founders' VRA would follow the original VRA in promoting individual rights, protecting all Americans, regardless of race, against racial discrimination in voting. A Founders' VRA would also return the federal judiciary to its traditional role of assessing rights-based claims rather than engaging in broad, highly speculative political judgments about what constitutes "fair" racial representation. As the preceding chapters have demonstrated, both the Court's use of a mathematical measure of representational fairness in the reapportionment cases— "one person, one vote"—and its determination under the VRA that "fair" representation equaled a right to minority office-holding in rough proportion to the racial demographics of the jurisdictions in question, were arbitrary decisions that had no support in the Constitution or the VRA. The rationalist presumption underlying the reapportionment cases and second-generation voting rights—that the judiciary has the intellectual wherewithal to review the political process and decide in a nonarbitrary way what constitutes "fairness" in the representational system—stands in stark contrast to what the Founders understood to be the proper role and capability of the judiciary.

By confining the judiciary to assessing whether an individual right to vote has been denied on the basis of race, a Founders' VRA would save courts from the intractability and embarrassment of trying to determine what constitutes fair representation. It would also respect the rule of law. All individuals would be treated equally rather than having their rights depend on the racial groups to which they belonged, as is currently the case with second-generation voting rights. In addition, by restricting the VRA to claims concerning individual rights, a Founders' VRA would save the judiciary from the simplistic and divisive orthodoxy it must invariably indulge in when attempting to assign group rights. This task has involved courts dividing the American electorate into racial classes largely on the basis of fashionable presumptions frequently predicated on thin, if not nonexistent, evidence consisting of determinations involving thousands, sometimes even millions, of voters and residents.

By restricting the judiciary to assessing the right to vote rather than the broader and intractable right to "fair" or "effective" representation, a Founders' VRA would preserve the separation of powers, which is violated when the Court arrogates to itself political decisions such as it has engaged in the reapportionment cases and under the VRA. Under the pretenses of following the VRA, the Court has imposed various forms of race-centric schemes of representation from congressional elections to local and even judicial elections.

Also preserved would be the principles of federalism. The guarantee clause of article 4 of the Constitution provides a guarantee to every state of "a Republican Form of Government." That clause, however, does not require any *specific* form of such government. As Madison emphasized in *Federalist* 43, the authority of the guarantee clause

> extends no further than to a *guarantee* of a republican form of government, which supposes a preexisting government of the form which is to be guaranteed. As long, therefore, as the existing republican forms are continued by the States, they are guaranteed by the federal Constitution. Whenever the States may choose to substitute other republican forms, they have a right to do so, and to claim the federal guaranty for the latter. The only restriction imposed on them is, that they shall not exchange republican for anti-republican Constitutions; a restriction which, it is presumed, will hardly be considered as a grievance.[10]

When the Court construed the guarantee clause for the first time in *Luther v. Borden* (1849), it concluded, in a manner consistent with Madison's remarks in *Federalist* 43, that the sovereignty of every state "resides in the people of the State." States were free to change their form of government as they saw fit. This tenet was a fundamental principle of the Constitution. Whether a state's change in its republican form comported with the guarantee clause was a rare question to be asked, but when it was asked it was a question "to be settled by the political power," not the judiciary.[11]

In 1849 the Court recognized that questions of representational form were purely political questions for the political branches of government to decide. As chapter 3 has emphasized, the Court apparently forgot this lesson in the reapportionment cases. It would forget it again in its construction of the VRA.

The Founders' Rejection of Multiculturalism and Democracy as "Victimization"

In addition to the changes outlined above, a Founders' VRA would not sanction or tolerate divisive notions of republicanism that threatened the concept of union and American citizenship—the concept of one "People of the United States"—that was the predicate for the emergence of the individual, political, and martial excellence discussed earlier. This concept was again reaffirmed in the Fourteenth Amendment, which provided that "all persons born or naturalized in the United States" were "citizens of the United States." The Fifteenth Amendment, the other source of the VRA's constitutional authority, similarly reaffirmed the concept of a single, national citizenship.

The multiculturalism of second-generation voting rights has worked at cross-purposes with this ideal of a uniform citizenship. Dividing Americans into an array of racial subclasses, it has institutionalized a vision of America as a nation of isolated racial minorities that deserve their own distinct representation because, presumably, they live within a racially divided society typified by classes of oppressors and oppressed.

However unfair the multiculturalist vision is to individual members of minority groups, its "democracy-as-victimization" concept of republicanism is of a piece with the Founders' characterization of minorities as groups generally unconcerned for the general welfare. Harvey Mansfield has written that "citizens are busy with what they can do for themselves and others; victims are concerned with what has been done to them and with what they can get from others."[12] If we accept Mansfield's distinction, we might say that today's VRA has converted the Founders' citizens' Constitution into a victims' Constitution, one in which blacks and Hispanics are presumed to have a right to electoral office independent of whether they lose elections due to discrimination.

The politics of multiculturalism assumes that "official minorities" are victim groups on account of their identity as official minorities; it assumes as a matter of course white guilt and minority victimhood. As we have seen in the preceding chapters, VRA law long ago abandoned the requirement of proof of intentional discrimination against blacks or Hispanics as a precondition for those groups' entitlement to electoral office. The VRA today assumes that blacks and Hispanics lose to whites and Anglos in elections only on account of discrimination—an assumption that holds even where racial discrimination likely has nothing to do with minority electoral losses.

If the "genius of the American system is that it requires factions and interests to take an enlarged view of their own welfare, to see, as it were, their own interests through the filter of the common good,"[13] today's VRA stands opposed to this system. The Founders hoped that the various institutional processes of the national government would involve reasoning on the merits of legislative proposals with a view to protecting individual rights and promoting the general welfare. These systems have been displaced by a republicanism in which the legislative process is seen as a power play among incompatible group interests, one in which logrolling, compromises, side payments, and other forms of bargaining are used to achieve not merely partisan gain[14] but also, in the case of the VRA, partisan racial gain. A Founders' VRA would abandon such an approach to American republicanism.

In *The Powers of War and Peace*, John Yoo described how the "conventional academic wisdom" about the Constitution's foreign affairs and war powers has led to serious misconceptions about the president's war-making prerogatives. That conventional wisdom has assumed that "the Constitution establishes defined processes for the regulation of foreign relations that makes them capable of judicial enforcement";[15] that there exists a formal, legalistic arrangement and "an intrusive judicial role in overseeing this legalistic arrangement to keep the presidency within its restricted bounds."[16] Yoo contests this conventional wisdom and suggests that the judiciary should stay out of war-powers disputes and leave the president and Congress to determine these issues on their own, as the Framers and the ratifiers of the Constitution intended.

The theme of this book is similar to Yoo's; only the constitutional issues are obviously different. The conventional wisdom in VRA law and its accompanying scholarship has assumed that the Founders' republicanism consists of a constellation of legally defined rules and regulations that can be readily enforced by a vigilant judiciary. This book argues, to the contrary, that the Founders' Constitution of republican liberty, like the Constitution's design for energetic government, was not intended to be tied down by fixed, legalistic rules imposed by an imperial judiciary that has little legal authority or competence to make assessments of "fair" representation and virtually no political accountability. In the Founders' view, judicial intervention into questions of representation, as the Constitution's provisions applicable to the issue make explicitly clear, would strangle American republican liberty. Theories of representation were inherently contestable because they were inherently political.

Accordingly, the Constitution's framers permitted only the political branches of government to address such questions. With few restrictions, questions of representational government were to be left to state legislatures to resolve because resolving questions at this level would facilitate greater local control, accountability, and freedom. We have seen how this conception of the Founders' republican liberty has been largely lost as a result of the judicial rationalism and multicultural politics that emerged with the reapportionment cases and second-generation voting rights.

The facts involving the VRA today are plain. The 1965 VRA arguably did more than any other federal initiative in history to fulfill the promise of American republicanism through the 1960s. Today, however, that same act has evolved into an initiative that arguably does as much as any other federal mandate to undermine that republicanism. The current VRA—the VRA of second-generation voting rights—requires legislators, judges, and administrators to think in racial terms, to count in racial terms, and to allocate political power in racial terms. Americans now have a choice between maintaining their longstanding Madisonian regime of equality and representation or continuing to undermine that regime with an ersatz multiculturalism that promises more intensified racial antagonism and racial bean-counting in election law in the years to come.

Publication Acknowledgments

Some of the material in this book, along with ideas and arguments advanced in it, have appeared in earlier publications of mine. I would like to thank the following publishers for their permission to reprint material from these earlier works:

Carolina Academic Press for Chapter 1, "Voting Rights, Representation, and the Problem of Equality," Chapter 5, "*Shaw v. Reno* and the Voting Rights Conundrum: Equality, the Public Interest, and the Politics of Representation," and Chapter 12, "The Supreme Court and the Future of Voting Rights," in *Affirmative Action and Representation:* Shaw v. Reno *and the Future of Voting Rights*, edited by Anthony A. Peacock (1997)

Greenwood Publishing Group for "Equal Representation or Guardian Democracy? The Supreme Court's Foray into the Politics of Reapportionment and Its Legacy," in *Voting Rights and Redistricting in the United States*, edited by Mark E. Rush (1998)

McGill-Queen's University Press for "Judicial Rationalism and the Therapeutic Constitution: The Supreme Court's Reconstruction of Equality and Democratic Process under the Charter of Rights and Freedoms," in *The Myth of the Sacred: The Charter, the Courts, and the Politics of the Constitution of Canada*, edited by Patrick James, Donald E. Abelson, and Michael Lusztig (2002)

Lexington Books for "The Voting Rights Act and the Politics of Multiculturalism: The Challenge to Commercial Republicanism at Century's Turn," in *Courts and the Culture Wars*, edited by Bradley C. S. Watson (2002); and "From *Beer* to Eternity: Why Race Will Always Predominate under the Voting Rights Act," in *Redistricting in the New Millennium*, edited by Peter F. Galderisi (2005)

Notes

Introduction

1. Reapportionment is the process that occurs after each decennial census, in which the 435 seats of the House of Representatives are redivided based on each state's share of the national population.

2. Associated Press, "Biden: Alito Filibuster Not Off the Table," November 20, 2005.

3. *Reynolds v. Sims*, 377 U.S. 533 (1964).

4. See *Lucas v. Colorado General Assembly*, 377 U.S. 713, 717–18, opinion of the Court, and 742–43, Clark, J., dissenting (1964).

5. *The National Voting Rights Act of 1965*, 79 Stat. 439, as renumbered and amended, 42 U.S.C., sec. 1973c.

6. *Allen v. State Board of Elections*, 393 U.S. 544 (1969).

7. See *Fannie Lou Hammer, Rosa Parks, and Coretta Scott King Voting Rights Act Reauthorization and Amendments Act of 2006*, secs. 5(b) and 5(d), hereinafter "VRA Reauthorization and Amendments Act," "VRA of 2006," or "2006 VRA."

8. F. A. Hayek, *Law, Legislation, and Liberty*, vol. 1, *Rules and Order* (Chicago: University of Chicago Press, 1973), 5, 8–34.

9. Hayek, *The Constitution of Liberty* (Chicago: University of Chicago Press, 1960), 22–24.

10. Hayek, *The Fatal Conceit: The Errors of Socialism*, in *The Collected Works of F. A. Hayek*, vol. 1, ed. W. W. Bartley III (Chicago: University of Chicago Press, 1989).

11. See James F. Blumstein, "Defining and Proving Race Discrimination: Perspectives on the Purpose vs. Results Approach from the Voting Rights Act," *Virginia Law Review* 69 (1983): 633, 635, 647, 689–701, 707–14.

12. Anthony A. Peacock, "The Voting Rights Act and the Politics of Multiculturalism: The Challenge to Commercial Republicanism at Century's Turn," in *Courts and the Culture Wars*, ed. Bradley C. S. Watson (Lanham, MD: Lexington Books, 2002), 168.

13. *Grutter v. Bollinger*, 123 S.Ct. 2325 (2003).

14. *Gratz v. Bollinger,* 123 S.Ct. 2411 (2003).

15. *Georgia v. Ashcroft*, 123 S.Ct. 2498 (2003).

16. See John D. Skrentny, *The Minority Rights Revolution* (Cambridge, MA: Belknap Press of Harvard University Press, 2002), 1–20, 85–142.

17. *Grutter v. Bollinger*, 2363, Thomas, J., concurring in part and dissenting in part, referring to *Holder v. Hall*, 512 U.S. 899 (1994), Thomas, J., concurring in judgment.

18. Alexander Hamilton, John Jay, and James Madison, *The Federalist: A Commentary on the Constitution of the United States*, ed. Robert Scigliano (New York: Modern Library, 2001), *Federalist* 10, 54.

19. *Baker v. Carr*, 369 U.S. 186 (1962).

20. *United Jewish Organizations of Williamsburgh, Inc. v. Carey*, 430 U.S. 144 (1977).

21. *City of Mobile v. Bolden*, 446 U.S. 55 (1980).

22. *Thornburg v. Gingles*, 106 S.Ct. 2752 (1986).

Chapter 1: Madisonian versus Multiculturalist Republicanism

1. Lance Banning, *The Sacred Fire of Liberty: James Madison and the Founding of the Federal Republic* (Ithaca, NY: Cornell University Press, 1995), 2.

2. Alexander Hamilton, John Jay, and James Madison, *The Federalist: A Commentary on the Constitution of the United States*, ed. Robert Scigliano (New York: Modern Library, 2001), *Federalist* 10, 57.

3. Ibid., 54. See also note 20.

4. See Jeremy Rabkin, *Judicial Compulsions: How Public Law Distorts Public Policy* (New York: Basic Books, 1989), 44–48.

5. *Federalist* 51, 330–35.

6. See Gordon S. Wood, *The Radicalism of the American Revolution* (New York: Alfred A. Knopf, 1992), 324–25.

7. *Colgrove v. Green*, 328 U.S. 549 (1946).

8. Ibid., 554–55.

9. Ibid., 552, emphasis added.

10. Ibid., 556.

11. Tom G. Palmer, "Madison and Multiculturalism: Group Representation, Group Rights, and Constitutionalism," in *James Madison and the Future of Limited Government*, ed. John Samples (Washington, D.C.: Cato Institute, 2002), 78.

12. *Federalist* 10, 57.

13. Comparing the representational theory of John Stuart Mill, one of the original proponents of proportional representation, with that of James Madison, Mark Rush has observed: "In fact, both Mill and Madison advocated their visions of government *not* to advance the discrete interests of the factional interests that comprised society but, instead, to promote the *public* interest *despite* the wishes of discrete or, worse, what Mill referred to as the 'uninstructed' minorities. Accordingly, a key goal of their prescriptions was to create a process by which the governing majority would be least likely to represent one discrete or uninformed interest. Furthermore, both sought to ensure that, ultimately, elites (presumably enlightened ones) would be insulated somewhat from the masses in order to be free to govern in the public interest." Mark E. Rush, "The Hidden Costs of Electoral Reform," in *Fair and Effective Representation? Debating Electoral Reform*

and Minority Rights, ed. Mark E. Rush and Richard L. Engstrom (Lanham, MD: Rowman and Littlefield, 2001), 104, emphasis in original. See also Joseph M. Bessette, *The Mild Voice of Reason: Deliberative Democracy and American National Government* (Chicago: University of Chicago Press, 1994), 56.

14. *Federalist* 10, 56.

15. Madison emphasizes this point in the first paragraph of *Federalist* 10: "Complaints are everywhere heard from our most considerate and virtuous citizens, equally the friends of public and private faith, and of public and personal liberty, that our governments are too unstable, that the public good is disregarded in the conflicts of rival parties, and that measures are too often decided, not according to the rules of justice and the rights of the minor party, but by the superior force of an interested and overbearing majority" (54).

16. In a letter to Thomas Jefferson dated October 17, 1788, Madison remarked: "Wherever the real power in a Government lies, there is the danger of oppression. In our Governments the real power lies in the majority of the community, and the invasion of private rights is *chiefly* to be apprehended, not from acts of Government contrary to the sense of its constituents, but from acts in which the Government is the mere instrument of the major number of the Constituents. This is a truth of great importance, but not yet sufficiently attended to." Cited in *The Mind of the Founder: Sources of the Political Thought of James Madison*, ed. Marvin Meyers (Hanover, NH: Brandeis University Press, 1981), 157, emphasis in original.

17. See Hamilton, *Federalist* 60, 384–85: "There is sufficient diversity in the state of property, in the genius, manners, and habits of the people of the different parts of the Union, to occasion a material diversity of disposition in their representatives towards the different ranks and conditions of society. And though an intimate intercourse under the same government will promote a gradual assimilation in temper and sentiments, yet there are causes, as well physical as moral, which may, in a greater or less degree, permanently nourish different propensities and inclinations in this particular. But the circumstance which will be likely to have the greatest influence in the matter, will be the dissimilar modes of constituting the several component parts of the government. The House of Representatives being to be elected immediately by the people, the Senate by the State legislatures, the President by electors chosen for that purpose by the people, there would be little probability of a common interest to cement these different branches in a predilection for any particular class of electors." The Seventeenth Amendment (1913) provided that federal senators would henceforth be "elected by the people" of the states rather than by state legislatures, as originally provided for in the Constitution.

18. As Hannah Pitkin notes, the mirror concept of representation, like that suggested by the Anti-Federalists, might require selection of candidates by lottery or random sampling if the ideal of representing as many segments or "classes" in society is to be achieved. See Hannah Fenichel Pitkin, *The Concept of Representation* (Berkeley, CA: University of California Press, 1972), 73. See also Will Kymlicka, *Multicultural*

Citizenship: A Liberal Theory of Minority Rights (New York: Oxford University Press, 1997), 139.

19. *Federalist* 17, 100–101 and *Federalist* 56, 360.

20. Lani Guinier, "The Triumph of Tokenism: The Voting Rights Act and the Theory of Black Electoral Success," *Michigan Law Review* 89 (March 1991): 1077.

21. See Thomas L. Pangle, *Montesquieu's Philosophy of Liberalism: A Commentary on the Spirit of the Laws* (Chicago: University of Chicago Press, 1973), 127.

22. See Ward E. Y. Elliott, *The Rise of Guardian Democracy: The Supreme Court's Role in Voting Rights Disputes, 1845–1969* (Cambridge, MA: Harvard University Press, 1974), 83.

23. Eric Metcalfe, "Illiberal Citizenship? A Critique of Will Kymlicka's Liberal Theory of Minority Rights," *Queen's Law Journal* 22 (1996): 194.

24. *Holder v. Hall*, 114 S. Ct. 2581 (1994). This case is discussed at length in Chapter 6.

25. Ibid., 2602.

26. Ibid., 2598. See also 2599. A majority-minority district (MMD) is an electoral district in which a majority of the residents are comprised of a minority protected by the VRA.

27. Ibid., 2599, citing *Wright v. Rockefeller*, 376 U.S. 52, 67, Douglas, J., dissenting (1964).

28. See *Shaw v. Reno*, 113 S.Ct. 2816, 2827–28, opinion of the Court (1993).

29. *Federalist* 10, 54.

30. See Linde, "When Initiative Lawmaking Is Not 'Republican Government,'" *Oregon Law Review* 72 (1993): 32: "Republican government must be responsive to the people, but what both history and recent experience in the states led the framers to fear was unbridled 'interest' and 'passion.' These were well-known terms in Enlightenment political theory, and nothing since has made them obscure. By the end of the seventeenth century, 'interest' had a specifically economic meaning. Individual 'passion' included noneconomic motives like pride and ambition. But only collective passion endangered a system built on collective action. . . . To the federalists, collective 'passion' was the antithesis of 'reason.'" See also *Federalist* 15: "Why has government been instituted at all? Because the passions of men will not conform to the dictates of reason and justice, without constraint. Has it been found that bodies of men act with more rectitude or greater disinterestedness than individuals? . . . A spirit of faction, which is apt to mingle its poison in the deliberations of all bodies of men, will often hurry the persons of whom they are composed into improprieties and excesses, for which they would blush in a private capacity" (91–92).

31. See David F. Epstein, *The Political Theory of the Federalist* (Chicago: University of Chicago Press, 1984), 80.

32. See Thomas C. Berg, "Religion, Race, Segregation, and Districting: Comparing *Kiryas Joel* with *Shaw/Miller*," *Cumberland Law Review* 26 (1996): 377.

33. See, for instance, Washington's Farewell Address, in *George Washington: A Collection*, ed. W.B. Allen (Indianapolis: Liberty Classics, 1988), 521–22.

34. Epstein, *Political Theory of the Federalist*, 159.

35. See Hiram Caton, *The Politics of Progress: The Origins and Development of the Commercial Republic, 1600–1835* (Gainesville, FL: University of Florida Press, 1988), 470. For a good survey of the centuries-old philosophical treatment of the distinction between interest and passion in classical liberal thought, see Albert O. Hirschman, *The Passions and the Interests: Political Arguments for Capitalism before Its Triumph* (Princeton, NJ: Princeton University Press, 1997). As Hirschman remarks: "Ever since the end of the Middle Ages, and particularly as a result of the increasing frequency of war and civil war in the seventeenth and eighteenth centuries, the search was on for a behavioral equivalent for the religious precept, for new rules of conduct and devices that would impose much needed discipline and constraints on both rulers and ruled, and the expansion of commerce and industry was thought to hold much promise in this regard" (129).

36. See Caton, *Politics of Progress*, 472; Hirschman, *Passions and the Interests*, 9–66. As Walter Berns has remarked, unlike other forms of faction, such as those based on religion, "property factions could be regulated (and accommodated) because, although divided from one another, they shared a common interest in economic growth, and to promote this growth would be the task of modern legislation. America's business would be (as Calvin Coolidge many years later said it was) business." Walter Berns, "Constitutionalism and Multiculturalism," in *Multiculturalism and American Democracy*, ed. Arthur M. Melzer, Jerry Weinberger, and M. Richard Zinman (Lawrence, KS: University Press of Kansas, 1998), 96.

37. *Federalist* 35, 211–12.

38. In *Federalist* 51 Madison reported, "It is of great importance in a republic not only to guard the society against the oppression of its rulers, but to guard one part of the society against the injustice of the other part" (333). The "greater number of citizens and extent of territory which may be brought within the compass of republican than of democratic government" was not only a key feature that distinguished these two forms of popular rule. It was "this circumstance *principally* which renders factious combinations less to be dreaded in the former than in the latter" (*Federalist* 10, 60, emphasis added). In other words, the noninstitutional features of the Constitution (for example, the size of the Founders' republic) rather than the Constitution's institutional structures were the principal bulwark against faction. See also Martin Diamond, *As Far as Republican Principles Will Admit*, ed. William A. Schambra (Washington, D.C.: AEI Press, 1992), 53; see also next note.

39. Madison and Hamilton specifically rejected the pleadings of Brutus, the *Federal Farmer* 7, and Melancton Smith, who, following Montesquieu, had claimed that only in small republics could true republican government exist. The critics claimed that large republics such as that proposed by the Constitution were recipes for despotism, particularly despotism from the center. Madison and Hamilton, both exemplary students of ancient history, disagreed. As the examples of Greek and Roman antiquity demonstrated, the very opposite of what the critics proposed was the case: It was in small

republics that tyranny dominated. The only inoculation against this danger was to be found in a large republic. See especially *Federalist* 9, 47–53. Recounting the misfortunes of ancient democracy and the more recent experience of the newly emancipated American states, Madison had this to say at the Constitutional Convention: "The lesson we are to draw from the whole is that where a majority are united by a common sentiment and have an opportunity, the rights of the minor party become insecure. In a Republican Govt. the Majority if united have always an opportunity. The only remedy is to enlarge the sphere, & thereby divide the community into so great a number of interests & parties, that in the 1st. place a majority will not be likely at the same moment to have a common interest separate from that of the whole or of the minority; and in the 2d. place, that in case they shd. have such an interest, they may not be apt to unite in the pursuit of it. It was incumbent on us then to try this remedy, and with that view to frame a republican system on such a scale & in such a form as will controul all the evils wch. have been experienced." Max Farrand, ed., *Records of the Federal Convention* (New Haven, CT: Yale University Press, 1966) 1:136.

40. Diamond, *As Far as Republican Principles Will Admit*, 53–57.

41. *Federalist* 10, 55–56, emphasis added.

42. Diamond, *As Far as Republican Principles Will Admit*, 55–56.

43. *Federalist* 51, 335. Diamond, *As Far as Republican Principles Will Admit*, 53, 56.

44. Diamond, *As Far as Republican Principles Will Admit*, 53, 56. For a critique of Diamond's interpretation of *The Federalist* and, specifically, Madison's thought concerning "commercial republicanism," see Banning, *Sacred Fire of Liberty*, 205–12. Banning rejects that Madison ever accepted Hamilton's understanding of "commercial republicanism" and points out that Madison himself never referred to "the United States as a 'commercial society' or a 'commercial republic,' as Hamilton did in *Federalist* no. 6" (212). Banning's interpretation is difficult to square with *Federalist* 10 and 51, in addition to other writings of Madison's. Moreover, the identity established between Hamilton's and Madison's writings in *The Federalist*, evidenced by the use of a single pseudonym, "Publius," suggests that Hamilton's and Madison's thought throughout *The Federalist* was intended to make up a single, coherent whole.

45. *Holder v. Hall*, 2598, Thomas, J., concurring.

46. *Shaw v. Reno*, 2832, opinion of the Court.

47. In "Triumph of Tokenism," Guinier wrote that "authentic leaders are those elected by black voters. In voting rights terminology, electoral ratification from majority-black, single-member districts establishes authenticity. These facts distinguish the authentic representatives from those officials who are handpicked by the 'establishment,' or who must appeal to white voters in order to get elected. Establishment endorsed blacks are unlikely to be authentic because they are not *elected* as the representatives of choice of the black community. In addition, these officials are often marginal community members whose only real connection with black constituents is skin color. Electoral support by a majority of black voters is thus a convenient proxy for political authenticity" (1103–4, emphasis in original). See also ibid.: "I . . . reject the criticism that authentic

black representation is meaningless. Authenticity reflects the group consciousness, group history, and group perspective of a disadvantaged and stigmatized minority. Authenticity recognizes that black voters are a discrete 'social group' with a distinctive voice . . . authentic representation also facilitates black voter mobilization, participation, and confidence in the process of self-government" (1108). Critics of Guinier's nomination in addition pointed to a 1991 law review article in which Guinier suggested that when applying the VRA, courts might consider whether "descriptively black representatives who were also Republicans [could] qualify as black representatives." Guinier, "No Two Seats: The Elusive Quest for Political Equality," *Virginia Law Review* 77 (November 1991): 1500n299. Interestingly, these comments were deleted from the reproduction of this essay in Lani Guinier, *The Tyranny of the Majority: Fundamental Fairness in Representative Democracy* (New York: Free Press, 1994), 71. See Palmer, "Madison and Multiculturalism," 79 and 110n29.

48. See Carol M. Swain, *Black Faces, Black Interests: The Representation of African Americans in Congress* (Cambridge, MA: Harvard University Press, 1993), 3–19; David T. Canon, *Race, Redistricting, and Representation: The Unintended Consequences of Black Majority Districts* (Chicago: University of Chicago Press, 1999), 20–59; and David Lublin, *The Paradox of Representation: Racial Gerrymandering and Minority Interests in Congress* (Princeton, NJ: Princeton University Press, 1997), 57–59, 69–70. See also Guinier, *Tyranny of the Majority*: "Blacks, as a poor and historically oppressed group, are in greater need of government sponsored programs and solicitude, which whites often resent and vigorously oppose" (37).

49. John C. Calhoun, *Union and Liberty: The Political Philosophy of John C. Calhoun* (Indianapolis: Liberty Fund, 1992), 23–4.

50. See, for instance, Swain, *Black Faces, Black Interests,* and Canon, *Race, Redistricting, and Representation.* As different as their approaches are to the question of race-based representation, both Swain and Canon attempt to define "black interests" and then proceed to assess how those interests have or have not been represented by members of Congress.

51. *Georgia v Ashcroft,* 123 S.Ct. 2498 (2003), especially 2512–13.

52. See Rainer Knopff, *Human Rights and Social Technology: The New War on Discrimination* (Ottawa: Carleton University Press, 1990), 205.

53. For a discussion of these bargaining theories of congressional process and their limits, see Bessette, *The Mild Voice of Reason,* especially 56–66. In *Ashcroft,* Justice O'Connor, writing for the Court, averred that "in a representative democracy, the very purpose of voting is to delegate to chosen representatives the power to make and pass laws. The ability to exert more control over that process is at the core of exercising political power. A lawmaker with more legislative influence has more potential to set the agenda, to participate in closed-door meetings, to negotiate from a stronger position, and to shake hands on a deal" (2513). Congressional policy formation, O'Connor suggests, is about deal-making and power politics. Because the VRA seeks to give greater access to minority viewpoints, it must enhance this process for minority constituencies.

VRA policy, in this light, assumes the posture that interest-group tradeoffs on behalf of particular constituencies are not merely *how* congressional policy unfolds, but how it *should* unfold—at least under the auspices of the VRA. To use Theodore Lowi's imagery, second-generation voting rights and related empirical literature tend to mirror the tenets of interest-group liberalism; they would transform *"access and logrolling from necessary evil to greater good."* Theodore J. Lowi, *The End of Liberalism: The Second Republic of the United States*, 2nd ed. (New York: W.W. Norton & Company, 1979), 55, emphasis in original. See also Bessette, *Mild Voice of Reason*, 57.

54. George W. Carey, *In Defense of the Constitution* (Indianapolis: Liberty Fund, 1995), 46–47. See also Lowi, *End of Liberalism*: "To the Madisonian, groups were a necessary evil much in need of regulation. To the modern pluralist, groups are good, requiring only accommodation. Madison went beyond his definition of the group to a position that 'the regulation of these various interfering interests forms the principal task of modern legislation'" (58). Bessette, in *Mild Voice of Reason*, describes how the dominant theories of congressional process in modern political science have similarly denigrated Madison's understanding of deliberative democracy: "Scholars of American government and politics seem increasingly drawn to an analytical framework that sees lawmaking and policymaking as the aggregation of individual interests and preferences—the rational actor, or self-interest, model—and not the result of argument, reasoning, and persuasion about common ends or goals" (xi). See also Rabkin, *Judicial Compulsions*, 23–26, 41; and Elliott, *Rise of Guardian Democracy*, 7–8.

55. The most comprehensive discussion of negative and positive liberty, from which the distinction between negative and positive rights derives, was originally developed by Isaiah Berlin. See Isaiah Berlin, "Two Concepts of Liberty," in *Four Essays on Liberty* (New York: Oxford University Press, 1969), 118.

56. The examples Alexander Hamilton provided in *Federalist* 78 of those rare instances in which the judiciary could find legislative acts constitutionally infirm—bills of attainder and ex post facto laws, for example—were cases involving *"reservations"* against government "of *particular* rights or privileges" (497, emphasis added). Hamilton's implication here, like Madison's frequent reference to rights under the Constitution as "private rights" (not public or group rights), was that the Constitution's original rights were individual rights that were negative in character; judicial review would focus on reservations against government of particular rights.

57. Karen Selick, "Rights and Wrongs in the Canadian Charter," in *Rethinking the Constitution: Perspectives on Canadian Constitutional Reform Interpretation, and Theory*, ed. Anthony A. Peacock (Toronto: Oxford University Press, 1996), 105.

58. *South Carolina v. Katzenbach*, 383 U.S. 301, 334, opinion of the Court (1966).

59. In *Federalist* 14, Madison remarked, "it is to be remembered that the general government is not to be charged with the whole power of making and administering laws. Its jurisdiction is limited to certain enumerated objects" (82). Madison also made clear his preference for "free markets" in a speech to Congress, April 9, 1789: "I own myself the friend to a very free system of commerce, and hold it as a truth, that commercial

shackles are generally unjust, oppressive and impolitic—it is also a truth, that if industry and labour are left to take their own course, they will generally be directed to those objects which are the most productive, and this in a more certain and direct manner than the wisdom of the most enlightened legislature could point out." Cited in Roger Pilon, "Madison's Constitutional Vision: The Legacy of Enumerated Powers," in *James Madison and the Future*, 28. As Pilon remarks: "Long before 20th century economists like Ludwig von Mises and Friedrich Hayek were explaining systematically the folly of social planning, there with the essential insight was Madison." Cited in ibid.

60. Canon, *Race, Redistricting, and Representation*, 254.

61. See Gordon Tullock, *The Rent-Seeking Society* (Indianapolis: Liberty Fund, 2005).

62. Canon, *Race, Redistricting, and Representation*, 141–42, emphasis in original.

63. *Federalist* 10, 58–59, emphasis added.

64. Sidney M. Milkis, *The President and the Parties: The Transformation of the American Party System since the New Deal* (New York: Oxford University Press, 1993), 14.

65. Carey, *In Defense of the Constitution*, 50.

66. Ibid., 49. See also note 53.

67. In his famous convention speech of June 6, 1787, the precursor to *Federalist* 10, Madison noted how religion could "become a motive to persecution & oppression" and that "we have seen the mere distinction of colour made in the midst of the most enlightened period of time, a ground of the most oppressive dominion ever exercised by man over man." James Madison, speech at the Constitutional Convention, June 6, 1787, in *Records of the Federal Convention*, ed. Max Farrand (New Haven, CT: Yale University Press, 1966), 1:135. Thus, for Madison, not just religious classifications might promote oppression and social disintegration, race classifications were equally ominous.

68. Scholarship on the VRA has noted how today's act has fragmented the American electorate, as well as the Democratic Party, into largely antagonistic ethnoracial constituencies. The necessity of creating majority-minority districts (MMDs) and even minority coalition districts under the act has pitted Democrats against Republicans in the most inflammatory racial terms. Racial redistricting has also tended to drive moderate white Democrats from office and replace them with generally more militant black Democrats, who can persist in their militancy with impunity because the VRA guarantees them political office in perpetuity, and it has pitted blacks against Hispanics in acrimonious political conflicts, such as those that have taken place in Illinois, California, and Florida. See David Lublin and D. Stephen Voss, "Boll-Weevil Blues: Polarized Congressional Delegations into the 21st Century," *American Review of Politics* 21 (Winter 2000): 427, 437, and 439; Stephen Thernstrom and Abigail Thernstrom, *America in Black and White: One Nation, Indivisible* (New York: Simon and Schuster, 1997), 288–312, especially 299–301, and 462–92; Lublin, *Paradox of Representation*, 52–53; Swain, *Black Faces, Black Interests*, 203–4, 220; Hugh Davis Graham, "Voting Rights and the American Regulatory State," in *Controversies in Minority Voting*, ed. Bernard Grofman and Chandler Davidson (Washington, D.C.:

Brookings Institution Press, 1992), 195–96; Susan A. MacManus, "The Appropriateness of Biracial Approaches to Measuring Fairness and Representation in a Multicultural World," *PS: Political Science & Politics* 28 (March 1995): 42–45; and Charles S. Bullock, "The South and the 1996 Elections," *PS: Political Science & Politics* 29, no. 3 (September 1996): 450. Compare Canon, *Race, Redistricting, and Representation*. For a good summary of some of the uglier racial incidents generated by the race preferences imposed through the administration of the VRA in the 1990s, see Maurice T. Cunningham, *Maximization, Whatever the Cost: Race, Redistricting, and the Department of Justice* (Westport, CT: Praeger, 2001), especially 157.

Chapter 2: Progressivism, Multiculturalism, and the Emergence of America's "Official Minorities"

1. James W. Ceaser, *Reconstructing America: The Symbol of America in Modern Thought* (New Haven, CT: Yale University Press, 1997), 126.

2. Ibid.

3. Arthur M. Melzer, Jerry Weinberger, and M. Richard Zinman, introduction to *Multiculturalism and American Democracy*, ed. Arthur M. Melzer, Jerry Weinberger, and M. Richard Zinman (Lawrence, KS: University Press of Kansas, 1998), 2, 3–4.

4. *Allen v. State Board of Elections*, 393 U.S. 544 (1969).

5. The right to proportional racial representation was the natural consequence of the theory of representation, adopted by the Court in *Allen*, to which democratic theorists have referred as "descriptive" representation. Descriptive representation, which allows voters to elect candidates "like" themselves, has its natural corollary in models of proportional representation, since the measure of justice for advocates of descriptive representation is how well representational systems "mirror" or mimic the interests of the nation as a whole. See Hannah Fenichel Pitkin, *The Concept of Representation* (Berkeley, CA: University of California Press, 1972), 60–91, and Maurice T. Cunningham, *Maximization, Whatever the Cost: Race, Redistricting, and the Department of Justice* (Westport, CT: Praeger, 2001), 150.

6. Thomas Sowell, *Civil Rights: Rhetoric or Reality?* (New York: Quill, 1984), 14, emphasis in original.

7. Peter Brimelow, "Time to Rethink Immigration?" in *Immigration: Debating the Issues,* ed. Nicholas Capaldi (Amherst, NY: Prometheus Books, 1997), 57. This essay was originally published in *National Review*, June 22, 1992.

8. Alexandre Kojève, *Introduction à la lecture de Hegel* (Paris: Gallimard, 1947). See also Barry Cooper, *The End of History: An Essay on Modern Hegelianism* (Toronto: University of Toronto Press, 1984).

9. Hegel, of course, was no relativist. He had indeed discovered truth that was both universal and eternal. But that truth could only be attained at the end of history, that endpoint that was required for the completion of Truth, which was all-comprehending.

10. Leo Strauss, *Natural Right and History* (Chicago: University of Chicago Press, 1953), 1–8, 35–80.

11. Harry V. Jaffa, *A New Birth of Freedom: Abraham Lincoln and the Coming of the Civil War* (Lanham, MD: Rowman and Littlefield, 2000), 84.

12. Harvey Mansfield contrasts the "old rights" of classical liberalism and *The Federalist* with the "new," self-expressive rights of the New Deal and the 1960s. He says of the latter: "As theory the new rights were born in Friedrich Nietzsche's doctrine of the creative self. How that doctrine came from Nietzsche's books of the late 1880s to American politics in the 1960s is a story that has not yet been fully told. One essential in the course of events is the historicism taken from German philosophy that was decisive in American pragmatism, for the pragmatists influenced the progressives and the progressives were predecessors of the New Deal." Harvey C. Mansfield, Jr., "Responsibility versus Self-Expression," in *Old Rights and New*, ed. Robert A. Licht (Washington, D.C.: AEI Press, 1993), 103.

13. See Jaffa, *New Birth of Freedom*, 85–96.

14. Carl Becker, *The Declaration of Independence: A Study in the History of Political Ideas* (New York: Vintage Books, 1922), 278–79.

15. Ibid., 277

16. Ibid., 265–66. See also Jaffa, *New Birth of Freedom*, 73–121.

17. Dennis J. Mahoney, *Politics and Progress: The Emergence of American Political Science* (Lanham, MD: Lexington Books, 2004), 75–87, 145–50.

18. Ibid., 75.

19. Theodore J. Lowi, *The End of Liberalism: The Second Republic of the United States*, 2nd ed. (New York: W. W. Norton & Company, 1979), xv.

20. See John Marini and Ken Masugi, introduction to *The Progressive Revolution in Politics and Political Science: Transforming the American Regime*, ed. John Marini and Ken Masugi (Lanham, MD: Rowman and Littlefield, 2005), 1; John Marini, "Progressivism, Modern Political Science, and the Transformation of American Constitutionalism," in *Progressive Revolution in Politics*, 221; and Jaffa, *New Birth of Freedom*, 73–152.

21. See Thomas G. West, "Progressivism and the Transformation of American Government," in *Progressive Revolution in Politics*, 28.

22. Marini and Masugi, introduction, *Progressive Revolution in Politics*, 2.

23. Strauss, "Restatement on Xenophon's *Hiero*," in *On Tyranny*, by Leo Strauss, rev. ed., ed. Victor Gourevitch and Michael S. Roth (Chicago: University of Chicago Press, 2000), 177.

24. Strauss, *Natural Right and History*, 4.

25. In the postmodernist and deconstructionist thought that would emerge as the offspring of historicism, thinking itself would be identified with power. In the work of one of the fathers of deconstructionism, Michel Foucault, knowledge itself is reduced to a species of the will to power. See, for example, Michel Foucault, *Power/Knowledge: Selected Interviews and Other Writings, 1972–1977*, ed. Colin

Gordon, trans. Colin Gordon, Leo Marshall, John Mepham, and Kate Soper (New York: Pantheon Books, 1980): "What makes power hold good, what makes it accepted, is simply the fact that it doesn't only weigh on us as a force that says no, but that it traverses and produces things, it induces pleasure, forms knowledge, produces discourse. It needs to be considered as a productive network which runs through the whole social body, much more than as a negative instance whose function is repression" (119).

26. Harry V. Jaffa, *Crisis of the House Divided: An Interpretation of Issues in the Lincoln-Douglas Debates* (Chicago: University of Chicago Press, 1982), 10.

27. Allan Bloom, *The Closing of the American Mind: How Higher Education Has Failed Democracy and Impoverished the Souls of Today's Students* (New York: Simon and Schuster, 1987), 30.

28. See Ceaser, *Reconstructing America*, 128.

29. Walter Berns, "Constitutionalism and Multiculturalism," in *Multiculturalism and American Democracy*, 92.

30. Bloom, *Closing of the American Mind*, 31.

31. Lowi, *End of Liberalism*, 55.

32. Mark E. Rush, "Representation in Theory and Practice," in *Voting Rights and Redistricting in the United States*, ed. Mark E. Rush (Westport, CT: Greenwood Press, 1998), 3.

33. Robert A. Dahl, *A Preface to Democratic Theory* (Chicago: University of Chicago Press, 1956), 133.

34. Ibid.

35. As noted above, Dahl simply refined earlier progressivist critiques of American government. Part of those critiques involved a new methodological approach to the science of politics. In *The Mild Voice of Reason: Deliberative Democracy and American National Government* (Chicago: University of Chicago Press, 1994), Joseph M. Bessette writes: "Deliberation, as . . . defined and . . . addressed by leading eighteenth- and nineteenth-century theorists and practitioners of liberal democracy, has not been the focus of the attention of scholars of American democracy throughout most of this century. Powerful alternative interpretations of legislative and governmental decisionmaking have replaced the earlier focus on the deliberative functions and capacities of governing institutions. . . . No idea is more responsible for this development than the view that politics reduces to the struggle of group interests. . . . No one presented this view more clearly and forthrightly than Arthur Bentley in his famous treatise, *The Process of Government* [1908]. . . . [According to Bentley,] the reality of the legislative process lies not in the presentation of information and arguments in public hearings, in a committee's reasoned defense of its proposals in a formal report to the full body, or in debate and persuasion on the floor of the House and Senate, but rather in the orchestration of deals, the trading of votes, and the hard-headed compromises that are arranged off-stage or through subtle manipulation of the formal process itself" (55–57). Bentley was one of the leading progressive

political scientists of his day who attempted to introduce a new, more rigorous methodological approach to political science that would replace the Founders' political science. Bentley's new approach, which attempted to allow for more ready quantification of political phenomena, focused predominantly on the interaction of groups. See Mahoney, *Politics and Progress*, 126–29, 147.

36. John P. Roche, "The Founding Fathers: A Reform Caucus in Action," *American Political Science Review* 55 (December 1961): 809.

37. Ibid., 804.

38. Ibid., 811.

39. Ibid., 804.

40. Alexander Hamilton, John Jay, and James Madison, *The Federalist: A Commentary on the Constitution of the United States*, ed. Robert Scigliano (New York: Modern Library, 2001), *Federalist* 1, 3.

41. Edward J. Erler, "Still Separate But Equal," *Claremont Review of Books* 4 (Summer 2004): 50. Justice Lewis Powell underlined the connection between individual rights and the rule of law in *University of California Regents v. Bakke*, 438 U.S. 265, 299 (1978): "If it is the individual who is entitled to judicial protection against classifications based upon his racial or ethnic background because such distinctions impinge upon his personal rights, rather than the individual only because of his membership in a particular group, then constitutional standards may be applied consistently. Political judgments regarding the necessity for the particular classification may be weighed in the constitutional balance."

42. Donald L. Horowitz, *The Courts and Social Policy* (Washington, D.C.: Brookings Institution Press, 1977), 45.

43. Herman Belz, *Equality Transformed: A Quarter-Century of Affirmative Action* (New Brunswick, NJ: Transaction Publishers, 1992), 3.

44. Ceaser, *Reconstructing America*, 126–28.

45. *Fullilove v. Klutznick*, 448 U.S. 448 (1980).

46. Ibid., 454, Burger, C. J., opinion of the Court.

47. Ibid., 537–38, Stevens, J., dissenting.

48. Ibid., 539.

49. Belz, *Equality Transformed*, 5, emphasis in original.

50. John D. Skrentny, *The Minority Rights Revolution* (Cambridge, MA: Belknap Press of Harvard University Press, 2002), 12 and 330; Hugh Davis Graham, *Civil Rights and the Presidency: Race and Gender in American Politics, 1960–1972* (New York: Oxford University Press, 1992), 162; Terry Eastland, *Ending Affirmative Action: The Case for Colorblind Justice* (New York: Basic Books, 1996), 56–57.

51. Skrentny, *Minority Rights Revolution*, 12, emphasis in original.

52. See Ceaser, *Reconstructing America*, 127.

53. See Graham, "Voting Rights and the American Regulatory State," in *Controversies in Minority Voting*, ed. Bernard Grofman and Chandler Davidson (Washington, D.C.: Brookings Institution Press, 1992), 180–82.

Chapter 3: The Reapportionment Cases and
the Origins of Judicial Rationalism

1. *Baker v. Carr*, 369 U.S. 186 (1962).

2. Robert G. Dixon, Jr., *Democratic Representation: Reapportionment in Law and Politics* (New York: Oxford University Press, 1968), 9–10, 13–14.

3. James Q. Wilson and John J. Dilulio Jr., *American Government: Institutions and Policies*, 10th ed. (Boston: Houghton Mifflin, 2006), 444.

4. See Ward E. Y. Elliott, *The Rise of Guardian Democracy: The Supreme Court's Role in Voting Rights Disputes, 1845–1969* (Cambridge, MA: Harvard University Press, 1974), 4, 55–88; Richard Cortner, *The Apportionment Cases* (Knoxville, TN: University of Tennessee Press, 1970), 96; and Dixon, *Democratic Representation*, 139–50.

5. *The Slaughter House Cases*, 83 U.S. 36 (1873). The Privileges or Immunities Clause applies the Bill of Rights to the states, or requires states to treat all citizens equally under law, and to provide all Americans, particularly newly freed blacks in the post–Civil War South, with basic rights to own and convey property, to enter into contracts, and to sue. For a good, succinct discussion, see Calvin Massey, "Privileges or Immunities," in *The Heritage Guide to the Constitution*, eds. Edwin Meese III, David F. Forte, and Matthew Spalding (Washington, D.C.: Regnery, 2005), 390.

6. *United States v. Reese*, 92 U.S. 214 (1876), and *United States v. Cruickshank*, 92 U.S. 542 (1876). The Enforcement Act of 1870, passed pursuant to Congress's authority under the Fifteenth Amendment "to enforce this article by appropriate legislation," was designed to provide black Americans in the South with the right to vote. The act gave federal officials the power to supervise southern elections and to punish violators of black voting rights.

7. *The Civil Rights Cases*, 109 U.S. 3, 17 (1883).

8. *Williams v. Mississippi*, 170 U.S. 213 (1898).

9. *Giles v. Harris*, 189 U.S. 475 (1903).

10. See Richard Claude, *The Supreme Court and the Electoral Process* (Baltimore: Johns Hopkins University Press, 1970), 73–74; and J. Morgan Kousser, "The Undermining of the First Reconstruction: Lessons for the Second," in *Minority Vote Dilution*, ed. Chandler Davidson (Washington, D.C.: Howard University Press, 1989), 40–41.

11. V. O. Key, Jr., *Southern Politics in State and Nation*, rev. ed. (Knoxville, TN: University of Tennessee Press, 1984), 576.

12. *Lassiter v. Northampton County Board of Elections*, 360 U.S. 45 (1959).

13. *South Carolina v. Katzenbach*, 383 U.S. 301 (1966) would affirm that the VRA's ban on southern literacy tests was a constitutional exercise of Congress's enforcement power under the Fifteenth Amendment.

14. *Breedlove v. Suttles*, 302 U.S. 277 (1937).

15. *Harper v. Virginia State Board of Elections*, 383 U.S. 663 (1966).

16. See Alexander M. Bickel, *The Supreme Court and the Idea of Progress* (New York: Harper & Row, 1970), 60.

17. *Newberry v. United States*, 256 U.S. 232 (1921).

18. *Smith v. Allwright*, 321 U.S. 649 (1944).

19. *Terry v. Adams*, 345 U.S. 461 (1953).

20. *Gomillion v. Lightfoot*, 364 U.S. 339 (1960).

21. Thomas Sowell, *Civil Rights: Rhetoric or Reality?* (New York: Quill, 1984), 61.

22. *Brown v. Board of Education*, 347 U.S. 483 (1954).

23. See chapter 1, pages 10–11.

24. *Luther v. Borden*, 48 U.S. 1 (1849).

25. Ibid., 47.

26. *Baker v. Carr*, 226.

27. Ibid., emphasis in original. In *Baker*, Justice Brennan did not specify what equal protection standards would apply in reapportionment disputes, but the Court would shortly answer that question in *Gray v. Sanders* (1963): "The conception of political equality from the Declaration of Independence, to Lincoln's Gettysburg Address, to the Fifteenth, Seventeenth, and Nineteenth Amendments can mean only one thing—one person, one vote." *Gray v. Sanders*, 372 U.S. 368, 381 (1963), opinion of the Court. The *Gray* holding would later translate into legislatures having to create electoral districts that had equal populations for both state and federal elections.

28. *Baker v. Carr*, 277, Frankfurter, J., dissenting.

29. Ibid., 300–2.

30. See ibid.: "Talk of 'debasement' or 'dilution' is circular talk. One cannot speak of 'debasement' or 'dilution' of the value of a vote until there is first defined a standard of reference as to what a vote should be worth. What is actually asked of the Court in this case is to choose among competing bases of representation—ultimately, really, among competing theories of political philosophy—in order to establish an appropriate frame of government for the State of Tennessee and thereby for all the States of the Union" (300).

31. *Wesberry v. Sanders*, 376 U.S. 1 (1964).

32. Ibid., 7–8.

33. Ibid., 10, citing Max Farrand, ed., *Records of the Federal Convention* (New Haven, CT: Yale University Press, 1966), 3: 472.

34. *Wesberry v. Sanders*, 14.

35. Quoted at ibid., 18.

36. Ibid.

37. Ibid., 21, Harlan, J., dissenting.

38. On Harlan's reading, the Court's claim that it derived support for its interpretation from the third paragraph of article 1, section 2 was based on a confusion of two issues: apportionment of representatives *among* the states and election of representatives *within* the states. Although delegates to the Convention indicated an intention to recognize the principle of allocating members of Congress to the states on the basis of population, providing for this with important exceptions in article 1, the Constitution did not require the allocation of representatives *within* the states on the basis of population. The

delegates did not, as Harlan put it, "surreptitiously slip their belief into the Constitution in the phrase 'by the People,' to be discovered 175 years later like a Shakespearian anagram." Ibid., 27.

39. See, for instance, Alexander Hamilton, John Jay, and James Madison, *The Federalist: A Commentary on the Constitution of the United States*, ed. Robert Scigliano (New York: Modern Library, 2001), *Federalist* 54. Here Madison speaks in the voice of "one of our Southern brethren" (349), but, as he indicates at the end of *Federalist* 54, he is in substantial agreement with his compatriot's argument: "It is a fundamental principle of the proposed Constitution, that as the aggregate number of representatives allotted to the several States is to be determined by a federal rule, founded on the aggregate number of inhabitants, so the right of choosing this allotted number in each State is to be exercised by such part of the inhabitants as the State itself may designate. The qualifications on which the right of suffrage depend are not, perhaps, the same in any two States" (350–51). See also Hamilton's discussion of article 1, section 4 in *Federalist* 59: "It will not be alleged, that an election law could have been framed and inserted in the Constitution, which would have been applicable to every probable change in the situation of the country; and it will therefore not be denied, that a discretionary power over elections ought to exist somewhere. It will, I presume, be as readily conceded, that there were only three ways in which this power could have been reasonably organized: that it must either have been lodged wholly in the national legislature, or wholly in the State legislatures, or primarily in the latter and ultimately in the former. The last mode has, with reason, been preferred by the convention. They have submitted the regulation of elections for the federal government, in the first instance, to the local administrations; which, in ordinary cases, and when no improper views prevail, may be both more convenient and more satisfactory; but they have reserved to the national authority a right to interpose, whenever extraordinary circumstances might render that interposition necessary to its safety" (379).

40. *Wesberry v. Sanders*, 23, Harlan, J., dissenting.

41. Ibid., 48.

42. *Reynolds v. Sims*, 377 U.S. 533 (1964).

43. Along with *Reynolds*, the other cases were *WMCA, Inc. v. Lomenzo* [New York], 377 U.S. 633 (1964), *Maryland Committee for Fair Representation v. Tawes*, 377 U.S. 656 (1964), *Roman v. Sincock* [Delaware], 377 U.S. 695 (1964), *Davis v. Mann* [Virginia], 377 U.S. 68 (1964), and *Lucas v. Forty-Fourth General Assembly of State of Colorado*, 377 U.S. 713 (1964).

44. *Reynolds v. Sims*, 545 and 553, Warren, C. J., opinion of the Court.

45. Ibid., 568–69, 579.

46. Ibid., 565–66.

47. Ibid., 565.

48. Ibid., 573.

49. Dixon, *Democratic Representation*, 272.

50. *Lucas v. Forty-Fourth General Assembly of the State of Colorado*, 731.

51. Dixon, *Democratic Representation*, 268–69.

52. 21 Wall. 162, 88 U.S. 162, cited in *Reynolds v. Sims*, 611–12, Harlan, J., dissenting. Harlan added that the majority was simply wrong to suggest that the original state constitutions had sanctioned an equal-population rule for both houses of their legislatures. Two-thirds of the "loyal" states and six of the ten "reconstructed" states that ratified the Fourteenth Amendment had constitutional provisions that explicitly departed from the rule established in *Reynolds*. As Harlan's argument demonstrated, the *Reynolds* holding led to the implausible conclusion that the vast majority of states in 1868 were willing to ratify a constitutional amendment that they knew—or should have anticipated—would have rendered their own state constitutions immediately unconstitutional. Ibid., 602–8.

53. The relevant language of the Fourteenth Amendment reads as follows: "But when the right to vote at any election . . . is denied to any of the male inhabitants of such State, being twenty-one years of age, and citizens of the United States, or in any way abridged, except for participation in rebellion, or other crime, the basis of representation therein shall be reduced in the proportion which the number of such male citizens shall bear to the whole number of male citizens twenty-one years of age in such State." According to Harlan, it was apparent that the second section of the Fourteenth Amendment "expressly recognizes the States' power to deny 'or in any way' abridge the right of their inhabitants to vote for 'the members of the [State] Legislature.'" It also expressly provides "a remedy for such denial or abridgment." *Reynolds v. Sims*, 594. As Stephen Presser has noted, this remedy is unambiguous: "The only manner in which the federal government could deal with perceived state recalcitrance on reapportionment was through altering a state's congressional representation." Stephen B. Presser, *Recapturing the Constitution: Race, Religion, and Abortion Reconsidered* (Washington, D.C.: Regnery Publishing, 1994), 172.

54. *Baker v. Carr*, 299, Frankfurter, J., dissenting.

55. Ibid., 267.

56. Timothy G. O'Rourke, "*Shaw v. Reno*: The Shape of Things to Come," in *Affirmative Action and Representation: Shaw v. Reno and the Future of Voting Rights*, ed. Anthony A. Peacock (Durham, NC: Carolina Academic Press, 1997), 52–53.

57. *Fortson v. Dorsey*, 379 U.S. 433 (1965).

58. *Burns v. Richardson*, 384 U.S. 73 (1966).

59. *Fortson v. Dorsey*, 436, Brennan, J., opinion of the Court, citing 228 F. Supp. 259, 263.

60. Ibid., 437.

61. Ibid., 438, quoting *Reynolds v. Sims*, 579.

62. *Fortson v. Dorsey*, 439, Brennan, J., opinion of the Court.

63. Ibid., 439–40.

64. *Reynolds v. Sims*, 586, quoted in *Burns v. Richardson*, 85.

65. The latter holding was due, in large measure, to the idiosyncratic demographics of the state. Hawaii had a large transient military and tourist population, making

census figures volatile and unreliable for purposes of districting (*Burns v. Richardson*, 94–95). It also exhibited an unusually high correlation between registered voters and citizen population figures: Approximately 90 percent of all registered voters turned out for elections between 1958 and 1962. Ibid., 96.

66. Ibid., 87–88.

67. Ibid., 88–89, emphasis added.

68. Ibid., 88.

69. *Avery v. Midland County*, 390 U.S. 474, 480–81 and 484–86 (1968); Claude, *Supreme Court and the Electoral Process*, 194.

70. *Kirkpatrick v. Preisler*, 394 U.S. 526 (1969).

71. *Wells v. Rockefeller*, 394 U.S. 542 (1969).

72. *Kirkpatrick v. Preisler*, 531; see also *Wells v. Rockefeller*, 546; *White v. Weiser*, 412 U.S. 783, 790 (1973).

73. *Karcher v. Daggett*, 462 U.S. 725, 734 (1983).

74. Ibid., 735–38.

75. *Vieth v. Pennsylvania*, 195 F. Supp. 2d 672 (M.D. Pa. 2002). See also Charles S. Bullock III, "Two Generations of Redistricting: An Overview," in *Extensions: A Journal of the Carl Albert Congressional Research and Studies Center* (Fall 2004): 9, 10.

76. *Karcher v. Daggett*, 766, White, J. dissenting.

77. Elliott, *Rise of Guardian Democracy*, 130. See also Gene Graham, *One Man, One Vote*: Baker v. Carr *and the American Levellers* (Boston: Little, Brown, 1972), 65.

78. See *Baker v. Carr*, 244–45, Douglas, J., concurring; *Reynolds v. Sims*, 577, opinion of the Court.

79. Dixon, *Democratic Representation*, 139.

80. *Reynolds v. Sims*, 543, Warren, C.J., opinion of the Court.

81. *Baker v. Carr*, 259, Clark, J., concurring.

82. Cited in Elliott, *Rise of Guardian Democracy*, 252n14.

83. Dixon, *Democratic Representation*, 289.

84. Daniel Hays Lowenstein and Richard L. Hasen, *Election Law: Cases and Materials* (Durham, NC: Carolina Academic Press, 2004), 102.

Chapter 4: From the Founders' Republicanism to the Politics of Multiculturalism

1. Quoted in Chandler Davidson, "The Voting Rights Act: A Brief History," in *Controversies in Minority Voting*, ed. Bernard Grofman and Chandler Davidson (Washington, D.C.: Brookings Institution Press, 1992), 17.

2. *Allen v. State Board of Elections*, 393 U.S. 544 (1969).

3. Between 1957 and 1960, for instance, the Justice Department filed only four lawsuits under the 1957 Civil Rights Act. As Barry Hawk and John Kirby observed in 1965, "Not a single Negro who had not been previously registered was enabled to register to vote by federal action during the three year period." Barry E. Hawk and John J. Kirby,

Jr., "Note: Federal Protection of Negro Voting Rights," *Virginia Law Review* 51 (1965): 1060. Things did not much improve despite changes to the civil rights acts of 1960 and 1964. See Abigail Thernstrom, *Whose Votes Count? Affirmative Action and Minority Voting Rights* (Cambridge, MA: Harvard University Press, 1987), 11–15. See also *South Carolina v. Katzenbach*, 383 U.S. 301, 313–14 (1966), pointing out how time-consuming and ineffective civil rights lawsuits were as a means of enhancing black voter registration in the South prior to the VRA.

4. The VRA would provide a battery of other remedies as well. To deal with the abuses of local registrars, for instance, the act authorized the attorney general to assign federal examiners to register voters (section 6). It also allowed the federal government to assign observers to oversee elections (section 8). It was a criminal offense to fail to register voters, intimidate voters, or to fail to count votes (section 11). It was also a crime to alter ballots or voting records or to conspire to interfere with the right to vote (section 12). Poll taxes were prohibited in state elections (section 10), although this provision became unnecessary after *Harper v. Virginia State Board of Elections*, 383 U.S. 663 (1966), which outlawed state poll taxes.

5. *South Carolina v. Katzenbach*, 301.

6. The U.S. Commission on Civil Rights reported in May 1968 that registration of the black voting-age population was more than 50 percent in every southern state. This situation had been the case in only three states prior to passage of the VRA: Florida, Tennessee, and Texas. Black registration figures between 1965 and 1968 rose in Mississippi from 6.7 to 59.8 percent; in Alabama from 19.3 to 51.6 percent; in Louisiana from 31.6 to 58.9 percent; in Georgia from 27.4 to 52.6 percent; in South Carolina from 37.3 to 51.2 percent; and in Virginia from 30.3 to 55.6 percent. U.S. Commission on Civil Rights, *Political Participation. A Study of the Participation by Negroes in the Electoral and Political Process in 10 Southern States since Passage of the Voting Rights Act of 1965* (Washington, D.C.: Government Printing Office, 1968), 12–13. Black office-holding also increased. Following the 1966 elections there were, altogether, 159 local black officeholders and legislators in the eleven southern states. Following the 1967 elections, that number exceeded 200, more than double the number serving when the VRA was passed in 1965. Ibid., 15. The Commission on Civil Rights further reported in 1975 that the total number of blacks elected to office in the seven southern states covered by the VRA had increased to 963 by April 1974. U.S. Commission on Civil Rights, *The Voting Rights Act: Ten Years After* (Washington, D.C.: Government Printing Office, 1975), 49. Although in 1972 gaps still existed between black registered voters and white registered voters in excess of 20 percent in Alabama and Louisiana, overall the difference between blacks and whites in the seven southern states declined by more than 30 percent between 1965 and 1972, dropping from 44.1 percent in 1965 to 11.2 percent by 1972. U.S. Commission on Civil Rights, *Voting Rights Act: Ten Years After,* 42–43.

7. Frank R. Parker, *Black Votes Count: Political Empowerment in Mississippi after 1965* (Chapel Hill, NC: University of North Carolina Press, 1990), 99.

8. *Holder v. Hall*, 114 S. Ct. 2581, 2593, Thomas, J., concurring opinion (1994).

9. *Allen v. State Board of Elections*, 569.

10. Ibid., 565.

11. *Perkins v. Matthews*, 400 U.S. 379 (1971). An annexation is where one jurisdiction annexes the land of another, thus adding whatever voters reside in the annexed land to the annexing jurisdiction.

12. *Georgia v. United States*, 411 U.S. 526 (1973).

13. *Dougherty County Board of Education v. White*, 439 U.S. 32 (1978).

14. Quoted in *Allen v. State Board of Elections*, 548–49, emphasis added. Although *Allen* did not address whether section 5 required changes to have a discriminatory effect and purpose, three months after *Allen* the Court determined that discriminatory effect was sufficient to deny a state's petition for exemption from the provisions of section 4(a). See *Gaston County, North Carolina v. United States*, 395 U.S. 285 (1969). Like section 5, section 4(a) allowed for exemption from section 4 if states could prove that literacy tests or similar devices had not "been used during the five years preceding the filing of the action for the purpose or with the effect of denying or abridging the right to vote on account of race or color." Eventually, as the Court determined in *Beer v. United States*, 425 U.S. 130 (1976), retrogressive effect on black electoral participation would be sufficient to preclude a state from an exempting declaratory judgment under section 5.

15. *Allen v. State Board of Elections*, 563, citing section 14(c)(1) of the VRA, emphasis added.

16. Andrew Kull, *The Color-Blind Constitution* (Cambridge, MA: Harvard University Press, 1992), 214.

17. *Allen v. State Board of Elections*, 583, Harlan, J., concurring in part and dissenting in part, hereinafter "dissenting."

18. Ibid., 583, 585.

19. Ibid., 589.

20. *Allen v. State Board of Elections*, 566, quoting *Reynolds v. Sims*, 377 U.S. 533, 555 (1964).

21. *Allen v. State Board of Elections*, 569.

22. As Andrew Kull has observed: "The Voting Rights Act was interpreted in *Allen* to reach what was undoubtedly discriminatory conduct, but of a kind to which the terms of the act did not apply, and by a rationale that excluded any reference to discrimination." *Color-Blind Constitution*, 215.

23. *Gomillion v. Lightfoot*, 364 U.S. 339 (1960).

24. Mark E. Rush, "The Hidden Costs of Electoral Reform," in *Fair and Effective Representation? Debating Electoral Reform and Minority Rights*, ed. Mark E. Rush and Richard L. Engstrom (Lanham, MD: Rowman and Littlefield, 2001), 116–17.

25. See *United Jewish Organizations of Williamsburgh, Inc. v. Carey*, 430 U.S. 144, 181 (1977), Burger, C. J., dissenting: "If *Gomillion* teaches anything, I had thought it was that drawing of political boundary lines with the sole, explicit objective of reaching a predetermined racial result cannot ordinarily be squared with the Constitution."

26. Nancy Maveety, *Representation Rights and the Burger Years* (Ann Arbor, MI: University of Michigan Press, 1991), 12–17, 97–145.

27. Ibid., 100.

28. *White v. Regester,* 412 U.S. 755, 765–66 (1973).

29. Gregory Caldeira, "Litigation, Lobbying, and the Voting Rights Bar," in *Controversies in Minority Voting,* 230, 242–43. See also Hugh Davis Graham, *Civil Rights and the Presidency: Race and Gender in American Politics, 1960–1972* (New York: Oxford University Press, 1992): "The voting rights bar drew its growth not from disputes over the right to vote, but instead from demands that minorities win elections" (140).

30. *United Jewish Organizations of Williamsburgh, Inc v. Carey,* 152–53, White, J., opinion of the Court.

31. In his dissenting opinion in *United Jewish Organizations of Williamsburgh, Inc. v. Wilson,* 510 F.2d 512, Judge Frankel emphasized that the decision of the Legislative Committee in New York to redistrict as it did, splitting the Hasidic Jewish community into separate electoral districts (the subject of the dispute discussed in detail below), was evidently the function of a firm racial quota advocated by the NAACP:

> While it was never said explicitly (a matter of some consequence for the decision herein), the Committee's staff director "got the feeling" that, to avoid disapproval, the 1972 Assembly district in which the *Hasidic* community was entirely embraced at the time would require revision to raise its nonwhite population from 61.5% to 65%. As he described the exchanges with the Department of Justice personnel, the upward revision from 61.5% resulted from conversations and inferences of the following character:
>
> "I said how much higher do you have to go?
>
> "Is 70 percent all right?
>
> "They didn't say yes or no, but they indicated it is more in line with the way we think in order to effect the possibility of a minority candidate being elected within that district.
>
> "I suggested 65 percent. It came out at that time that is a figure used by the NAACP in numerous briefs and other documents.
>
> "I got the feeling, and I cannot vouch for this as a matter of having been specifically said, but I left that meeting indicating that 65 per cent would be probably an approved figure.
>
> The upshot of the talks, the director said, was: "I thought it was logical for me to assume anything under 65 would not be acceptable" (527, emphasis in original).

See also *United Jewish Organizations of Williamsburgh, Inc. v. Carey,* 164n22.

32. *United Jewish Organizations of Williamsburgh, Inc. v. Wilson,* 510 2d., at 518n10, opinion of court. The NAACP was arguing, in short, that the appellants' claim was based on their religious identity, not their racial identity, and that the VRA only permitted claims based on racial identity.

33. *United Jewish Organizations of Williamsburgh, Inc. v. Carey,* 165.

34. Ibid., 167.

35. This was later affirmed in *Voinovich v. Quilter,* 113 S.Ct. 1149 (1993).

36. *United Jewish Organizations of Williamsburgh, Inc v. Carey*, 166, White, J., opinion of the Court.

37. *City of Richmond v. United States*, 422 U.S. 358, 370 (1975). The majority here, speaking through Justice White, is explaining its per curiam decision in *City of Petersburg v. United States*, 410 U.S. 962 (1973).

38. Summarizing *City of Richmond* in *UJO*, the Court wrote: "The proscribed 'effect' on voting rights can be avoided by a post-annexation districting plan that 'fairly reflects the strength of the Negro community as it exists after the annexation' and which 'would afford [it] representation reasonably equivalent to [its] political strength in the enlarged community'" (*United Jewish Organizations of Williamsburgh, Inc. v. Carey*, 160, citing *City of Richmond v. United States*, 370–71).

39. *Beer v. United States*, 141. Cited at *United Jewish Organizations of Williamsburgh, Inc. v. Carey*, 159.

40. An MMD is a single-member electoral district in which a majority of the voting-age population or residents consists of a minority group recognized by the VRA.

41. *United Jewish Organizations of Williamsburgh, Inc. v. Carey*, 161.

42. Ibid., opinion of the Court: "Unless we adopted an unconstitutional construction of § 5 in *Beer* and *City of Richmond*, a reapportionment cannot violate the Fourteenth or Fifteenth Amendment merely because a State uses specific numerical quotas in establishing a certain number of black majority districts. Our cases under § 5 stand for at least this much" (162).

43. As Abigail Thernstrom has remarked, by identifying New York with places like Neshoba County, Mississippi, which was also covered by the 1970 VRA, and where three civil rights workers had been murdered in 1964 for promoting black voter registration, the preclearance provision of the VRA "had come to have a validity independent of the proven presence of wrongs requiring it." By 1970 the original purpose of the VRA—to ensure the black vote—was already becoming obscured. See Thernstrom, *Whose Votes Count?*, 40–41.

44. *United Jewish Organizations of Williamsburgh, Inc. v. Carey*, 186, Burger, C. J. dissenting.

45. Ibid., 187.

46. Ibid., 186.

47. *United Jewish Organizations of Williamsburgh, Inc. v. Wilson*, 529, Frankel, D. J., dissenting

48. Ibid., 530.

49. Ibid., 533.

50. *United Jewish Organizations of Williamsburgh, Inc. v. Carey*, 184–85.

51. Ibid, 185.

52. Ibid., 154–55, White, J., opinion of the Court, quoting *United Jewish Organizations of Williamsburgh, Inc. v. Wilson*, 525, emphasis in original.

53. Ibid., 178, Brennan, J., concurring in part.

54. Ibid., 166, White, J., opinion of the Court.

55. See Samuel Issacharoff, "The Redistricting Morass," in *Affirmative Action and Representation: Shaw v. Reno and the Future of Voting Rights*, ed. Anthony A. Peacock (Durham, NC: Carolina Academic Press, 1997), 211–12.

56. See *United Jewish Organizations of Williamsburgh, Inc. v. Carey*, 158–9; see also House of Representatives, *Voting Rights Act Extension*, 97th Cong., 1st sess., 1981, H. Rep. 97-227, 6, hereinafter House report.

57. 42 USC sec. 1973 [1994], sec. 14(c)(3).

58. U.S. Commission on Civil Rights, *Voting Rights Act: Ten Years After*, 345.

59. Ibid., 67.

60. *White v. Regester*, 755.

61. See *United Jewish Organizations of Williamsburgh, Inc. v. Carey*, 158n17; see also J. Morgan Kousser, *Colorblind Injustice: Minority Voting Rights and the Undoing of the Second Reconstruction* (Chapel Hill, NC: University of North Carolina Press, 1999), 56.

62. *White v. Regester*, 768, quoting *Graves v. Barnes*, 343 F. Supp. 704, 731 (WD Tex. 1972).

63. Section 4(9)(f)(4).

64. Section 4(9)(f)(3).

65. See, for instance, Thomas M. Boyd and Stephen J. Markman, "The 1982 Amendments to the Voting Rights Act: A Legislative History," *Washington and Lee Law Review* 40 (1983): 1378–79, describing testimony during the 1982 House hearings on the VRA extension and amendments regarding the costs of the bilingual ballot requirements: "[Congressman] McClory stated that in California, officials reported that $645,754.23 was spent in thirty-eight counties for this purpose, and a similar amount in the primaries, for a total of more than $1.2 million in 1980. In San Francisco alone, McClory claimed, the cost for printing Chinese ballots was $40,542. In Wyoming, the bilingual ballot provisions of the Act allegedly doubled the printing costs to the State. Scotts Bluff County, Nebraska, allegedly spent $17,673.26 in the 1980 primary and $16,044.68 in the general election to print ballots which no one ever requested."

66. See John Silber, "One Nation, One Language, One Ballot," *Wall Street Journal*, April 30, 1996, A14.

67. According to Abigail Thernstrom, who emphasizes the omission of González from the evidence referred to in *White v. Regester*, the Court's "opinion rested on 'factual findings' that, in reality, were unexplained assertions of indeterminate weight" (*Whose Votes Count?*, 72–73). See also Peter Skerry, *Mexican Americans: The Ambivalent Minority* (Cambridge, MA: Harvard University Press, 1993): "It would be a mistake to overlook the significant level of office-holding enjoyed by Mexican Americans in San Antonio [prior to 1971]. For example, in 1970 Mexican Americans had achieved more than 50 percent of parity in office-holding. . . . Even during the heyday of the Anglo-elite dominated Good Government League in the 1950s and 1960s, Mexican Americans won important elective offices. In 1955, Henry B. González ran countywide and got elected

to the State Senate. Six years later he went to Congress, becoming the nation's first Mexican-American congressman. Also in 1955 Albert Peña was elected as one of four Bexar County commissioners, and he, too, went on to become a nationally prominent Mexican-American leader" (105).

68. "Statement of Commissioner Stephen Horn on the Minority Language Provisions of the Voting Rights Act," in *U.S. Commission on Civil Rights, The Voting Rights Act: Unfulfilled Goals* (Washington, D.C.: Government Printing Office, 1981), 94.

69. House report, 59–60.

70. Silber, "One Nation," A14.

71. See Skerry, *Mexican Americans*, 332.

72. Ibid., 330–31.

73. "By multiplying the number of residentially concentrated ethnic groups that can assert claims to a limited number of safe legislative seats," Peter Schuck has written, "immigration has intensified intergroup conflict and made negotiated solutions to these inevitably bitter disputes much more difficult" (Peter H. Schuck, "Alien Rumination," in *Immigration: Debating the Issues*, ed. Nicholas Capaldi [Amherst, NY: Prometheus Books, 1997], 85).

74. Thernstrom, *Whose Votes Count?*, 62.

75. Timothy G. O'Rourke, "The 1982 Amendments and the Voting Rights Paradox," in *Controversies in Minority Voting*, 87–89. See also Caldeira, "Voting Rights Bar," 248.

76. Rainer Knopff, *Human Rights and Social Technology: The New War on Discrimination* (Ottawa: Carleton University Press, 1990), 211–12.

77. Knopff, "The Statistical Protection of Minorities: Affirmative Action Policy in Canada," in *Minorities and the Canadian State*, ed. Neil Nevitte and Allan Kornberg (Oakville, Ontario: Mosaic Press, 1985), 99–104, especially 102–3. See also Kull, *Color-Blind Constitution:* "The meaning of the word *discrimination*, in 1964, was not yet ambiguous. As explained by Hubert Humphrey during the Senate debate on the civil rights bill, it meant 'a distinction in treatment given to different individuals because of their different race.' A prohibition of discrimination against individuals necessarily barred 'preferential treatment for any particular group.' The ordinary understanding of 'discrimination,' moreover, was such that a violation of the legal prohibition 'would seem already to require intent'" (182, emphasis in original, quoting U.S. Congress, *Congressional Record* 110 (1964): S 5423, 11848, 12723 (remarks of Sen. Humphrey).

78. See Chapter 2, pages 39–40, notes 49–51.

79. "Statement of Commissioner Stephen Horn," 94.

80. Thernstrom, *Whose Votes Count?*, 8.

81. Graham, *Civil Rights and the Presidency*, 162.

82. Ibid., 151–2; see also Maurice T. Cunningham, *Maximization, Whatever the Cost: Race, Redistricting, and the Department of Justice* (Westport, CT: Praeger, 2001), 94–95.

Chapter 5: The 1982 Amendments to the
Voting Rights Act and Their Aftermath

1. See Samuel Issacharoff, Pamela S. Karlan, and Richard H. Pildes, *The Law of Democracy: Legal Structure of the Political Process*, 2nd ed. (Westbury, NY: The Foundation Press, 2001), 580n4.

2. Abigail Thernstrom, *Whose Votes Count? Affirmative Action and Minority Voting Rights* (Cambridge, MA: Harvard University Press, 1987), 45.

3. Keith J. Bybee, *Mistaken Identity: The Supreme Court and the Politics of Minority Representation* (Princeton, NJ: Princeton University Press, 1998), 20n35, citing U.S. Commission on Civil Rights, *The Voting Rights Act: Unfulfilled Goals* (Washington, D.C.: Government Printing Office, 1981), 66.

4. David T. Canon, *Race, Redistricting, and Representation: The Unintended Consequences of Black Majority Districts* (Chicago: University of Chicago Press, 1999), 65n4.

5. *Miller v. Johnson*, 115 S. Ct. 2475, 2493 (1995), opinion of the Court, quoting HR Rep. 91-397 (1969), 8, emphasis added.

6. See, for instance, *Washington v. Davis*, 426 U.S. 229, 240 (1976): "The basic equal protection principle [is] that the invidious quality of a law claimed to be racially discriminatory must ultimately be traced to a racially discriminatory purpose." See also *Village of Arlington Heights v. Metropolitan Housing Dev. Corp.*, 429 U.S. 252, 265 (1977); *Personnel Administrator of Mass. v. Feeney*, 442 U.S. 256, 274–79 (1979); *City of Mobile v. Bolden*, 446 U.S. 55, 66–68 (1980); *Wygant v. Jackson Board of Education*, 476 U.S. 267, 274 (1986); and *Richmond v. Croson*, 488 U.S. 469, 492, 498–506 (1989).

7. See *Guinn v. United States*, 238 U.S. 347, 359, 365 (1915); *Lane v. Wilson*, 307 U.S. 268, 275–77 (1939); *Smith v. Allwright*, 321 U.S. 649, 664 (1944); *Terry v. Adams*, 345 U.S. 461, 473 (1953); *Lassiter v. Northampton Election Bd.*, 360 U.S. 45 (1959); *Gomillion v. Lightfoot*, 364 U.S. 339, 341, 347 (1960); and *Wright v. Rockefeller*, 376 U.S. 52, 56, 58 (1964).

8. *Allen v. State Board of Elections*, 393 U.S. 544, 572 (1969), opinion of the Court.

9. *City of Rome v. United States*, 446 U.S. 156, 172 (1980).

10. Ibid., 172–73.

11. At issue in *Rome* were changes to the city commission and board of education elections, as well as thirteen annexations. The electoral changes involved switching from plurality to majority vote requirements, staggered terms, a residency requirement for board of education candidates, and the reduction of the city's wards from nine to three with numbered posts in each. Because Rome was predominantly white and had a history of racial bloc voting, the electoral changes proposed, combined with whites and blacks voting differently, could have an adverse effect on the ability of blacks to elect candidates of their choice. Also important, however, the thirteen parcels of land that had been annexed by the city had been acquired for nondiscriminatory purposes and had caused a net decline of only 1 percent in the city's black electorate (*City of Rome v. United States*, 194, Powell, J., dissenting opinion). In

addition, the three-judge district court that heard the case in the original instance had found that Rome had not employed any discriminatory barriers impeding black voter registration for seventeen years. Nor had the city used any other barriers to impede black voting or black candidates' running for office. White-elected officials had encouraged blacks to run for office and had been responsive to the black community. No discrimination had been found against blacks in the provision of municipal services, and efforts had been made to improve black neighborhoods (Ibid., 208, Rehnquist, J., dissenting opinion).

12. *City of Rome v. United States*, 177. See also *Beer v. United States*, 425 U.S. 130, 140 (1976).

13. *City of Rome v. United States*, 216–17, 219–21, Rehnquist, J., dissenting opinion.

14. Ibid., 217.

15. Ibid., 218.

16. *City of Mobile v. Bolden*, 446 U.S. 55 (1980).

17. *White v. Regester*, 412 U.S. 755 (1973).

18. *Zimmer v. McKeithen*, 485 F.2d 1297 (5th Cir.). See House of Representatives, *Voting Rights Act Extension*, 97th Cong., 1st sess., 1981, H. Rep. 97-227, 6, hereinafter House report, 30 and 43. The totality of circumstances test developed by Justice White in *Regester* is referred to in section 2(b). The provision, "to participate in the political process and to elect representatives of their choice," is a direct paraphrase of Justice White's opinion in *White v. Regester*, 766, the word "representatives" replacing White's "legislators." Section 2(a) was amended in 1982 by striking out "to deny or abridge," where it appeared and inserting in its place "in a manner which *results* in a denial or abridgement of" (emphasis added; see House report, 71).

19. House report, 2.

20. See Chandler Davidson and Bernard Grofman, "The Voting Rights Act and the Second Reconstruction," in *Quiet Revolution in the South: The Impact of the Voting Rights Act, 1965–1990*, ed. Chandler Davidson and Bernard Grofman (Princeton, NJ: Princeton University Press, 1994), 385: "After the amendment of section 2, numerous suits attacking local at-large elections were filed. The number of section 2 cases between 1982 and 1989 dwarfed the number of constitutional challenges brought during the 1970s in the pre-*Bolden* period. Indeed, from 1982 through 1989 (1990 in Georgia) we found over 150 section 2 challenges to municipal elections in the eight states of our study [Alabama, Georgia, Louisiana, Mississippi, North Carolina, South Carolina, Texas, and Virginia]."

21. In "The 1982 Amendments of Section 2 and Minority Representation," in *Controversies in Minority Voting*, ed. Bernard Grofman and Chandler Davidson (Washington, D.C.: Brookings Institution Press, 1992), Laughlin McDonald notes that "since it was amended in 1982," section 2 "has become one of the most powerful weapons for protecting voting rights" (66). "In addition to the increase in the number of voting rights cases being brought and the jurisdictions affected, the scope of section 2 litigation has broadened." Ibid., 72. Writing in the same volume, Timothy

G. O'Rourke remarks that "the introduction of the [section 2] results test brought a surge in voting rights litigation, with most cases being won by plaintiffs"; O'Rourke, "The 1982 Amendments and the Voting Rights Paradox," 99–100. In Virginia, for example, prior to 1982, there were no successful constitutional challenges to vote-dilution claims. Following the 1982 amendments, at least twenty-two section 2 suits were brought by mid-1990 disputing county, city, and town electoral practices, with plaintiffs winning no less than nineteen of these cases. Ibid., 100n44. Abigail Thernstrom has also documented that during the first four years following the 1982 amendments, "the success rate of plaintiffs in section 2 cases exceeded 90 percent." Indeed, she writes, these figures "only hint at the magnitude of [plaintiffs'] success" since "an uncounted but unquestionably large number of suits are settled out of court by jurisdictions reluctant to commit scarce funds to an almost hopeless cause or to take a stand that might be interpreted as 'anti-black'" (*Whose Votes Count?* 228–9).

22. James F. Blumstein, "Minority Voting Rights and Voting," *Wall Street Journal*, May 27, 1982, 28, cited in Blumstein, "Defining and Proving Race Discrimination: Perspectives on the Purpose vs. Results Approach from the Voting Rights Act," *Virginia Law Review* 69 (1983): 691.

23. Report of the Subcommittee on the Constitution to the Committee on the Judiciary of the Voting Rights Act, S. Sub. Rep., 97th Cong., 2nd sess., 1982, 79, hereinafter Senate Subcommittee report.

24. *Voting Rights Act Extension*, Report of the Committee on the Judiciary, United States Senate, 97th Cong., 2nd sess., 1982, S. Rep. 97-417, 35, hereinafter Senate report.

25. Writing in 2001, Issacharoff, Karlan, and Pildes observed

that the amended § 2 has spawned a torrent of litigation that has dramatically reshaped the American electoral landscape. As late as 1982 a sizeable majority of municipal elections were conducted at large, and most southern states elected at least some state legislators from multimember districts. But by the mid-1990s most jurisdictions with substantial minority populations had switched to using at least some single-member districts, and state legislatures were elected entirely from single-member districts, at least some of which were majority nonwhite (*Law of Democracy*, 859).

26. Senate Subcommittee report, 30.

27. Ibid., 3–4.

28. Ibid., 43.

29. Ibid., 33.

30. See Thomas M. Boyd and Stephen J. Markman, "The 1982 Amendments to the Voting Rights Act: A Legislative History," *Washington and Lee Law Review* 40 (1983): 1428.

31. This was the final language of section 2(b) of the 1982 VRA.

32. See House report, 29.

33. Senate report, 36.

34. House report, 29.

35. Frank R. Parker, "The 'Results' Test of Section 2 of the Voting Rights Act: Abandoning the Intent Standard," *Virginia Law Review* 69 (1983): 737.

36. Boyd and Markman, "1982 Amendments," 1355.

37. During the hearings leading up to the 1982 VRA, Republicans in both the Senate and House had complained of intimidation by the "Civil Rights Industry"; Senate report, 210. Senator East objected that "supporters of HR 3112, [the House bill containing the proposed changes to the VRA], let it be known that any questioning of or deviation from its language constituted a punishable lapse from orthodoxy, and would justify the vicious charge of racism." Ibid., 212. Congressman Hyde had also complained of the reluctance of witnesses to appear in the House who were not going to testify "in accordance with the zeit geist" (Hearings on the Voting Rights Act before the Senate Subcommittee on the Constitution of the Committee on the Judiciary, 97th Cong., 2nd sess., 1982, 404). Hyde further criticized "the intimidating style of lobbying" that had curtailed serious debate on the House floor of the proposed bill's language (Ibid., 394).

38. Blumstein, "Defining and Proving Race Discrimination," 647.

39. House report, 29, emphasis added.

40. Ibid., 691, 696.

41. Ibid., 692. As Blumstein noted, during the 1981–82 "voting rights debate, no one was prepared to embrace the racial entitlements concept" (635).

42. *Zimmer v. McKeithen*, 1304–5 and 1304n16.

43. The primary factors included a lack of minority access to a candidate-slating process, legislators who were unresponsive to minority interests, "tenuous state policy" that had given an underlying preference to multimember or at-large districting, and a history of discrimination that precluded effective minority electoral participation. The court added that proof of these factors could be "enhanced by a showing of the existence of large districts, majority vote requirements, anti–single shot voting provisions, and the lack of provision for at-large candidates running from particular geographical subdistricts." Vote dilution was established on proof "of an aggregate of these factors," although *White v. Regester* made clear that not all of the factors had to be proved to obtain relief (*Zimmer v. McKeithen*, 1305).

44. *Washington v. Davis*, 229.

45. Although it was an employment law case, *Davis* had used the same evidentiary principle that had been applied in cases involving zoning (*Village of Arlington Heights v. Metropolitan Housing Dev. Corp.*, 252), public schools (*Keyes v. School District No. 1, Denver, Colo.*, 413 U.S. 189 [1973]), and jury selection (*Akins v. Texas*, 325 U.S. 398 [1945]). Moreover, the *Davis* Court had explicitly indicated that the principle of purposeful discrimination applied to voting rights cases as much as to claims involving other forms of racial discrimination (*City of Mobile v. Bolden*, 67, opinion of the Court, referring to *Washington v. Davis*, 240).

46. *City of Mobile v. Bolden*, 61.

47. This was true for cases such as *Guinn v. United States* (see especially 359 and 365 [1915]), which dealt with a "grandfather" clause for a literacy test, and a host of racial gerrymandering cases such as *Gomillion v. Lightfoot* (see especially 341 and 347 [1960]), and *Wright v. Rockefeller* (see especially 56 and 58 [1964]). See also *Lassiter v. Northampton Election Bd.*, 360 U.S. 45 (1959) and *Lane v. Wilson*, 307 U.S. 268, 275–77 (1939). The intent standard also applied to the white primary cases, *Smith v. Allwright*, see especially 664, and *Terry v. Adams*, see especially 473.

48. Here Stewart cited *Washington v. Davis* in addition to cases dealing with multi-member districts, such as *White v. Regester, Whitcomb v. Chavis*, 403 U.S. 124 (1971), *Burns v. Richardson*, 384 U.S. 73 (1966), and *Fortson v. Dorsey*, 379 U.S. 433 (1965).

49. *City of Mobile v. Bolden*, 114, Marshall, J., dissenting.

50. Ibid., 108, quoting *Fortson v. Dorsey*, 439, emphasis removed.

51. *City of Mobile v. Bolden*, 120, Marshall, J., dissenting.

52. Ibid., 111n7.

53. Ibid., 75n22, Stewart, J. opinion of the Court, quoting Marshall, J., dissenting.

54. Ibid., 75, Stewart, J., opinion of the Court.

55. See *City of Mobile v. Bolden*, 79–80, Stewart, J., opinion of the Court: "Reversing the trial court, this Court [in *Whitcomb v. Chavis*] said: 'The District Court's holding, although on the facts of this case limited to guaranteeing one racial-group representation, is not easily contained. It is expressive of the more general proposition that any group with distinctive interests must be represented in legislative halls if it is numerous enough to command at least one seat and represents a majority living in an area sufficiently compact to constitute a single-member district. This approach would make it difficult to reject claims of Democrats, Republicans, or members of any political organization in Marion County who live in what would be safe districts in a single-member district system but who in one year or another, or year after year, are submerged in a one-sided multi-member district vote'" (citing *Whitcomb v. Chavis*, 156–57).

56. *City of Mobile v. Bolden*, 78n26, Stewart, J., opinion of the court.

57. House report, 29–30.

58. Senate Subcommittee report, 72.

59. The Supreme Court of Canada, for instance, formally adopted a results test as the measure of equality rights infractions in civil rights law in 1985 and in constitutional law in 1989. See *Re. Ontario Human Rights Commission v. Simpsons-Sears Ltd.* [1985] 2 S.C.R. 536, *Re. Bhinder v. Canadian National Railway Co.* [1985] 2 S.C.R. 56, and *Andrews v. Law Society of British Columbia* [1989] 1 S.C.R. 143. I have discussed these cases in Anthony A. Peacock, "Judicial Rationalism and the Therapeutic Constitution: The Supreme Court's Reconstruction of Equality and Democratic Process under the Charter of Rights and Freedoms," in *The Myth of the Sacred: The Charter, the Courts, and the Politics of the Constitution in Canada*, ed. Patrick James, Donald E. Abelson, and Michael Lusztig (Montreal: McGill-Queen's University Press, 2002), 17; and Peacock, "Strange Brew: Tocqueville, Rights, and the Technology of Equality," in *Rethinking the*

Constitution: Perspectives on Canadian Constitutional Reform, Interpretation, and Theory, ed. Anthony A. Peacock (Toronto: Oxford University Press, 1996), 122. See also Rainer Knopff, *Human Rights and Social Technology: The New War on Discrimination* (Ottawa: Carleton University Press, 1990).

60. As Steven Markman has written: "The new [1982] Voting Rights Act was the first civil-rights law to expressly provide for a 'protected class' of American citizens, the first to endorse the idea that civil rights were grounded in group rather than individual entitlements, the first explicitly to focus upon equality of results rather than upon fairness of process, and the first in which coherent legal standards were replaced by a standardless weighing of the 'totality of circumstances' by the federal judiciary" ("Minority Rules," *National Review*, March 21, 1994, 66).

61. *Thornburg v. Gingles*, 106 S.Ct. 2752, 2759, citing Senate report, 28–29.

62. *Thornburg v. Gingles*, 2763–4, 2772. See also Paul W. Jacobs II and Timothy G. O'Rourke, "Racial Polarization in Vote Dilution Cases under Section 2 of the Voting Rights Act: The Impact of *Thornburg v. Gingles*," *Journal of Law and Politics* 3 (Fall 1986): 311–17.

63. *Thornburg v. Gingles*, 2772, Brennan, J., opinion of the Court, emphasis in original.

64. Ibid., 2773, emphasis added.

65. Ibid., 2763, citing Senate report, 28.

66. *Thornburg v. Gingles*, 2777, Brennan, J., opinion of the Court.

67. Ibid., 2766–67.

68. Ibid., 2791, O'Connor, J., concurring. See also ibid., 2765n15, Brennan, J., opinion of the Court, referring to Senate report, 30n120. See also Jacobs and O'Rourke, "Racial Polarization," 311.

69. *Thornburg v. Gingles*, 2783, White, J., concurring.

70. Ibid., 2787, O'Connor, J., concurring, emphasis in original.

71. See ibid., 2765n15, Brennan J., opinion of the Court, referring to Senate report, 30n120. See also Jacobs and O'Rourke, "Racial Polarization," 311–17, 353.

72. *Holder v. Hall*, 114 S.Ct. 2581, 2597 (1994), Thomas, J., concurring.

73. Issacharoff, Karlan, and Pildes, *Law of Democracy*, 860.

74. *Thornburg v. Gingles*, 2764, Brennan, J., opinion of the Court.

75. See Bernard Grofman, "Expert Witness Testimony and the Evolution of Voting Rights Case Law," in *Controversies in Minority Voting*, 197, 221, 223–24.

76. See *Thornburg v. Gingles*, 2764n13, citing James Blacksher and Lawrence Menefee, "From *Reynolds v. Sims* to *City of Mobile v. Bolden*," *Hastings Law Journal* 34 (1982): 1. Blacksher had been a cooperating attorney for the NAACP's Legal Defense and Educational Fund and lead counsel for the plaintiffs in *Bolden*. Menefee, Blacksher's law partner in Mobile, had also been a co-counsel acting on behalf of the plaintiffs in *Bolden*. See also *Thornburg v. Gingles*, 2765–7, 2772–8; Grofman, "Expert Witness Testimony," 209–10; and Maurice T. Cunningham, *Maximization, Whatever the Cost: Race, Redistricting, and the Department of Justice* (Westport, CT: Praeger, 2001): "The [three] preconditions [in *Gingles*] are largely drawn from Justice

Brennan's reading of the social science literature; they are only marginally part of the then existing case law and the Court cites no consideration of them within the legislative history" (72).

77. In 1985, voting rights activists had lobbied Congress and the Department of Justice to incorporate the section 2 results test into section 5 preclearance. Although the voting rights bar found a sympathetic ear with liberal congressman Don Edwards, whose House subcommittee had held hearings on this issue in November of that year, President Reagan's assistant attorney general for civil rights, William Bradford Reynolds, refused the request. In January 1987, however, the DOJ relented, requiring the attorney general to withhold preclearance from those jurisdictions whose proposed electoral changes were "free of discriminatory purpose and retrogressive effect" but which nevertheless constituted "a clear violation of amended section 2" (*Procedures for the Administration of Section 5 of the Voting Rights Act of 1965*, as amended, 28 C.F.R. sec. 51.55[2]); see also Cunningham, *Maximization, Whatever the Cost*, 26–77, 73. When combined with the *Gingles* ruling mandating something approximating proportional representation for geographically compact, politically cohesive minorities, the DOJ's 1987 regulation would help set the stage for what Justice Kennedy would refer to in *Miller v. Johnson* (1995) as the Justice Department's "max black" redistricting agenda (115 S. Ct., 2475, 2484, opinion of the Court). The DOJ would impose this agenda on a host of jurisdictions covered by sections 4 and 5 following the 1990 census. Although the Supreme Court would eventually find the DOJ's 1987 regulation illegal in *Reno v. Bossier Parish School Board*, 520 U.S. 471 (1997), by then the damage wrought by the regulation had been done. Jurisdictions forced to comply with the racial maximization policies had had to respond to constitutional challenges to their decennial redistricting, and many of these cases had already reached the Supreme Court.

Chapter 6: The 1990s: *Shaw v. Reno* and the
Resurrection of the Founders' Republicanism?

1. Abigail Thernstrom, *Whose Votes Count? Affirmative Action and Minority Voting Rights* (Cambridge, MA: Harvard University Press, 1987), 9.

2. Hugh Davis Graham, "Voting Rights and the American Regulatory State," in *Controversies in Minority Voting*, ed. Bernard Grofman and Chandler Davidson (Washington, D.C.: Brookings Institution Press, 1992), 195.

3. *Allen v. State Board of Elections*, 393 U.S. 544 (1969). Like other voting rights scholars, Lani Guinier believed that once the *Allen* Court conceded that the VRA provided a right to an undiluted vote, this right could only be vindicated by some form of proportional representation. Yet proportional representation could not be satisfied in a system of geographic districting because geographic districting required that racial interests be compressed into territorial districts, an intractable problem that went a long way to explaining the unseemliness of racial redistricting. The solution, according to Guinier, was to abandon geographic districting altogether: "It is the assumption that a territorial

district can accurately approximate a fixed racial group identity—and not the assumption of racial group identity itself—that is problematic." Lani Guinier, "Groups, Representation, and Race-Conscious Districting: A Case of the Emperor's Clothes," *Texas Law Review* 71 (1993): 1624. Guinier added that if, on the basis of *Allen*, minorities had a right to elect their candidates of choice because a predominantly white electorate consistently defeated their preferred candidates, it seemed to follow that minorities should have a commensurate right to control policy where a predominantly white legislature consistently defeated their preferred legislative initiatives. What would be the point of the first right if minorities did not also enjoy the second?; Guinier, "The Triumph of Tokenism: The Voting Rights Act and the Theory of Black Electoral Success," *Michigan Law Review* 89 (March 1991): 1102. See also Guinier, "No Two Seats: The Elusive Quest for Political Equality," *Virginia Law Review* 77 (November 1991): 1459, and Guinier, "Race-Conscious Districting": "Voting is not simply about winning elections. The purpose of voting is to influence public policy" (1613). What Guinier termed "third-generation" voting rights would require, then, not merely the abandonment of geographic districting but the repudiation of the core republican principle of majority rule itself. Adopting a theory of "concurrent" or "constitutional" majorities originally developed by John C. Calhoun, Guinier advocated a doctrine of "fundamental fairness" or "proportionate interest representation," in which minorities and majorities would trade turns making policy. "[T]hose in the majority do not lose," Guinier wrote in 1994, "they simply learn to take turns." Lani Guinier, *The Tyranny of the Majority: Fundamental Fairness in Representative Democracy* (New York: Free Press, 1994), 7; see also, ibid., 1–20, and Guinier, "Triumph of Tokenism," 1080, 1102, 1140n303, 1136–44. See as well John C. Calhoun, *Union and Liberty: The Political Philosophy of John C. Calhoun* (Indianapolis: Liberty Fund, 1992), 23–78, especially 28–29. Needless to say, Guinier's academic writings were controversial and gave her critics plenty of fodder to work with in 1993. Whether Guinier's advocacy was inconsistent with second-generation voting rights was a different matter. What virtually no one in the controversy over her nomination was prepared to admit was that Guinier's proposals, however radical they might have seemed, were perfectly consistent with the logic of second-generation voting rights as they had evolved through the 1990s.

4. *Shaw v. Reno*, 113 S.Ct. 2816, 2820, opinion of the Court (1993).

5. Ibid., 2821. See also *Pope v. Blue*, 809 F. Supp. 392, 394 (W.D.N.C. 1992).

6. Tinsley E. Yarborough, *Race and Redistricting: The Shaw-Cromartie Cases* (Lawrence, KS: University Press of Kansas, 2002), 97, referring to the testimony of Thomas Hofeller.

7. Richard H. Pildes and Richard G. Niemi, "Expressive Harms, 'Bizarre Districts,' and Voting Rights: Evaluating Election-District Appearances after *Shaw v. Reno*," *Michigan Law Review* 92 (December 1993): 566. "Dispersion" refers to establishing "how tightly packed or spread out the geography of a district is" (Ibid., 554). "Perimeter" examines "the extent to which district borders wander in irregular ways" (Ibid., 555).

8. *Shaw v. Reno*, 2827.

9. See, for instance, Guinier, "Triumph of Tokenism," 1101–34. See also chapter 1n47 and note 3 above.

10. *Holder v. Hall*, 114 S.Ct. 2561 (1994).

11. *Miller v. Johnson*, 115 S.Ct. 2475 (1995).

12. *United States v. Hays*, 115 S.Ct. 2431 (1995).

13. *Shaw v. Hunt (Shaw II)*, 517 U.S. 899 (1996).

14. *Bush v. Vera*, 517 U.S. 952 (1996).

15. Bernard Grofman, "High Court Ruling Won't Doom Racial Gerrymandering," *Chicago Tribune*, July 9, 1993, sec. 1, 19.

16. Pildes and Niemi, "Expressive Harms," 495.

17. *Miller v. Johnson*, 2488.

18. *Bush v. Vera*, 1001, Thomas, J., concurring.

19. *City of Richmond v. J.A. Croson Co.*, 488 U.S. 469 (1989).

20. See Katharine Inglis Butler, "Affirmative Racial Gerrymandering: Rhetoric and Reality," *Cumberland Law Review* 26 (1996): 331.

21. *City of Richmond v. J.A. Croson Co.*, 506, opinion of the Court.

22. Ibid., 502.

23. Ibid., 495–96. See also T. Alexander Aleinikoff and Samuel Issacharoff, "Race and Redistricting: Drawing Constitutional Lines after *Shaw v. Reno*," *Michigan Law Review* 92 (December 1993): 598.

24. See, for example, *Grove City College v. Bell*, 465 U.S. 555 (1984), where the Court narrowly construed Title VI of the 1964 Civil Rights Act. In the late 1980s the Court modified the legal doctrines applicable to race-conscious affirmative action under Title VII of the Civil Rights Act. Disparate impact analysis was altered, making it more difficult for employees to assert claims. *Watson v. Fort Worth Bank*, 108 S.Ct. 2777 (1988) and *Wards Cove Packing Co. v. Antonio*, 490 U.S. 642 (1989). In 1989 the Court also allowed for judicial review of affirmative action consent decrees to which white plaintiffs were not a party (*Martin v. Wilks*, 109 S.Ct. 2180 [1989]). These decisions were subsequently overturned by Congress in the Civil Rights Act of 1991, P.L. 102-66.

25. *University of California Regents v. Bakke*, 438 U.S. 265, especially 294 (1978).

26. Ibid., 324–79. Brennan, J., concurring in the judgment in part and dissenting in part.

27. Ibid., 294–7.

28. *City of Richmond v. J.A. Croson Co.*, 493.

29. See *Shaw v. Reno*, 2816, 2821. See also ibid., 2828: "Classifying citizens by race, as we have said, threatens special harms that are not present in our vote-dilution cases. It therefore warrants different analysis."

30. See *Miller v. Johnson*, 2486, opinion of the Court. See also James F. Blumstein, "*Shaw v. Reno* and *Miller v. Johnson*: Where We Are and Where We Are Headed," *Cumberland Law Review* 26 (1996): 503–6.

31. *Shaw v. Reno*, 2826, emphasis in original.

32. *United Jewish Organizations of Williamsburgh, Inc. v. Carey*, 430 U.S. 144, 155 (1977), White, J., opinion of the Court, emphasis in original.

33. Ibid., 161, emphasis added.

34. Ibid., 162.

35. *Shaw v. Reno*, 2830.

36. Ibid., 2829. See also *United Jewish Organizations of Williamsburgh, Inc. v. Carey*, 168, White, J., opinion of the Court.

37. Ibid., 155, emphasis added.

38. Ibid., 154n14, citing the Brief for Petitioners, emphasis in original.

39. *Holder v. Hall*, 2592, Thomas, J. concurring.

40. Ibid.

41. Ibid., 2611.

42. Ibid., 2592–97 and 2604–7.

43. Ibid., 2619.

44. Ibid., 2596, 2602.

45. Ibid., 2594.

46. Ibid., 2597.

47. Ibid., 2597.

48. Ibid., 2598.

49. Prior to *Grutter v. Bollinger*, the only racial classifications permitted by the Court were those necessary to ensure national security or to remedy past discrimination for which government was responsible. See *Grutter v. Bollinger*, 123 S.Ct. 2325, 2351, Thomas, J., concurring in part and dissenting in part (2003).

50. *Adarand Constructors, Inc. v. Pena*, 115 S. Ct. 2097 (1995).

51. See Blumstein, "*Shaw v. Reno* and *Miller v. Johnson*," 505.

52. *Metro Broadcasting, Inc. v. FCC*, 497 U.S. 547 (1990).

53. *Adarand Constructors, Inc. v. Pena*, 2111, opinion of the Court.

54. *Shaw v. Hunt*, 909–10, emphasis in original.

55. *Miller v. Johnson*, 2491.

56. *Adarand Constructors, Inc. v. Pena*, 2112–13, emphases in original.

57. *Miller v. Johnson*, 2486, quoting *Metro Broadcasting, Inc. v. FCC*, at 602, O'Connor, J., dissenting.

58. *Miller v. Johnson*, 2486.

59. Ibid., 2506, Ginsburg, J., Souter, J., dissenting.

60. Ibid.

61. Ibid.

62. *University of California Regents v. Bakke*, 295.

63. *Bush v. Vera*, 1051, Souter, J., dissenting.

64. *Miller v. Johnson*, 2497, Stevens, J., dissenting.

65. *United States v. Hays*, 115 S.Ct. 2431, 2435.

66. Ibid., 2436.

67. Ibid.

68. *Miller v. Johnson*, 2497–98, Stevens, J., dissenting.

69. *Brown v. Board of Education*, 347 U.S. 483 (1954).

70. *Shaw v. Hunt*, 924, 928, Stevens, J., dissenting; see also *Bush v. Vera*, 1052–54, Souter, J., dissenting.

71. *Plessy v. Ferguson*, 163 U.S. 537 (1896).

72. *Brown v. Board of Education*, 492–95, Warren, C.J., opinion of the Court.

73. Ibid., 495, emphasis added.

74. See *Shaw v. Reno*, 2835, White, J., dissenting.

75. *Miller v. Johnson*, 2486, Kennedy, J., opinion of the Court.

76. Ibid., 2488.

77. Ibid., 2486.

78. William Van Alstyne, "Rites of Passage: Race, the Supreme Court, and the Constitution," *University of Chicago Law Review* 46 (1979): 783. Van Alstyne points out that the specific case that had overruled *Plessy* was *Gayle v. Broweder*, 352 U.S. 903 (1956), Ibid., 783n24, a case cited by Justice Kennedy in *Miller* in support of the *Shaw* claim (*Miller v. Johnson*, 2486). See also Thomas C. Berg, "Religion, Race, Segregation, and Districting: Comparing *Kiryas Joel* with *Shaw/Miller*," *Cumberland Law Review* 26 (1996): "Some critics of *Shaw* and *Miller* assert that the plaintiffs in such cases have no standing to object to majority-minority districts. As several contributors to this symposium have argued, the 'representational harm' theory of standing propounded in *Shaw* and *Miller* suffers from flaws. But the Court might have found a more coherent basis for standing in the principle that there is standing to sue for any individual who has been subjected to racial 'sorting' (that is, who has been classified into one institution over another because of race), regardless of whether the individual or his group suffers any independent or distinctive harm (in the voting cases, regardless of whether the vote of the plaintiffs or their racial group is diluted). As some of *Shaw's* supporters have noted, such a theory seems necessary to explain the Court's actions in the 1950s and 1960s cases concerning segregation of public facilities. While *Brown v. Board of Education* might be explicable on the ground (explicitly stated in the *Brown* opinion) that segregated schools in fact caused psychological harm to African-American children, the Court made no such specific finding in later segregation cases, which it decided mostly by per curiam orders. Moreover, the Court has treated 'sorting' itself as a cognizable injury in recent affirmative action cases, holding that plaintiffs can raise challenges based on differential treatment whether or not they can prove that they ultimately would have been admitted to the school or hired for the job" (370).

79. Van Alstyne, "Rites of Passage," 781. See also Stephen B. Presser, "A Conservative Comment on Professor Crump," *University of Florida Law Review* 56 (July 2004): 789, 800–1.

80. Van Alstyne, "Rites of Passage," 775, 782, 792.

81. See, for instance, *Washington v. Davis*, 426 U.S. 229 (1976), *Village of Arlington Heights v. Metropolitan Housing Development Corporation*, 429 U.S. 252 (1977), and *City of Mobile v. Bolden*, 446 U.S. 55 (1980). See also Blumstein, "*Shaw v. Reno* and *Miller v. Johnson*," 506–8. In *Miller* the threshold question became whether "race was the *predominant factor*

motivating the legislature's decision to place a significant number of voters within or without a particular district" (2488, Kennedy, J., opinion of the Court, emphasis added).

82. *Bush v. Vera*, 999, Thomas, J., concurring.

83. Ibid., 990, O'Connor, J., concurring.

84. Ibid., 1073, Souter, J., dissenting.

Chapter 7: The Supreme Court and the Voting Rights Act after 2000

1. *Bush v. Vera*, 517 U.S. 952, 990 (1996), O'Connor, J., concurring.

2. *Easley v. Cromartie*, 532 U.S. 234 (2001).

3. *Shaw v. Hunt (Shaw II)*, 517 U.S. 899 (1996).

4. *Cromartie v. Hunt*, 133 F. Supp. 2d 407 (E.D.N.C. 2000).

5. *Easley v. Cromartie*, 259–60, Thomas, J., dissenting.

6. *Shaw v. Hunt (Shaw II)*, 907, Rehnquist, C.J., opinion of the Court, emphasis added.

7. *Easley v. Cromartie*, 262–63, Thomas, J., dissenting.

8. *Miller v. Johnson*, 115 S.Ct. 2475, 2484–85, 2491–93, opinion of the Court (1995).

9. Ibid., 2493.

10. *Reno v. Bossier Parish School Board (Bossier II)*, 528 U.S. 320 (2000).

11. Notices, *Federal Register* 66, no. 12 (January 18, 2001): 5412, hereinafter Redistricting Guidance.

12. *Beer v. United States*, 425 U.S. 130 (1976).

13. Redistricting Guidance, 5412.

14. Ibid.

15. I have discussed these cases and other post-2000 redistricting issues in Anthony A. Peacock, "From *Beer* to Eternity: Why Race Will Always Predominate under the Voting Rights Act," in *Redistricting in the New Millennium*, ed. Peter F. Galderisi (Lanham, MD: Lexington Books, 2005), 119.

16. *Georgia v. Ashcroft*, 123 S.Ct. 2498 (2003).

17. Fannie Lou Hammer, Rosa Parks, and Coretta Scott King Voting Rights Act Reauthorization and Amendments Act of 2006.

18. *League of United Latin American Citizens v. Perry*, 126 S.Ct. 2594 (2006).

19. Texas Democratic Senator Judith Zaffirini said that according to nine minority senators in the state, the congressional redistricting map originally passed by the Texas Senate September 23, 2003, was "discriminatory" (see Natalie Gott, "Texas Senate Gives Tentative OK for Map," http://www.findlaw.com, September 24, 2003). When the redistricting plan was passed during a third special legislative session October 12, 2003, Zaffirini was again quoted by the Associated Press as remarking that "the map would disenfranchise millions of minority voters" (April Castro, "GOP pushes through Texas redistricting," *Salt Lake Tribune*, October 13, 2003, A8). Attending a reception for the National Hispanic Caucus in Salt Lake City on July 17, 2004, Texas senate minority leader Leticia Van de Putte, chairwoman of the National Latino Caucus of State

Legislators, remarked that Texas's redistricting plan "disfranchised many minorities because it stacked them into fewer 'supermajority' districts while scattering smaller pockets of ethnic groups into a greater number of districts" (Paul Rolly, *Salt Lake Tribune*, July 18, 2004, A10). Van de Putte was one of the Democrats who fled to New Mexico in 2003 to avoid voting on the Texas Republicans' redistricting plan.

20. Social scientists generally agree that the Democrats paid a steep price for the MMDs that were created in the South during the 1990s as a result of section 5 enforcement. Carol Swain and David Bositis, for instance, have found that racial redistricting cost the Democrats at least five congressional seats in 1992 and at least twelve more in 1994. Lisa Handley, Bernard Grofman, and Wayne Arden determined that Democrats may have lost as few as two but as many as ten to eleven seats during that time. Charles Bullock was less precise in his estimates but suggested that there were six Democratic losses in 1992 and three more in 1994. David Lublin, who summarized the above findings, himself surmised that at a minimum the Democrats lost five seats in 1992 to racial redistricting and two more in 1994, although the Democrats likely lost four more than this conservative estimate suggests. See David Lublin, *The Paradox of Representation: Racial Gerrymandering and Minority Interests in Congress* (Princeton: Princeton University Press, 1997), 111–14.

21. An MID is simply an electoral district in which a legally recognized minority comprises less than 50 percent of the voting-age population or residents, but where that minority nevertheless exercises sufficient influence as to be able to elect its preferred candidate.

22. *Georgia v. Ashcroft*, 195 F. Supp. 2d 25, 39, opinion of the court (D.C. 2002).

23. Ibid., 41. In its jurisdictional statement before the U.S. Supreme Court, the state of Georgia remarked, "In the Senate, only one African American Senator (S.D. 2) voted against the Senate plan . . . and she did so simply because of her personal desire for a district exactly as she wanted it—which ignored the fact that 56 Senate districts had to be drawn with no one incumbent getting just what they wanted. One African American House member also voted against the House plan. . . . Such near unanimous support is a rarity in any political endeavor" (11n2).

24. *Georgia v. Ashcroft*, 195 F. Supp. 2d at 40, 42, opinion of the court.

25. See ibid., 77, 96.

26. The trial in *Ashcroft* highlighted the exceedingly technical and speculative nature of section 5 evidentiary investigations. The majority and minority in *Ashcroft* clashed on a host of evidentiary questions: whether expert or lay witness testimony should be primary; which expert's testimony should prevail, given that both the federal government's and the state's experts provided inadequate evidence to assess retrogression accurately; what was the extent and meaning of white crossover voting in local and statewide electoral contests; and how should the voting patterns of racial groups be measured (should black voter registration be used or black voting-age population). There was even dispute over how to count up multirace respondents to the 2000 census. The DOJ had argued that census respondents who self-identified as black or as black and white

should be counted as black. Those who self-identified as black in combination with another nonwhite racial or ethnic group should not be counted as black. Georgia, by contrast, had contested that all those voters who identified themselves as either exclusively black or as black in combination with some other racial or ethnic group should be counted in the black voting-age population. How one counted black voters made a significant difference. Using the DOJ's method, Georgia's senate plan was retrogressive. Using Georgia's method, it was nonretrogressive. The majority accepted the DOJ's method of counting. Judge Oberdorfer accepted the state of Georgia's.

27. "Descriptive" representation occurs where voters are entitled to elect representatives "like" themselves; in the case of the VRA, where minorities can elect other minorities. Descriptive representation of blacks and Hispanics generally requires MMDs. "Substantive" representation occurs where jurisdictions are free to draw districts in which minorities make up less than half of the voting-age population or residents in a district (an MID), but where the district will nevertheless result in biracial coalitions that will, in Justice O'Connor's words, "help to achieve the electoral aspirations of the minority group." *Georgia v. Ashcroft*, 2512, O'Connor, J., opinion of the Court. See also Hannah Fenichel Pitkin, *The Concept of Representation* (Berkeley: University of California Press, 1972), 60–91; and Maurice T. Cunningham, *Maximization, Whatever the Cost: Race, Redistricting, and the Department of Justice* (Westport, CT: Praeger, 2001), 150.

28. See chapter 5 for discussion of "totality of circumstances."

29. *Georgia v. Ashcroft*, 2511.

30. Ibid., 2512–14.

31. Ibid., 2518, Souter, J., dissenting.

32. Ibid.

33. Ibid., 2520.

34. *South Carolina v. Katzenbach*, 383 U.S. 301 (1996).

35. *Georgia v. Ashcroft*, 123 S. Ct., 2517, Kennedy, J., concurring opinion.

36. Ibid., Thomas, J., concurring opinion, referring to *Holder v. Hall*, 114 S. Ct. 2581, Thomas, J., concurring (1994).

37. *City of Boerne v. Flores*, 521 U.S. 507, 519–20, opinion of the Court (1997).

38. Ibid., 533.

39. Ibid., 532.

40. See *Lopez v. Monterey County*, 525 U.S. 266, 294n6, Thomas, J., dissenting (1999): "Although *City of Boerne* involved the Fourteenth Amendment enforcement power, we have always treated the nature of the enforcement powers conferred by the Fourteenth and Fifteenth Amendments as coextensive. See, e.g., *City of Boerne*, 518–528; *James v. Bowman*, 190 U.S. 127 [1903]."

41. See Charles S. Bullock III and Ronald Keith Gaddie, "Assessments of Voting Rights Progress in Georgia, South Carolina, Louisiana, Virginia, Texas, and Florida" (unpublished manuscript, prepared for the Project on Fair Representation, American Enterprise Institute, 2006).

42. See Samuel Issacharoff, "Is Section 5 of the Voting Rights Act a Victim of Its Own Success?" *Columbia Law Review* 104 (October 2004): 1714.

43. Ibid., 1720.

44. Ibid., 1712.

45. Some defenders of the VRA's temporary provisions claim that sections 4 and 5 are saved, among other reasons, by the act's "bailout" provision in section 4(a)(1). See, for instance, Paul Winke, "Why the Preclearance and Bailout Provisions of the Voting Rights Act Are Still a Constitutionally Proportional Remedy," *New York University Review of Law and Social Change* 28 (2003): 69. The evidentiary burdens that jurisdictions must meet under section 4(a)(1), however, are so high as to be virtually insuperable. This situation has been the case for over thirty-five years now, and the barriers were raised, not lowered, by the 1982 amendments to the act (as Winke concedes at ibid., 72). See Abigail Thernstrom, *Whose Votes Count? Affirmative Action and Minority Voting Rights* (Cambridge, MA: Harvard University Press, 1987), 27–29.

46. *Bush v. Vera*, 990, O'Connor, J., concurring.

47. *League of United Latin American Citizens v. Perry*, 2594.

48. VRA of 2006, sections 5(b) and 5(d).

49. Ibid., section 5(c), emphasis added.

50. *League of United Latin American Citizens v. Perry*, 2594.

51. See *Session v. Perry*, 298 F. Supp. 2d 451, 470–73 (2004).

52. 241 F. Supp. 2d 478 (2003).

53. *Session v. Perry*, 241 F. Supp. 2d at 472, emphasis added.

54. *League of United Latin American Citizens v. Perry*, 2622, opinion of the Court.

55. Ibid., 2663, Roberts, C.J., concurring in part, concurring in the judgment in part, and dissenting in part.

56. Ibid., 2624, Kennedy, J., concurring.

57. Ibid., 2625.

58. Ibid., Souter, J., concurring in part and dissenting in part.

59. Ibid., 2648n3.

60. Ibid., 2645n16, Stevens, J., concurring in part and dissenting in part.

61. Ibid.

62. *Bush v. Vera*, 1000, Thomas, J., concurring, emphasis added.

63. *League of United Latin American Citizens v. Perry*, 2667, Scalia, J., concurring in the judgment in part and dissenting in part.

64. Ibid., 2665.

65. Ibid., 2667.

66. On the concept of rational and durable liberty, see Alexander Hamilton, "The Continentalist No. I," in *The Papers of Alexander Hamilton 1779–1781*, eds. Harold C. Syrett and Jacob E. Cooke (New York: Columbia University Press, 1961), 2: 649, esp. 651; see, also, Peter McNamara, *Political Economy and Statesmanship: Smith, Hamilton, and the Foundation of the Commercial Republic* (DeKalb, IL: Northern Illinois University Press, 1998), 96–7.

Conclusion

1. See, for instance, Jean-Jacques Rousseau, *Discours sur les sciences et les arts* [Discourse on the Sciences and the Arts] and *Discours sur l'origine, et les fondements de l'inégalité parmi les hommes* [Discourse on the Origin and the Foundations of Inequality Among Men], in *Oeuvres complètes* (Paris: Gallimard, 1964), 3: 1, 109, respectively.

2. See Robert Kagan, *Dangerous Nation* (New York: Alfred A. Knopf, 2006): "Even as they fretted about the dangers of luxury and avarice that a multiplying commerce produced, the members of the founding generation, from Federalists like Hamilton to Republicans like Jefferson and Madison, questioned neither the commercial nature of the American people nor the vast benefits to the nation that would be gained by unleashing the forces of commercial liberalism. Their grand scheme was to harness the material ambitions of men and women into a mammoth self-generating engine of national wealth and power. American foreign policy in the first decade of the republic aimed, above all other goals save the preservation of the nation itself, at feeding the ravenous appetites of a generation of Americans whom Gouverneur Morris recognized as 'the first-born children of the commercial age'" (72–73). Drew McCoy has also observed that during the Revolutionary period "most Americans had no choice but to adopt the deceptively simple and perhaps chimerical proposal that John Brown had offered in his widely read tract from the 1750s—'that Commerce and Wealth not be discouraged in their Growth; but checked and controuled in their Effects'—for very few of them, including Benjamin Franklin, ever seriously anticipated a republican America without commerce and the wealth and refinement it would inevitably bring. Franklin's vision of an expanding agricultural republic was not a call for Americans to retreat to a social simplicity that was primitive or barbarous—indeed, no one appreciated more than he the advantages of Hume's version of civilized cultural progress. And above all, Franklin's republican vision was hardly that of a Spartan, self-contained society of hermit yeomen, for it was closely tied to a much broader international commercial vision." Drew R. McCoy, *The Elusive Republic: Political Economy in Jeffersonian America* (Chapel Hill, NC: University of North Carolina Press, 1980), 75.

3. Alexander Hamilton, Letter to Robert Morris, April 30, 1781, in *The Papers of Alexander Hamilton 1779–1781*, ed. Harold C. Syrett and Jacob E. Cooke (New York: Columbia University Press, 1961), 2:618.

4. Anthony A. Peacock, "The Voting Rights Act and the Politics of Multiculturalism: The Challenge to Commercial Republicanism at Century's Turn," in *Courts and the Culture Wars*, ed. Bradley C. S. Watson (Lanham, MD: Lexington Books, 2002), 167, 185–86; see also McCoy, *Elusive Republic*; Karl-Friedrich Walling, *Republican Empire: Alexander Hamilton on War and Free Government* (Lawrence, KS: University Press of Kansas, 1999); and Michael D. Chan, *Aristotle and Hamilton: On Commerce and Statesmanship* (Columbia, MO: University of Missouri Press, 2006).

5. Alexander Hamilton, John Jay, and James Madison, *The Federalist: A Commentary on the Constitution of the United States*, ed. Robert Scigliano (New York: Modern Library, 2001), 3.

6. Ibid., 47.

7. *Federalist* 22, 139.

8. Ibid.

9. Ibid., 86.

10. *Federalist* 43, 278–79, emphasis in original. Nothing in the Fourteenth Amendment to the Constitution altered this freedom to choose republican forms of government under the guarantee clause. See Hans A. Linde, "When Initiative Lawmaking Is Not 'Republican Government': The Campaign Against Homosexuality," *Oregon Law Review* 72 [1993]: 33. The Fifteenth Amendment did require states to cease discrimination against voters on the basis of race, but this merely affirmed the republican principle contained in the guarantee clause.

11. *Luther v. Borden*, 48 U.S. 1, 47 (1849).

12. Harvey C. Mansfield, Jr., *America's Constitutional Soul* (Baltimore: Johns Hopkins University Press, 1993), 86.

13. "Prepared Statement of Dr. Edward J. Erler," Subcommittee on the Constitution of the Committee on the Judiciary, U.S. Senate, 97th Congress, 2nd session, hearings on S. 53, S. 1761, S. 1975, S. 1992, and HR 3112, Bills to Amend the Voting Rights Act of 1965, January 27–March 1, 1982, 490, 509–10.

14. See Joseph M. Bessette, *The Mild Voice of Reason: Deliberative Democracy and American National Government* (Chicago: University of Chicago Press, 1994), 58–63.

15. John Yoo, *The Powers of War and Peace: The Constitution and Foreign Affairs after 9/11* (Chicago: University of Chicago Press, 2005), 6.

16. Ibid., viii.

About the Author

Anthony A. Peacock is an associate professor of political science at Utah State University, where he teaches courses on law, politics, and war. He has a Ph.D. from The Claremont Graduate School and a law degree from Osgoode Hall Law School, York University. He practiced civil litigation in Toronto from 1989 to 1992. In addition to editing *Affirmative Action and Representation: Shaw v. Reno and the Future of Voting Rights* (Carolina Academic Press, 1997), and *Rethinking the Constitution: Perspectives on Canadian Constitutional Reform, Interpretation, and Theory* (Oxford University Press, 1996), Peacock has published numerous articles, book chapters, and book reviews on American and Canadian law and politics. His work has been cited by the Supreme Court of Canada. He has provided radio commentary on state and national politics and has lectured on American politics and law both nationally and internationally. Peacock's scholarship focuses on American constitutionalism and the theory and history of political economy and war, with particular emphasis on their relationship to law and free government. He is currently working on a book about Thucydides and *The Federalist* as well as an edited volume on freedom and the rule of law. Peacock lives with his wife, Gretchen, and their three children in Logan, Utah.

Index